MYTH

Second edition

Laurence Coupe offers students a comprehensive overview of the development of 'myth', showing how mythic themes, structures and symbols persist in literature and entertainment today. This introductory volume:

- illustrates the relation between myth, culture and literature with discussions of poetry, fiction, film and popular song
- explores uses made of the term 'myth' within the fields of literary criticism, anthropology, cultural studies, feminism, Marxism and psychoanalysis
- discusses the association between modernism, postmodernism, myth and history
- familiarizes the reader with themes such as the dying god, the quest for the grail, the relation between 'chaos' and 'cosmos', and the vision of the end of time
- demonstrates the growing importance of the green dimension of myth.

Fully updated and revised in this new edition, *Myth* is both a concise introduction and a useful tool to students first approaching the topic, while also a valuable contribution to the study of myth.

Laurence Coupe is Senior Lecturer in English at Manchester Metropolitan University. He is the author of *Kenneth Burke on Myth* (Routledge, 2005), *Marina Warner* (2006) and *Beat Sound, Beat Vision* (2007), and he is the editor of *The Green Studies Reader* (Routledge, 2000).

THE NEW CRITICAL IDIOM

SERIES EDITOR: JOHN DRAKAKIS, UNIVERSITY OF STIRLING

The New Critical Idiom is an invaluable series of introductory guides to today's critical terminology. Each book:

- provides a handy, explanatory guide to the use (and abuse) of the term;
- offers an original and distinctive overview by a leading literary and cultural critic;
- relates the term to the larger field of cultural representation.

With a strong emphasis on clarity, lively debate and the widest possible breadth of examples, *The New Critical Idiom* is an indispensable approach to key topics in literary studies.

Also available in this series:

The Author by Andrew Bennett
Autobiography by Linda Anderson
Adaptation and Appropriation by Julie Sanders
Class by Gary Day
Colonialism/Postcolonialism (Second edition) by Ania Loomba
Comedy by Andrew Stott
Crime Fiction by John Scaggs
Culture/Metaculture by Francis Mulhern
Difference by Mark Currie
Discourse by Sara Mills
Drama/Theatre/Performance by Simon Shepherd and Mick Wallis
Dramatic Monologue by Glennis Byron
Ecocriticism by Greg Garrard
Elegy by David Kennedy
Genders by David Glover and Cora Kaplan
Genre by John Frow
Gothic by Fred Botting
Historicism by Paul Hamilton
Humanism by Tony Davies
Ideology by David Hawkes
Interdisciplinarity by Joe Moran
Intertextuality by Graham Allen
Irony by Claire Colebrook
Literature by Peter Widdowson
Magic(al) Realism by Maggie Ann Bowers
Memory by Anne Whitehead
Metaphor by David Punter
Metre, Rhythm and Verse Form by Philip Hobsbaum
Mimesis by Matthew Potolsky
Modernism by Peter Childs
Narrative by Paul Cobley
Parody by Simon Dentith
Pastoral by Terry Gifford
Performativity by James Loxley
The Postmodern by Simon Malpas
Realism by Pam Morris
Rhetoric by Jennifer Richards
Romance by Barbara Fuchs
Romanticism by Aidan Day
Science Fiction by Adam Roberts
Sexuality by Joseph Bristow
Stylistics by Richard Bradford
Subjectivity by Donald E. Hall
The Sublime by Philip Shaw
The Unconscious by Antony Easthope

MYTH

Second edition

Laurence Coupe

LONDON AND NEW YORK

First edition published 1997
by Routledge

Second edition published 2009
by Routledge
2 Park Square, Milton Park, Abingdon, Oxon OX14 4RN

Simultaneously published in the USA and Canada
by Routledge
270 Madison Ave, New York, NY 10016

Routledge is an imprint of the Taylor & Francis Group, an informa business

Typeset in Adobe Garamond and Scala Sans by
Florence Production Ltd, Stoodleigh, Devon

British Library Cataloguing in Publication Data
A catalogue record for this book is available from the British Library

Library of Congress Cataloging in Publication Data
Coupe, Laurence, 1950–.
Myth/Laurence Coupe. – 2nd ed.
p. cm.
Includes bibliographical references and index.
1. Myth. I. Title.
BL304.C68 2008
201′.3 – dc22 2008030181

ISBN10: 0–415–44241–9 (hbk)
ISBN10: 0–415–44284–2 (pbk)
ISBN10: 0–203–88808–1 (ebk)

ISBN13: 978–0–415–44241–1 (hbk)
ISBN13: 978–0–415–44284–8 (pbk)
ISBN13: 978–0–203–88808–7 (ebk)

For Margaret

Contents

Series Editor's Preface

The New Critical Idiom is a series of introductory books which seeks to extend the lexicon of literary terms, in order to address the radical changes which have taken place in the study of literature during the last decades of the twentieth century. The aim is to provide clear, well-illustrated accounts of the full range of terminology currently in use, and to evolve histories of its changing usage.

The current state of the discipline of literary studies is one where there is considerable debate concerning basic questions of terminology. This involves, among other things, the boundaries which distinguish the literary from the non-literary; the position of literature within the large sphere of culture; the relationship between literatures of different cultures; and questions concerning the relation of literary to other cultural forms within the context of interdisciplinary studies.

It is clear that the field of literary criticism and theory is a dynamic and heterogeneous one. The present need is for individual volumes on terms which combine clarity of exposition with an adventurousness of perspective and a breadth of application. Each volume will contain as part of its apparatus some indication of the direction in which the definition of particular terms is likely to move, as well as expanding the disciplinary boundaries within which some of these terms have been traditionally contained. This will involve some re-situation of terms within the larger field of cultural representation, and will introduce examples from the area of film and the modern media in addition to examples from a variety of literary texts.

Acknowledgements

I am grateful to the following people: Talia Rodgers for encouraging me to write the first edition and Polly Dodson for encouraging me to write the second; John Drakakis for his thoughtful editorship; Don Cupitt for providing the initial inspiration; Marina Warner for her example; Robert Segal for his indispensable advice; Patrick Curry for his ideas and encouragement; Susan Rowland for helping me clarify my own thinking; Jonathan Bate for reminding me of the 'green' dimension of myth.

I am grateful to the following publishers: Faber & Faber for permission to quote from the UK editions of T. S. Eliot's *Collected Poems* (1963) and Philip Larkin's *Collected Poems* (1988); Harcourt Brace & Co. for permission to quote from the US edition of T. S. Eliot's *Collected Poems* (1963); Farrar, Strauss & Giroux for permission to quote from the US edition of Philip Larkin's *Collected Poems* (1988); Carcanet Press for permission to quote from Edgell Rickword's *Behind the Eyes: Collected Poems and Translations* (1976).

INTRODUCTION

PARADIGM, PERFECTION AND POSSIBILITY

The word 'myth' is used so frequently that one can expect to come across it not only in most books on literary or cultural studies, but also in most forms of popular entertainment. The usage is often rather loose, however. In literary and cultural studies 'myth' is frequently used as synonymous with 'ideology', as in 'the myth of progress' or 'the myth of the free individual'. In entertainment it is frequently used as synonymous with 'fantasy', as in 'Enter the mythical world of *Dungeons and Dragons*!' In either case, it is being used to imply some sort of illusion, whether one is an academic exposing the hidden agenda of a literary or cultural text, or one is a games manufacturer trying to attract customers. While it is true that there is some overlap between myth and ideology, and between myth and fantasy, it is not helpful to use them interchangeably. As I hope to show, there is a lot more to myth than deception or distraction. We will come to a provisional definition of 'myth' in due course, but let us first consider four kinds of narrative that can legitimately be described as mythic.

Here is a story from ancient Egypt. Osiris, god of vegetation, being the object of universal love and admiration, provokes the envy of his brother Set. Set has him buried alive in a coffin, which is then thrown out to sea. Isis, goddess of vegetation, finds his body, washed up at the Lebanese port of Byblos and caught in a tree. She hides the corpse, but Set finds it and cuts it into pieces, scattering it over the land of Egypt. Isis recovers all the parts except one, the genitals. Even so, having the gift of magic, she is able to make Osiris father a child, Horus. Thereafter, on ceremonial occasions the reigning king of Egypt represents Horus and the deceased king is referred to as Osiris. This story might serve as an example of the kind of narrative known as *fertility myth*.

Here is a second story, from ancient Mesopotamia, at the time when it was dominated by the city of Babylon. Tiamat is the primeval mother goddess; she is the sea, the origin of all life; she may be imagined as a huge dragon. A younger god, Marduk, sets out to prove himself as warrior by waging war against her. Triumphing, he cuts her body into two and out of it he makes the universe, with a heaven above and an earth below, set amidst the ocean. Thereafter, he is the supreme god, and the Babylonian king represents him in the annual new year festival, which takes place after the floods have subsided. This story might serve as an example of the kind of narrative known as *creation myth*.

Here is a third story, from ancient Israel. The Hebrews, later known as the Israelites, are being held captive as slaves in Egypt, and the pharaoh refuses to let them go. Their god Yahweh visits the pharaoh's land with ten plagues, culminating in the death of every firstborn son of every Egyptian household. The pharaoh relents, and the Hebrews' leader Moses is instructed by Yahweh to lead the people to freedom through the Red Sea. No sooner have the Hebrews left Egypt, however, than the pharaoh changes his mind, and sends his army after them. The waves of the sea part for the Hebrews, but join together again as the Egyptians pursue them. All the pharaoh's army is drowned, while the Hebrews are able to go forward towards their promised land. Thereafter, the liberated slaves begin to understand that their god Yahweh is the one, universal and all-powerful God. They celebrate the feast of 'the Passover' to commemorate the two saving acts of Yahweh: making death 'pass over' their own households, and enabling his people to 'pass over' the Red Sea from bondage to freedom. This story might serve as an example of the kind of narrative known as *deliverance myth* (Frye 1982: 49).

Here is a fourth story, from ancient Greece. King Acrisius does not want his daughter Danae to produce any children, having been told by an oracle that his grandson will grow up to kill him, and imprisons her so that she cannot possibly conceive. But the sky father Zeus enters her cell and impregnates her, and a male child is born. When the king discovers this, he shuts both his daughter and his grandson in a chest and has it thrown into the sea. Thanks to the intervention of Zeus, the chest lands safely on an island, and both mother and child are given a home by its ruler, Polydectes. As the boy Perseus grows up, he and Polydectes, who is a tyrant, become enemies. Unable to marry Danae while Perseus is present, Polydectes sends him on the almost impossible task of obtaining the head of a much feared female monster, the Medusa or Gorgon, whose gaze can turn humans to stone. With divine help he succeeds. While returning, he rescues the young woman Andromeda from a sea-dragon and takes her back with him. Upon arrival, he finds his mother in hiding from Polydectes, who is now her husband, and who has been treating her violently. Perseus turns him to stone by means of the severed head. His mother rejoices at his victory, and approves his marriage to Andromeda. Later, he does indeed kill Acrisius, throwing a discus at him by accident in the public games. This story might serve as an example of the kind of narrative known as *hero myth*.

Here, then, we have four main kinds of myth: fertility myth, creation myth, deliverance myth and hero myth. Our purpose in this book, however, is not only to understand the significance of such stories, but also to trace their persistence, as they continue to be retold in novels, plays, poems and films with which we may already be familiar. So let us move straight on to another story, this time from early modern England.

Prospero, duke of Milan, is deposed by his brother Antonio, who puts him and his baby daughter Miranda to sea in a rotten boat. Fortunately, they land safely on an island, where Prospero trains himself to become a magician. He frees an 'airy spirit', Ariel, from the tree where he has been imprisoned by Sycorax the witch, and he subordinates the witch's monstrous son, Caliban. Having acquired the magic arts, Prospero stages a shipwreck off the coast of the island, thus bringing his brother and his travelling companions into his power. Among these are Alonso, king of Naples, who helped Antonio in the act of deposition, and Alonso's son Ferdinand. The young man falls in love with Miranda, but before he can marry her he has to prove his worth by undergoing a kind of rite of initiation, which involves performing the hardest of menial tasks. Meanwhile, his father Alonso narrowly escapes murder by his own brother Sebastian, urged on by the wicked Antonio. Moreover, he and they see a banquet appear and then disappear, thanks to Ariel, who denounces them as 'three men of sin'. Finally Alonso, who has been chastened by his experiences on the island, asks and receives forgiveness from Prospero, who also extends forgiveness to his own unrepentant brother. The king's son marries the rightful duke's daughter, and the goddesses Iris, Ceres and Juno descend to perform in the wedding masque.

I have included this last example, Shakespeare's play *The Tempest* (1611), to demonstrate that the mythic and the literary are not so far apart as is often supposed. Indeed, in the chapters that follow, we will discover that 'mythology' – the body of inherited myths in any culture – is an important element of literature, and that literature is a means of extending mythology. That is, literary works may be regarded as 'mythopoeic', tending to create or re-create certain narratives which human beings take to be crucial to their understanding of their world. Thus cultural and literary criticism may involve 'mythography', or the interpretation of myth, given that the mythic is an important dimension of cultural and literary experience.

But for now, it is enough to recognize that the stories told above – four myths and one literary work – are both similar and dissimilar. The obviously common factor is the symbolism of the sea, in each case associated paradoxically with both death and new life – as with the Christian ritual of adult baptism, in which participants feel they are dying to their former existence and being reborn from out of the water. Such a symbol is recurrent enough to be called an 'archetype' (literally, an original image, or founding figure). Equally important, though, is the narrative variation. In the first and second stories, the protagonists are divine, and their re-emergence from the waters is a sign of power. In the third and fourth stories, the protagonists are human, though either inspired or fathered by a deity, and their re-emergence from the waters is a sign of divine approval. In the fifth narrative, the protagonists are again human, but rather more so than in the third and fourth narratives: hence we might want to concentrate much more on individual characters and their interaction.

However, it should be stressed that this kind of narrative presupposes the other kinds, and we are constantly aware of an overarching framework of fertility, cosmology, deliverance and superhuman heroism. Shakespeare's play draws its power from the existence of such paradigms, and from its imaginative reworking of their themes. Moreover, where hero myth differs from fertility, creation and deliverance in not normally being associated with any rites, if literary myth takes the form of drama, it cannot escape the suggestion of ritual. Indeed, as with *The Tempest*, it may draw our attention to the importance of ceremony, such as Ferdinand and Miranda's wedding masque. It may well incorporate primitive ritual patterns into its own structure, such as Ferdinand's rite of initiation and Alonso's process of expiation.

We have just considered four kinds of narrative which we can identify as myths, and tried to relate them briefly to a familiar literary work. It is worth anticipating here a point I will elaborate upon later: that mythographers are fond of privileging one particular example as the paradigm of one kind of myth, and more importantly, one particular kind as the paradigm of myth generally. For Sir James Frazer, fertility myth is the key to all mythologies; for Mircea Eliade, it is creation myth. Here we will try and avoid such selectivity, adopting the 'family-resemblance' approach outlined by the theologian Don Cupitt. He considers that there are so many conflicting definitions of myth – usually based on the choice of one particular example or kind – that it is least misleading to list a number of 'typical features' and then act on the assumption that a narrative is mythic if it has most, but not necessarily all, of these features. There is, in fact, no pure paradigm of myth:

> So we may say that a myth is typically a traditional sacred story of anonymous authorship and archetypal or universal significance which is recounted in a certain community and is often linked with a ritual; that it tells of the deeds of superhuman beings such as gods, demigods, heroes, spirits or ghosts; that it is set outside historical time in primal or eschatological [i.e. last, ultimate] time or in the supernatural world, or may deal with comings and goings between the supernatural world and the world of human history; that the superhuman beings are imagined in anthropomorphic [i.e. humanly formed] ways, although their powers are more than human and often the story is not naturalistic but has the fractured, disorderly logic of dreams; that the whole body of a people's mythology is often prolix [i.e. lengthy, wordy], extravagant and full of seeming inconsistencies; and finally that the work of myth is to explain, to reconcile, to guide action or to legitimate. We can add that myth-making is evidently a primal and universal function of the human mind as it seeks a more-or-less unified vision of the cosmic order, the social order, and the meaning of the individual's life. Both for society at large and for the individual, this story-generating function seems irreplaceable. The individual finds meaning in his life by making of his life a story set within a larger social and cosmic story.
>
> (Cupitt 1982: 29)

This 'family-resemblance' approach avoids the inevitable dogmatism of any mythography that insists on bringing to the fore one or other example or kind of myth, and which is determined to state its necessary features.

It is, then, advisable for the mythographer to acknowledge that his or her own chosen emphasis is only one of many. For example, though fertility myths are often linked with a ritual, not all myths are linked with a ritual; though fertility and creation myths are about gods, not all myths are about gods. Moreover, though fertility, creation and most hero myths take place outside of historical time, deliverance myth involves the fusion of myth and history, and some hero myths (the story of Odysseus, for example) have their roots in historical events (the Trojan War). Exceptions to, and contradictions of, any particular paradigm are endless.

However, according to the literary critic Kenneth Burke, there is something about human language that encourages the absolutism which Cupitt advises us to avoid. Both making myths and reading myths imply a drive towards completion, an insistence on seeing things through to as near their full development as is practicable. Burke relates this tendency to the Greek philosopher Aristotle's principle of 'entelechy', or 'actualization of potential', the process by which an acorn insists, as it were, on becoming a full-grown oak, or a child insists on becoming a mature adult. Burke's equivalent term is 'perfectionism', but he is much more sceptical about the principle than the casual reader might think. Above all, he insists that in considering myth we trace the stages by which the idea of perfection is generated and sustained. This will inevitably involve some hypothesis, since few people can claim to have been present when a myth was invented.

Thus, the first stage might be 'some material operation to be performed, such as the planting, cultivating and harvesting of crops', involving a 'strictly pragmatic use of speech', a simple 'saying' to accompany the 'doing' (such as 'Pass me those seeds'). The second stage might be the completed harvest. The third stage might be the desire to 'double' or 'round out' the experience through story and symbolism, to charge it with significance, which finds expression in myth and ritual. If the context is that of planting and reaping, then we will get fertility myth and ritual, involving a god of vegetation and a sacrifice. The fourth stage might be the designation by the community of certain 'myth men' or 'mythic specialists' (priests, for example), who conserve and communicate the myth and who supervise the ritual in its apparently pure form. Fifth, the readers of the myth, distant in time and space from its creators, might take the myth to be the complete answer to their theoretical problems. Thus for both originators and interpreters, myth might offer, for the duration of the narrative, not just an effective narrative, but an approximation to totality (Burke 1971: 100–5).

Burke does not argue against this hypothetical process, but reminds us that it is usually a good idea when dealing with a myth to consider what it is 'doing' as well as what it is 'saying': that is, to bear in mind the pragmatic impulse which would have occasioned it in the first place. The same applies when we are dealing with an interpretation of myth: if the interpreter has decided in advance one dominant meaning of myth, then she has projected a certain idea of perfection onto material that may have more practical functions. But then, all this is to be expected, and to be understood rather than condemned outright, for the human being is 'the symbol-using animal' who, as such, is 'goaded by the spirit of hierarchy': that is, 'moved by a sense of order', having 'the incentives of organization and status'.

Put more strongly, this same animal is 'rotten with perfection', a condition which is both a blessing and a curse. It is a blessing because it allows us to conceive of the 'perfect' season, and so the 'perfect' harvest, and so, if that is what we want, the 'perfection' of myth. It is a curse because it also allows us to conceive of the 'perfect' victim or scapegoat, and so the 'perfection' of sacrifice. Pushed further, it may result in such phenomena of our century as the 'perfect' enemy to be exterminated by the master race (as in the rhetoric of Adolf Hitler) or the construction of the 'perfect' thermonuclear warhead (Burke 1966: 15–22). Thus, the drive towards completion and unity can create not only powerfully imaginative stories, but also systematic violence. Myth may imply totality, but 'perfectionism' is to be resisted where it becomes totalitarian.

So far we have given examples of kinds of myth, each of which may serve as a definitive paradigm, and gone on to address the question of perfection. But there is a third aspect to be considered, perhaps less sceptically than the first two – that of possibility. Here we take our cue from the philosopher Paul Ricoeur, who argues that we must go beyond the modern view of myth as 'false explanation' to a sense of its 'exploratory significance and its contribution to understanding'. He speaks of the 'symbolic function' of myth, its power of discovery and revelation. Though he agrees with Burke that the impetus of myth can be explained, he does not agree with the more usual assumption of the modern age, that myth as such can be explained away. For its purpose may always exceed its origin; as a stimulus to speculation, it is a genuine 'dimension of modern thought' (Ricoeur 1967: 5). Moreover, myth may imply a hierarchy, but it also implies a horizon: it is 'a disclosure of unprecedented worlds, an opening on to other *possible* worlds which transcend the established limits of our *actual* world' (Ricoeur 1991: 490). In other words, while myth may be paradigmatic, and while it may imply a given social and cosmic order, or perfection, it also carries with it a promise of another mode of existence entirely, a possible way of being just beyond the present time and place. It is not only foundational (as in fertility and creation narratives), but also liberating (as in deliverance and in many heroic and literary narratives).

THE MYTH OF MYTHLESSNESS

Paradigm, perfection and possibility: these, then, are three terms to bear in mind when approaching myth. But the third raises in turn another issue, for Ricoeur is only having to defend myth because it is being attacked. In short, he is countering that movement known as 'demythologization'. We usually associate this with modernity, but as Jean-Pierre Vernant explains, it goes back a good deal further:

> The concept of myth that we have inherited from the Greeks belongs, by reason of its origins and history, to a tradition of thought peculiar to Western civilisation in which myth is defined in terms of what is not myth, being opposed to reality (myth is fiction) and, secondly, to what is rational (myth is absurd). If the development of the study of myth in modern times is to be understood it must be considered in the context of this line of thought and tradition.
>
> (Vernant 1982: 186)

It was the second opposition, that of myth and rationality, which proved the more decisive. 'Myth' originally meant 'speech' or 'word', but in time what the Greeks called *mythos* was separated out from, and deemed inferior to, *logos*. The former came to signify fantasy; the latter, rational argument. This process was a tortuous one, but the result was crucial:

> Between the eighth and fourth centuries B.C. a whole series of interrelated conditions caused a multiplicity of differentiations, breaks and internal tensions within the mental universe of the Greeks which were responsible for distinguishing the domain of myth from other domains: the concept of myth peculiar to classical antiquity thus became clearly defined through the setting up of an opposition between *muthos* [sic] and *logos*, henceforth seen as separate and contrasting terms.
>
> (Vernant 1982: 187)

However, we are not to infer that late antiquity witnessed a wholesale demythologization. The need for myth was clearly evident in the 'higher' religions, as we can tell from their numerous narratives of creation, fertility and (in the case of Judaism) deliverance. Moreover, if there was an attempt by classical Greek philosophy to distinguish itself from myth, it was ambivalent: Plato is justly famous for his fables (one of which will feature in Chapter 4).

It was during the Enlightenment, that glorification of reason which dominated the later seventeenth and early eighteenth centuries in Europe, that a systematic attempt was made to explain away mythology. But demythologization also enjoyed a revival in the twentieth century. The German theologian Rudolf Bultmann (1884–1976) wanted to rescue the Christian Bible, which was for him the scripture of the very highest religion, from the misconceptions and fantasies of a 'pre-scientific' outlook. What he advised was, first recognizing the debt which St Paul and the Gospel-writers owed to mythology, then separating out the saving message or *kerygma* of Jesus Christ hidden beneath or behind it.

In his long essay, 'New Testament and Mythology', Bultmann explains that the mythic cosmos informing the Epistles and the Gospels is a 'three-storied structure', consisting of a heaven above, a hell below and an earth in the middle:

> The earth is the scene of the supernatural activity of God and his angels on the one hand, and of Satan and his demons on the other. These supernatural forces intervene in the course of nature and in all that men think and will and do.
>
> (Bultmann 1953: 1)

Like Burke, Bultmann emphasizes the hierarchical aspect of mythic thinking; but unlike Burke, he thinks it can be disposed of. Modern humanity does not need to think in terms of a cosmic battle between God and Satan. Of course, to be fair to Bultmann, he is not simply repudiating *mythos* in the name of *logos:* rather, he is updating it in order that the *Logos,* the Word of God, is not obscured. That is, he is seeking to translate the mythological content of the Gospels into modern, existential meaning. The *kerygma,* the hidden message concerning the *Logos,* is what matters, and the narrative medium must be rendered in non-narrative, immediate terms for it to speak anew to the individual Christian of today. Thus, what we end up with is an imaginatively impoverished text, consisting of only what accords neatly with the modern reader's worldview.

Only a year or two after a theologian had been arguing for an attitude of suspicion towards ancient myth, a poet was expressing his distaste for that literary legacy which he called the 'myth-kitty'. His approach to the writing of poetry may be seen to parallel Bultmann's approach to the reading of scripture. The idea is to achieve authenticity, whether as writer or as reader, beyond inherited associations: 'As a guiding principle I believe that every poem must be its own sole freshly created universe, and therefore have no belief in "tradition" or a common myth kitty or casual allusions in poems to other poems . . .' (Larkin 1983: 79).

However, the interesting, and endearing, thing about Philip Larkin is that as poet he rarely practises what he preaches. We may note how often his poems culminate in a mood of extreme yearning for some saving paradigm which has been sanctioned by tradition. 'The Whitsun Weddings' begins as a matter-of-fact observation of young couples boarding the train for their honeymoons, but ends by invoking the spirit of fertility, from which the speaker feels painfully alienated – the sexual image of 'an arrow-shower' merging with the prospect of 'rain' (Larkin 1988: 116). The short lyric 'The Trees' makes the same appeal to the fertility paradigm, only more explicitly. The speaker, conscious of growing older, wants to believe that the trees signify regeneration, that they are urging us to 'Begin afresh, afresh, afresh' (Larkin 1988: 166). Here the fertility overlaps with the creation paradigm, by which a new world is felt to begin. In 'High Windows' the latter dominates: disgusted by the shallow pleasures of this world, the speaker seems to ask to be lifted up into a higher realm. The cosmology here is spatial, indeed hierarchical: the 'thought of high windows' implies, beyond the 'sun-comprehending glass' a 'deep blue air' which, being 'nowhere' on this earth, is 'endless' (Larkin 1988: 165).

Accepting Proust's observation that the only paradise is indeed the one that has been lost, it would not perhaps be inappropriate to regard Larkin's poetry as mythic in the sense of seeking to evoke a desired plenitude of being. It is about the lack of the sacred, the desire for totality. It is haunted by what Larkin himself names in another poem 'The Importance of Elsewhere'. It reeks of myth as surely as the kind of allusive writing, so circumspect about tradition, that he explicitly repudiates. Mythology informs his poetry in the form of absence. Where he appears to be expressing himself directly in the first person on a personal matter, he is really reproducing an inherited narrative of longing. Myth and mythopoeia have survived the individual attempt at demythologization.

If we need a phrase to sum up the error of modernity, represented here by Bultmann and (as critic) by Larkin, we might do worse than use that of Robert Jewett and John Shelton Lawrence: 'the myth of mythlessness'. By this they mean the unexamined belief which arose in the Enlightenment and which still survives: the belief that humanity has successfully transcended the need for mythical forms of thought (Jewett and Lawrence 1977: 250). This arrogant view, already thrown into doubt by Cupitt, Burke and Ricoeur, will be further challenged in the chapters that follow.

PART I

Reading myth

INTRODUCTION TO PART I

It is always possible to read a literary or cultural text for its mythic interest. This inevitably presupposes that other texts are of related interest, since one is chiefly involved in tracing commonly accepted paradigms. Comparison and contrast thus come into play. But, of course, these activities in turn depend on how one reads myth in the first place: depend, that is, on which paradigms are of interest, and on how to interpret them. What is called 'myth criticism' is inseparable from what is called 'mythography'. The latter has usually been a matter of giving priority to one particular paradigm; here I will be drawing attention to the implications of doing so.

In this part, I offer an exercise in myth criticism which begins and ends with Francis Ford Coppola's film about the Vietnam war, *Apocalypse Now* (1979). By the logic just outlined, we will find that, rather than inviting a lengthy and detailed analysis, this work will soon lead us to others. For we cannot understand *Apocalypse Now* as a mythic text unless we refer it back to *The Golden Bough*; and it is almost impossible to deal with Frazer's major work of mythography in this context without referring to the poem on which it had the most famous influence, Eliot's *The Waste Land* (1922). Nor can the latter be situated without taking note of Eliot's own case for 'the mythical method'; which in turn makes more sense when we juxtapose it with the mythopoeic programme of his contemporary, Edgell Rickword.

Rickword's interest in the Symbolist poet and visionary, Arthur Rimbaud, connects him with Jim Morrison, lyricist of the Doors. Moreover, the presence of their music on the soundtrack of *Apocalypse Now* invites us to ponder the relation between contemporary popular culture and mythopoeia. And by connotation our enquiry will extend to encompass also Michael Herr's *Dispatches,* which explores the Vietnam war as a myth, and the theories of Mircea Eliade, which help situate both Eliot and Morrison.

Eventually, we will return to where we started, with *Apocalypse Now*, this time concentrating on the significance of its title. This will necessitate a brief account of the Book of Revelation and its influence. That will take us to the end of Part I, and in Part II we will reconsider some of the theoretical issues raised in a wider historical perspective. We will move from 'reading myth' to 'mythic reading': that is, we will make explicit the intimate connection between 'mythography', the interpretation of myth, and 'mythopoeia', the making of myths.

Broadly, Chapter 1 will focus on the paradigm of fertility myth, as expounded by Frazer, and on the way it is put at the service of a particular view of hierarchy in the poetry and criticism of Eliot. In Chapter 2 we will consider the resonance of the paradigm of creation myth, as expounded by Eliade; but we will approach this topic dialectically, by addressing the 'chaos' which is presupposed by 'cosmos'. This dimension will be mainly represented by the poems and songs of Jim Morrison of The Doors. In Chapter 3, the paradigm will be that of the myth of deliverance, as variously expressed and explored in ancient and modern narrative, and in creative and critical work. Throughout, hero myths will be addressed where appropriate. Always the emphasis will be on the relation of all these to literary and cultural texts.

In what follows, it will be as well to bear in mind some distinctions which are normally observed in literary and cultural history: in particular, that between modernity and modernism, and that between postmodernity and postmodernism. We have already said that demythologization is associated with 'modernity'. The name for the aesthetic movement which resisted this trend is 'modernism'. Though the two terms are often used interchangeably, it makes much more sense to see them rather as dialectical opposites. Wherever myth has been pronounced dead, artists have risen up to proclaim it alive. One such was T. S. Eliot. But of course *The Waste Land* was a long time ago, and with the emergence of 'postmodernity', or 'the postmodern condition', we have witnessed, not a retreat from myth, but a much more pervasive sense of myth. Where Eliot sought to counter history by invoking antique form, for the 'postmodernist' artist such as Francis Ford Coppola the response demanded by contemporary culture is to blur the distinction between history and myth, as in *Apocalypse Now.*

1

ORDER

DYING GODS

Coppola's *Apocalypse Now* was inspired initially by Joseph Conrad's *Heart of Darkness* (1902), which indeed informs the film throughout. The narrator, in the former named Willard and in the latter Marlow, takes a terrifying river journey. In the novella this is along the Congo in the days of the imperialist scramble for Africa; in the film it is through Vietnam to Cambodia during the American war against the Vietcong. He is trying to locate a mysterious figure, in both cases called Kurtz, whose mind has apparently been deranged by his years in the wilderness. Kurtz has become the object of native worship, and has encouraged the most barbaric practices. The film goes beyond Conrad's tale in that Captain Willard of the US Army has received instructions to 'terminate with extreme prejudice' the command of Colonel Kurtz – that is, kill him – because his 'methods' are 'unsound'. In other words, his mission is the murder of a man who has set himself up as a god. This murder is performed in parallel with the natives' sacrifice of a buffalo. In both novella and film, Kurtz's last words are: 'The horror! the horror!' But where Marlow returns to England to persuade the fiancée of this 'universal genius' that his final utterance was her name, Willard leaves Kurtz's temple to be faced by his followers' bowing down before him, as the new god. Refusing this role, he leaves the settlement; the final sequence, seen over the closing credits, shows it being bombed by American helicopters.

Coppola, then, gives to Conrad's narrative the power of a mythic paradigm. Here the choice is that of fertility myth, and his guides are Sir James Frazer and Jessie L. Weston. Thus, it is no coincidence that his Kurtz, the man-god condemned to die, has in his possession those two works by them which deal with that very topic. Conveniently, when the camera pans the interior of Kurtz's temple, it lingers on these volumes, ensuring the viewer registers their relevance. They are Frazer's *The Golden Bough* and Weston's *From Ritual to Romance.* If Conrad's novella provides Coppola with his storyline, it is these exercises in mythography that provide him with his structure. We will call this the pattern of the dying and reviving god.

The Golden Bough appeared in twelve volumes between 1890 and 1915, and was subsequently abridged in one volume in 1922. Its subtitle, 'A Study in Magic and Religion', may suggest a straightforward work of documentation; but there is a lively narrative at work here. This monumental work is, one might say, structured like a detective novel, since it begins with a murder and then sets out to identify the murderer and, more importantly for Frazer, the motive and the method. Sabine McCormack, editor of an abridgement of Frazer's lengthy and tortuous account, sets the scene:

> At Nemi, near Rome, there was a shrine where, down to imperial times, Diana, goddess of woodlands and animals and giver of offspring, was worshipped with a male consort, Virbius. The rule of the shrine was that any man could be its priest, and take the title of the King of the Wood, provided he first plucked a branch – the Golden Bough – from a certain sacred tree in the temple grove and then killed the priest. This was the regular mode of succession to the priesthood. The aim of *The Golden Bough* is to answer two questions:

> why did the priest have to kill his predecessor, and why did he first have to pluck the branch? Because there is no simple answer to either question, Frazer collects and compares analogies to the custom of Nemi. For by showing that similar rules existed all over the world and throughout history, he hopes to reach an understanding of how the primitive mind works, and then to use his understanding to shed light on the rule of Nemi. In collecting analogies, Frazer does not look for total parallels, but breaks up the custom of Nemi into its component parts and examines each in turn. Indeed, one piece of evidence may be used for more than one aspect of the question.
>
> (McCormack as in Frazer 1978: 18)

Thus, Frazer's anthropology may be categorized as belonging to the 'myth and ritual' school of interpretation. As the epithet suggests, this approach to mythology explains the narrative in terms of the ceremony which, it is assumed, it either arose from or accompanied. As the kind of ceremony Frazer is most interested in is that of vegetation, the kind of myth he is most interested in is that concerning a fertility god and goddess.

Having chosen that model, he then chooses as the main example of his paradigm the Phoenician/Greek story of Adonis – which he takes to be analogous to a story that we have already encountered, that of Osiris. The myth tells us that, as a man, Adonis is mortally wounded by a wild boar, to be subsequently revived as a god by Aphrodite, the goddess of love and fertility (the Roman Venus). The idea is that she wishes to ensure that each year he will be reborn in the spring to be with her. Frazer describes the ritual interest of this story:

> At the festivals of Adonis, which were held in Western Asia and in Greek lands, the death of the god was annually mourned, with a bitter wailing, chiefly by women; images of him, dressed to resemble corpses, were carried out as to burial and then thrown into the sea or into springs; and in some places his revival was celebrated on the following day. At Alexandria images of Aphrodite and Adonis were displayed on two couches; beside them were set ripe fruits of all kinds, cakes, plants growing in flower-pots, and green bowers twined with anise. The marriage of the lovers was celebrated one day, and on the

> morrow women attired as mourners, with streaming hair and bared breasts, bore the image of the dead Adonis to the sea-shore and committed it to the waves. Yet they sorrowed not without hope, for they sang that the lost one would come back again.
>
> (Frazer 1978: 130)

The meaning of such a ritual, and such a myth, is fertility. This, as we shall see, is what links it with the rule of Nemi.

If Frazer's 'myth and ritual' theory is the basis of his anthropology, that theory is applied in a particular kind of procedure, known as the 'comparative method'. All places and times, any odd scraps of evidence of ritual practice, are grist to the mill. Material may be gleaned from ancient Greece and ancient Egypt alike, and from ancient Greece and nineteenth-century rural England alike, without bothering with detailed contextualization or reservation. Anywhere there is evidence of something like a fertility ritual (for example, an effigy thrown into a river then fished out again), the overall pattern of death and regeneration may be inferred. Frazer is, that is to say, a 'universalist': he believes that we can make comparisons across cultures because the primitive human urge to myth-making is essentially the same.

Of course, his very claim to be able to do so suggests something of the spirit of modernity. The ceremonies and stories documented belong either to our archaic past or to the residual barbarism of the 'folk' imagination. Thus, though Frazer's ostensible interest is mythographic not mythopoeic, his very condescension towards the evidence he universalizes betrays the myth at work: derived from the Enlightenment, it is the story of progress via rationality. We have already named this as the 'myth of mythlessness'. That is one paradox at the heart of Frazer's work. A related one is that, despite subscribing to his own narrative of improvement, he betrays a nostalgia for the world which produced the ceremonies and stories he recovers in such painstaking detail. That is, while Frazer's official position is something very close to positivism, envisaging humanity as having progressed from magic, through religion, and so to science, he seems almost as fascinated by what he calls the 'folly' of the first two stages as by the supposed truth of the third.

But let us be sure how 'myth and ritual' interpretation and universalist comparativism work in practice. In short, we must register Frazer's answers to Frazer's own questions. Why does the King of the Wood have to die? Why does the successor have to pluck the branch? After twelve volumes, we have the answers. The god, or his impersonator, has to die precisely because his business is fertility. The community depends on him, or so it believes, for its own survival. If the god does not die he cannot be reborn to fertilize the goddess, and so there will be no new crops. The underlying principle is that of magic, which for Frazer is the origin of all myth-making and all religion. Indeed, he goes further, and credits magic with the beginnings of secular authority, and so of civilization itself; not only the first priests, but the first kings were evidently magicians. The succession to the title of King of the Wood was a matter of magic, elaborated as religious ritual.

According to Frazer, at the early, magical stage of thinking, nature is conceived as an impersonal force, to be manipulated. As magic evolves into religion, nature takes on the form of anthropomorphic deities, who must be allowed full scope to exercise their powers. Everything comes to hinge on guaranteeing the god his fertility. The residual logic is twofold. By 'sympathetic' magic, the death and revival of the god parallels or, to put it more strongly, causes the renewal of the land. (Frazer compares this with the act of pouring water on the ground in order to induce rain.) By 'contagious' magic, the god becomes a 'scapegoat' figure who carries away the sterility which might otherwise blight the crops. (Strictly speaking, this is 'anti-contagious' magic. Frazer illustrates contagious magic itself by the lover winning power over the beloved by casting a spell on clippings of her hair.) The logic is foolproof. And it tells us also why the King of the Wood must pluck 'the Golden Bough'. This part of the tree, which is an oak, is clearly the mistletoe. It contains the power of Jupiter, Roman god of sky and storm, who periodically casts his full force into the tree in the course of a lightning flash. The successor to the title must pluck it in order to prove he has acquired the divine energy. It is only through this violent succession, anticipated by the violence of the thunderstorm, that the fertility of the land can be ensured. There is a magical connection between the drama of the dying and reviving god on the one hand, and the seasonal cycle on the other. The king is dead; long live the king.

If the basis of religion is the pattern of death and regeneration, then it is possible to conclude that the 'higher' faiths cannot claim exemption from this paradigm. Indeed, in the first edition of *The Golden Bough* it is quite obvious that Frazer began by regarding Jesus Christ as just another variant upon the model of the dying and reviving god. As the work progressed, however, he became increasingly evasive on this issue – as though Frazer, a mild agnostic, were fearful of excessive controversy. But the connection between fertility religion and Christianity did need spelling out, and his disciple Jessie L. Weston broached the issue directly. Or rather, she sought to demonstrate that narratives which had previously been taken to be purely Christian had in fact originated in vegetation ceremonies, or what she called 'Nature Cults'.

Reading Weston's *From Ritual to Romance* (1920), we see how Frazer's anthropology can help solve long-standing puzzles of literary interpretation – in this case, that the medieval legend of the Holy Grail is not anticipated by Christian orthodoxy:

> Some years ago, when fresh from the study of Sir J. G. Frazer's epoch-making work, *The Golden Bough*, I was struck by the resemblance existing between certain features of the Grail story, and characteristic details of the Nature Cults described. The more closely I analysed the tale, the more striking became the resemblance, and I finally asked myself whether it were not possible that in this mysterious legend – mysterious alike in its character, its sudden appearance, the importance apparently assigned to it, followed by as sudden and complete a disappearance – we might not have the confused record of a ritual, once popular, later surviving under conditions of strict secrecy?
>
> (Weston 1920: 3–4)

Weston's assumption is that the fertility ritual documented by Frazer was transformed in time into a 'Mystery Cult'. Certainly, it is true that in the centuries immediately before and after Christ, the ancient Near East and the Mediterranean region witnessed a religious displacement. The collective festival ensuring the revival of the crops, and so the survival of the community, was intermittently adapted into a new kind of ceremony. In this kind, the individual initiate sought liberation from the chains of earthly life, putting trust not in a fertility god such as Adonis or Osiris, but in a 'mystery' god such as Attis.

The story of Attis, which originated in the ancient land of Phrygia (eastwards across the Aegean Sea from Greece, and north-west of Syria), may be easily summarized. He is a shepherd driven mad by the goddess Cybele's love for him; in his frenzy he castrates himself, only to be taken up by her as her eternal consort (often depicted riding with her on a chariot drawn by lions). The cult, which spread throughout Greece and then to Rome, centred on an annual, spring ritual in honour of Attis: this would involve devotees' castrating themselves, and there would also be group flagellation by priests dressed as women. After this, the participants would celebrate the rebirth of the god. Recounted like this, the ritual seems more bizarre than that of Adonis, but Weston's main concern is that there was a much stronger emphasis on initiation. Those dedicated to Attis were distinguished from the populace generally by their willingness to emasculate themselves. In other words, there were two levels of worship: 'exoteric' (by which the community at large benefited from Attis' rebirth) and 'esoteric' (by which the chosen few participated in the secret of his divinity). In this respect, the worship of Attis brought it very close to 'the Eleusian mysteries' – Eleusis being the site of a temple in honour of Demeter, goddess of corn, where a two-stage initiation was held. The first involved symbolism of vegetation; the second took a less tangible form, but supposedly led to a profounder, more spiritual insight.

For some time, evidently, Jesus Christ was identified as a mystery god, effecting salvation on two levels. For the many he would be just another dying god of vegetation; for the few he would be the object of secret devotion. The link between the two levels would be the 'Messianic' or 'Eucharistic' feast, in which the bread and wine could be regarded not only as the harvest and the vintage, but also as spiritual nourishment. Hence the symbolism of the Grail:

> It has taken me nine or ten years longer to complete the evidence, but the chain is at last linked up, and we can now prove by printed texts the parallels existing between each and every feature of the Grail story and the recorded symbolism of the Mystery Cults. Further, we can show that between these Mystery Cults and Christianity there existed at one time a close and intimate union, such a union as of itself involved the practical assimilation of the central rite, in each case a 'Eucharistic' Feast, in which the worshippers partook of the Food of Life from the sacred vessels.
>
> (Weston 1920: 4–5)

Weston's conclusion, made with due acknowledgement to Frazer, is that the Grail legend derived from the 'Mystery Cult' just as surely as the 'Mystery Cult' derived from the 'Nature Cult'. The later literary form of romance, which in the case of the Grail narratives involved the quest of a knight for the lost cup containing Christ's sacrificial blood, was firmly rooted in fertility religion – only it had developed by way of a detour through mystery. What was constant was the idea of the body and blood of the saviour offering new life, whether the communal life of fertility or the individual life of enlightenment.

The parallel with Frazer's material is striking. We know from Frazer that there is no question that the existing King of the Wood has to be replaced by a violent usurper – probably a desperate, runaway slave – full of new potency for the fertilization of the goddess. Otherwise life will not come out of death, spring out of winter. Similarly, Weston argues, the questing knight is given a definite series of tasks in a definite order. He has to undergo terrible ordeals, such as that of the 'Chapel Perilous'. He has to find the Grail castle. He has to ask the ritual question of the chalice: 'Whom does it serve?' He has to understand the answer: that the wounded 'Fisher King' and the 'Waste Land' are one. Only by his doing so will the healing powers of the Grail be effective: the waters freed, the monarch healed and fertility restored. Finally, with the Waste Land redeemed, its ruler is able to die in peace, and the quester can become the new Fisher King.

Nor is it a matter simply of ensuring the regeneration of the land. What has ailed the king has, it seems, been a crisis of spirit, a lack of faith in the efficacy of the Grail. The successful knight, usually named Perceval or Parsifal, represents the power of innocent wisdom. He replaces Anfortas, the wounded or impotent monarch, suffering from the infirmity of misunderstanding. Thus we have glimpsed a mysterious initiation, founded in vegetation ceremony and embellished by not only the folk imagination, but also by centuries of spiritual speculation. We have moved thereby from sacred ceremony ('Ritual') to secular literature ('Romance').

Coppola's Kurtz may be understood in the light of both *The Golden Bough* and *From Ritual to Romance.* He may be identified with the ageing King of the Wood, killed by the younger man, namely Willard. However, here the usurpation does not lead to renewal; death does not lead to new life. Willard refuses the role of king, and departing from Kurtz's community, effectively gives the all-clear for its destruction. The 'myth and ritual' structure has been used, but with severe irony. Moreover, in this mythic text, the pattern does not include the goddess. If she is present at all, it is in the triple form of three *Playboy* models whose entertainment for the troops only leaves them sexually frustrated. The Vietnam war is the antithesis of fertility. As for Weston's questing knight and Fisher King: Willard and Kurtz may play these parts, the former undergoing all manner of ordeals during his quest for Kurtz's temple and the latter displaying all the signs of spiritual sickness; but again, no succession takes place, and from Willard's traumatized expression at the end of the film, no enlightenment has been gained. Again, the mythic material is used ironically. Yet the irony, judging by the cult status of Coppola's film, only intensifies the mythic appeal. One meets few devotees of the film who are also advocates of demythologization.

WORDS AND THE WORD

> I decided that the ending could be the classic myth of the murderer who goes up the river, kills the king and then himself becomes the king – it's the Fisher King, from The Golden Bough. Somehow it's the granddaddy of all myths. . . . [In] reading some of The Golden Bough and then From Ritual to Romance I found a lot concerning

> that theme. T. S. Eliot's The Wasteland also seemed so apt for the conclusion of the story.
>
> (Coppola, cited in Cowie 1990: 123)

Whatever the confusions in Coppola's acknowledgement of influence, quoted by Peter Cowie in his study of the director, this recollection of making the film is a useful indicator of the link he had understood between Frazer, Weston and Eliot before finding an appropriately mythic conclusion for *Apocalypse Now*. Here we will not be trying to demonstrate the influence of Eliot on Coppola, which is evident enough from Kurtz's recitation from 'The Hollow Men' in the darkness of his temple, but simply making sure that *The Waste Land* is understood in its own right, as the poem at the heart of modernist mythopoeia. Then, when we come to consider Coppola's film again, at the end of Part I, we will be in a position to appreciate how Eliot's project differs, despite its undoubted influence, from the more diffuse sense of myth that characterizes postmodernism.

Eliot, taking his cue perhaps from Conrad, argued that literature had to face the 'horror' of modern life. And, since 'horror' could only be appreciated intermittently, it had to alternate with 'boredom'. But beyond both, there was a need for what he called 'glory' (Eliot 1964: 106). The work which best illustrates this thinking is *The Waste Land* itself. Its irony, its depiction of 'boredom' and 'horror', only articulates the loss of, and need for, 'glory'. It is a poem which, despite its reputation for obscurity and experimentation, is thoroughly informed by what Burke calls 'perfectionism': it centres on the need for hierarchy, completion, order. The means to this for Eliot is the paradigm of fertility. As he himself confirms in the notes accompanying the poem, it is informed by the 'myth and ritual' school of interpretation. He explicitly acknowledges his debt to *The Golden Bough* and *From Ritual to Romance*, the latter in particular suggesting not only 'the title', but also 'the plan and a good deal of the incidental symbolism'. He adds that anyone acquainted with Frazer's and Weston's books 'will immediately recognise in the poem certain references to vegetation ceremonies' (Eliot 1963: 80).

Perhaps we should emphasize here the deliberateness of the poet's choice of paradigm and of mythographic approach. Eliot, whose interest in anthropology had begun at university, knew that the comparative, universalist method employed in *The Golden Bough* only represented one possible mode of interpretation. He was fully aware of new work carried out in the area of ethnography, that is, the recording and analysis of a particular culture, including its myths and rituals, based on field research. Indeed, in the year of the publication of *The Waste Land*, there also appeared an important ethnographic work by Bronislaw Malinowksi, *Argonauts of the Western Pacific*. This was self-evidently the product of direct experience and documentation, and so ran contrary to the armchair expertise of Frazer. *Argonauts* thus focused the growing disenchantment with Frazerian comparativism, now found by many anthropologists to be too generalizing, too insensitive to specific communities.

However, in various papers, articles and reviews in the years before *The Waste Land*, and even as late as his *Notes towards the Definition of Culture* (1948), Eliot resisted the cultural particularism of this modern 'functionalist' anthropology, as it was called. Where it referred to 'cultures' and the way they worked, he inferred from *The Golden Bough* the existence of 'culture', essential and universal. It was the unifying pattern that attracted him in Frazer's enterprise. The regrettably evolutionist proposal of an advance beyond magic and religion to science could be discarded, leaving only the idea of a global myth the 'roots' of which were the basis of a collective legacy. Devoid of such a paradigm, the imaginative logic of the poem would lack its resonance. The cultural breakdown which it conveys could not be recognized as such without a basis of primitive harmony. Modernism, unlike modernity, needed its 'roots'.

Informed by the 'myth and ritual' school, then, *The Waste Land* is, despite appearances, a story; and the tale it tells is a deliberate fusing and updating of two other stories – that of the dying and reviving god (Frazer), and that of the quest for the Grail (Weston). Once this is realized, apparently disconnected images and incidents assume their mythic meaning; negative phenomena imply positive essences; confusion implies the need for enlightenment. However, the 'glory' of reviving god and of completed quest remains tragically elusive.

The unnamed narrator glimpses, early in the poem, a vision of beauty associated with a 'hyacinth girl' and a 'hyacinth garden'. He feels himself to be looking into 'the heart of light, the silence' (Eliot 1963: 64). In seeking to regain this vision, and to understand its meaning, he is forced to confront also the vision of Conrad's *Heart of Darkness*, of alternating 'boredom' and 'horror'. Much of the poem takes place in the wilderness and the metropolis, each symbolizing the Waste Land of modernity. The question implicitly posed is, in Frazer's perspective, what sacrifice could redeem this arid world and reaffirm the fertility cycle? In Weston's, it is a matter of whether the quester, our unnamed protagonist, can reaffirm the sacred link with the Grail and so cure the Fisher King, in a land which does not even know itself to be waste.

Taking Frazer's perspective first, we may say that the reader of the poem is left in no doubt that the fertility god has died. But the community depicted here is hardly ready for his revival. Spring brings only anxiety not rejoicing. April is 'the cruellest month' precisely because it is then that 'lilacs' emerge from 'the dead land', disturbing the habitual death-in-life of the inhabitants, winter having covered earth in 'forgetful snow'. These people may well be asked what 'roots' they know, for they are, spiritually, in a desert (Eliot 1963: 63). But they can give no answer: the 'crowds of people walking round in a ring' glimpsed by the clairvoyant Madame Sosostris are oblivious to the need for true ceremony (Eliot 1963: 64). Theirs is an empty ritual. A corpse is buried in a garden, suggesting a link with the ancient cult of Osiris, but there is no mention of any rebirth. 'Phlebas the Phoenician' drowns, suggesting a link with the cults of both Osiris and Adonis, but the waters of death are not transformed into the waters of life (Eliot 1963: 75).

As for Weston's perspective, the role of the Fisher King has been denied and degraded. Where once the fish symbolized fertility – abundant life brought out of the waters – it is now associated chiefly with desolation. The protagonist recalls fishing on a winter evening in 'the dull canal', musing upon 'the king my father's death' (Eliot 1963: 70). Again, even at the very end of the poem, the Grail monarch is still waiting to be healed, as he sits on the shore 'Fishing, with the arid plain behind me' (Eliot 1963: 79).

However, to remain with Weston's perspective, it should not escape our attention that, in the case of the phrase 'the king my father's death' (in the original, 'the King my father's wreck'), the notes refer us to *The Tempest*, the mythopoeic work of literature which I referred to in the introductory chapter, and which has much in common with Grail romance. Like Perceval, Prince Ferdinand at this moment of the play (Act I, Scene 2) may be seen as on a quest: ultimately, though he does not know it, for his bride Miranda and for the inheritance of Prospero's dukedom; immediately for King Alonso, his father, whom he believes to have been drowned. No sooner has he uttered his words, however, than he hears Ariel's 'ditty'. Significantly, though the 'airy spirit' sings of death by water, he also sings of a 'sea-change / Into something rich and strange' (I. ii. 490–1). This cryptic promise will be fulfilled when Ferdinand does indeed find his father Alonso again, alive and very much changed.

Again, though Eliot's quester does not discover the healing knowledge of the Grail, the symbolism is a consistent and informing presence. Further references to the legend, such as a quotation from Verlaine's poem 'Parsifal', though juxtaposed ironically with the bawdy refrain of a music-hall ballad, do remind us that in the traditional romance the king is cured. Though we have lost all assurance of that healing moment, and though we do not even hear the ritual question of the Grail, we may begin to intuit the distant beginning of some new way of life. Indeed, this is suggested, albeit desperately, by the words quoted from the Book of Isaiah: 'Shall I at least set my lands in order?' (Eliot 1963: 79).

Returning to Frazer's perspective: though the poem offers no decisive transition from dying god to reviving god, the invocation of effective sacrifice is too strong for the poem to be merely a documentation of 'boredom' and 'horror'. Though the inhabitants of the Waste Land are oblivious to the need for 'vegetation ceremonies', *The Waste Land* itself is obsessed with them. Though Madame Sosostris cannot find in her Tarot pack the card of The Hanged Man, the sign of sacrifice, the noted absence of the card has its resonance. Moreover, in both Frazer's and Weston's perspectives, the Tarot image suggests not only a 'Life Cult' but also a 'Mystery Cult', and not only a 'Mystery Cult' but also Christianity itself. Thus later in the poem, we hear of 'frosty silence in the gardens' and 'agony in stony places', of 'shouting' and 'crying' in 'Prison and palace': allusions to the crucifixion narrative. Though the inhabitants of the Waste Land can only reflect that 'He who is living is now dead', thus failing to understand that what matters about the crucifixion is the resurrection which follows it, the Gospel story is still able to be invoked to telling effect (Eliot 1963: 76).

Eliot's poem, then, while conveying 'boredom' and 'horror', gains its power from its reminder of the 'glory' which has been lost and which needs to be regained. According to Burke's thinking, this ideal is only implicit in language itself, which is 'rotten with perfection'. More particularly, it is the very nature of 'words' to suggest the one, perfect, universal 'Word' (Burke 1970: 7). And indeed, *The Waste Land*, on first sight a bewildering array of words, does insistently gesture towards some absolute, if absent, Word. By the end of the poem it has even been named: it is the Sanskrit 'Shantih', translated into Christian terms by the notes as 'The Peace which passeth understanding' (Eliot 1963: 86). Having named it, the poem invites us to lament the very distance between words and Word which it enacts. It is thus that the poem itself stands as a tragic indictment of an age that seems content to leave the Word unheard. It is against the spirit of that age that the poem works: despite its demonstration of chaos, *The Waste Land* is really about the need for order. It uses the paradigm of fertility as the framework for a transcendent vision. For, no matter how lacking the age may seem in hierarchical principles and in ideas of perfection, the aesthetic ordering of words which the poem achieves is intended to stand as a reminder of the power of the all-embracing Word.

THE MYTHICAL METHOD

Eliot's quest for a saving paradigm persisted. Reviewing James Joyce's recently published novel in 1923, in an article entitled

'*Ulysses*, Order and Myth', he reflected on the possibilities of 'the mythical method':

> In using the myth, in manipulating a continuous parallel between contemporaneity and antiquity, Mr Joyce is pursuing a method which others might pursue after him. They will not be imitators, any more than the scientist who uses the discoveries of Einstein in pursuing his own, independent investigations. It is simply a way of controlling, of ordering, of giving a shape and a significance to the immense panorama of futility and anarchy which is contemporary history. . . . Instead of the narrative method, we may now use the mythical method. It is, I seriously believe, a step toward making the modern world possible for art. . . . And only those who have won their own discipline in secret and without aid, in a world which offers very little assistance to that end, can be of any use in furthering this advance.
>
> (Eliot 1975: 177–8)

Before considering how far this does justice to Joyce's achievement, we might pause to note the continuity between this review and a slightly earlier, and seemingly unrelated, article. In 'Tradition and the Individual Talent' (1919) the same concepts are evident, though they are couched in slightly different terms. Thus we are told that 'tradition' involves 'aesthetic, not merely historical matters'. Only by converting historical experience into art, and then the sequence of works of art into a canon, do we become aware 'not only of the pastness of the past, but of its presence'. For the 'existing monuments' form 'an ideal order', which is modified slightly every time a fresh artefact appears and is added to it; 'and this is conformity between the old and the new.'

According to Eliot, though this or that poem appears in time, 'tradition' is best depicted as a spatial, a 'simultaneous', arrangement of 'monuments'. He implies that the effect for the contemporary reader is that of walking round what André Malraux, and after him Donald Davie, will call 'the imaginary museum'. Moreover, the task of 'the individual talent' is not to produce an 'expression' of 'emotion' and 'personality', but to attain 'impersonality'. The poet must serve 'the mind of Europe', which is 'much more important than his own private mind': 'it is a mind which . . . abandons nothing *en route,* which does not superannuate either Shakespeare, or Homer, or the rock drawing of the Magdalenian draughtsmen' (Eliot 1975: 37–44). The contemporary artist, the artist working in or around 1920, must treat as contemporary not only the author of *The Tempest* (early seventeenth century), but also the author of the *Odyssey* (eighth century BC), and must treat them both as contemporaries of the anonymous cave artists of the later Palaeolithic period. For what matters is the 'simultaneous' and 'ideal order', which transcends history.

Thus, Eliot is using the word 'myth' in his *Ulysses* review as synonymous with the word 'tradition' in this earlier article. The fact that the common denotation is not immediately obvious only helps to render the critical rhetoric more effective. It seems only too appropriate, then, that Joyce is praised for having applied the inherited form of Homer's text to the all too diverse material of the world around him. He has, we are persuaded, managed to comprehend the chaos of modernity by utilizing an ancient paradigm. That is, he has invoked the spatial, impersonal tradition rather than expressed his temporal, personal interests. It would be wrong to infer, though, that Eliot has totally missed the point of Joyce's enterprise. The Homeric model is there, and the novel would not have its 'shape' without it. *Ulysses* certainly does match the *Odyssey* episode by episode; and though Eliot does not give examples, the alert reader soon recognizes the parallels.

Homer's text, itself loosely based on hero myths of early antiquity (specifically, the era which saw the rise of the warrior class), tells the following story. Odysseus, ruler of Ithaca, has been helping in the Greek army's siege of Troy. His quest is to return home and to reaffirm his identity as a man, a king and a husband. His wife Penelope is being pestered by suitors who wish her to declare herself a widow and marry one of them. His son Telemachus, believing him to be alive, sets out to find him even as he himself makes his journey. It is while Odysseus rests *en route* at the court of King Alcinous of the Phaeacians that he recounts his more marvellous adventures. These include: the encounter with the monstrous one-eyed Cyclops; the narrow escape from the charms of Circe, who can turn men into swine; the visit to Hades, or the Underworld; and the evasion of the Sirens, whose charming song can beguile sailors to their death. Eventually, Odysseus returns to Ithaca, where he is reunited with Telemachus, who has also come home. He overcomes the suitors and is restored to the bed of Penelope.

Apart from using the Roman version of Odysseus' name, Ulysses, Joyce keeps assiduously close to Homer. The Cyclops becomes the aggressive, one-eyed landlord of a Dublin tavern; Circe's island becomes a modern brothel; Hades becomes an urban graveyard; the Sirens become barmaids. As for Odysseus' desire to be reunited with his son Telemachus, that is realized in the encounter towards the end of the novel between Leopold Bloom, the commercial failure, and young Stephen Daedalus, the frustrated artist. Here are two men cast adrift in the modern metropolis, finding archetypal status in their meeting, informed as it is by the Homeric context.

Eliot wants to go further than noting parallels, however. He claims that Joyce is not here merely making clever connections, but imposing an order on 'the immense panorama of futility and anarchy which is contemporary history'. In other words, 'the mythical method', made possible only by a discipline both severe and 'secret', is the necessary counterpoint to the vulgar chaos of the twentieth century. Again, we may recall parallel phrasing from 'Tradition and the Individual Talent': 'ideal order'; 'presence' of the 'past'; 'conformity between the old and the new'; 'the mind of Europe'; 'impersonality' (as opposed to 'emotion' and 'personality').

It should be obvious, then, that Eliot, in reviewing Joyce's novel, is effectively describing and commending his own poetic practice in *The Waste Land.* If for Homer we substitute the material documented by Frazer and Weston, then 'certain references to vegetation ceremonies' are what give 'a shape and a significance' to the disorder discovered. In justifying himself, he attributes to the author of *Ulysses* an affinity with his own austere principles. Whether the paradigm is heroism or fertility, it offers a means to perfection.

Two reservations have to be made, however. First, Eliot uses Joyce's fiction as the opportunity to oppose 'the mythical method' to 'the narrative method'. He assumes that what matters most about *Ulysses* is the paradigm inherited from Homer rather than the actual tale it tells, the protagonist of which is a modest middle-aged Irishman and not a Greek warrior. That is, Eliot privileges form over matter, structure over story. It is as if he has forgotten what the classical Greek philosopher Aristotle (in other respects a strong influence upon him) meant when in his *Poetics* he used *mythos* in the sense of 'emplotment'. As Paul Ricoeur explains, this means 'both "fable" (in the sense of imaginary story) and "plot" (in the sense of well-constructed history)'. He adds: 'What Aristotle calls plot is not a static structure but an operation, an integrative process which . . . confers on the narrated story an identity one can call dynamic' (Ricoeur 1991: 426). It is precisely this 'dynamic' identity which Eliot overlooks, thus failing to give due weight to the dialectical nature of plot, which mediates between the temporal flow of events and the human need for hierarchy, stability, order. Eliot wants only the order, and tries to abstract the 'pure' myth informing Joyce's novel from the given sequence of events and interaction of characters. In attempting this, Eliot is treating both the *Odyssey* and *Ulysses* in the same static and externalizing manner as Bultmann treats the Bible. Only, where the latter wants to separate out the doctrine from the narrative, the *kerygma* or *logos* from the Gospel *mythos,* Eliot wants to distinguish myth proper from the mere telling of tales. He takes the notion of myth as paradigm to the point of an arid formalism. The *mythos* of Homer becomes the *logos* which Joyce is credited with forcing upon his material. Thus Eliot effects his own kind of demythologization even as he proclaims the indispensability of myth; and in the process Joyce's novel is enlisted for most un-Joycean aims.

The second reservation concerns the opposition of myth and history, of 'shape and significance' on the one hand and 'futility and anarchy' on the other. Put simply, this is a simple misreading of the novel. It is as if Eliot has attributed the sentiment of Stephen Daedalus – 'History is a nightmare from which I am trying to awake' – to his creator. The most superficial acquaintance with Joyce's novel will reveal that Dublin, which indeed may be said to represent history, is very far from being chaotic. On the contrary, its network of churches and brothels, libraries and bars, may be said to cater very efficiently for the needs of its citizens. What they themselves do may border on confusion, but it would misrepresent the modern metropolis to say that in itself it embodies 'anarchy and futility'.

Consider in this context the 'Ithaca' or 'catechism' episode, in which Bloom draws water from the tap to make cocoa for himself and Stephen Daedalus at the end of their adventurous day. The water, we are told, flowed

> from Roundwood reservoir in county Wicklow of a cubic capacity of 2,400 million gallons, percolating through a subterranean aqueduct of filter mains of single and double pipeage constructed at an initial plant cost of £5 per linear yard.
>
> (Joyce 1960: 782–3)

As Fredric Jameson has noted, here is order, and here is mythic power: 'the transformation of Nature by human and collective praxis' (Jameson 1982: 140–1). That is, to adapt Eliot's terms, the 'order and myth' in this chapter of *Ulysses* are focused on a revelation concerning the hidden effects of human labour, deliberately invoked by the apparent banality of the way water reaches the average Dublin house, rather than on the empty form of 'a shape and a significance' imposed from above.

The only human labour which Eliot in his review wishes to connect with myth is aesthetic. For him, 'the mythical method' is 'a step toward making the modern world possible for art'. There is his agenda in brief. 'The modern world', a world of 'futility and anarchy', is what is given. It must await 'art', identified with the 'ideal order' of 'myth', if it is to be redeemed. The possibility that human life is already structured, and already symbolic, before the artist begins his or her work, is precluded. It is as if mythopoeia, the capacity to produce myths and to provide a model of the world, belongs only to an exclusive elite. We may, of course, posit the emergence in every community of one particular 'myth man' or 'mythic specialist', to use Kenneth Burke's terms. But, as Burke insists, we misconceive this role if we take the specialization for granted, and forget the source of its power: the general, pragmatic need to 'complete' or 'perfect' crucial events such as planting and harvesting, by way of symbolism and story (Burke 1971: 103–5).

In this elitism, which goes with his aestheticism or formalism, Eliot is a representative figure. His is the voice of a distinct, uncompromising strain in modernism. His 'mythical method' is one way – one extreme way – of expressing an urge which a poem by his contemporary Wallace Stevens presents paradoxically as the 'blessed rage for order'. By contrasting the ways in which Stevens and Eliot exemplify this 'rage', we might manage, provisionally, to place the latter's mythic interests. In his poem, 'The Idea of Order at Key West', Stevens begins by contrasting the strength of the sea with the fragility of a woman's song. By the end he has demonstrated that, if we need the sea, or reality, for the imagination to work upon, then so does the sea attain consciousness, as it were, through the human ability to 'sing', to produce art (Stevens 1986: 65–6).

Stevens' intuition might be seen as a reaffirmation of a theme in Romantic poetry. After all, Wordsworth and Coleridge made the relationship between reality and imagination the very subject of their verse. In *The Prelude* and 'Kubla Khan', in odes such as 'Intimations of Immortality' and 'Dejection', they sought to vindicate the ideal of poetry as illumination rather than mere reflection, and the poet as visionary rather than scribe. Stevens in 'Key West' is perhaps benefiting from this legacy, and within the poem endorsing their faith. In his whole body of work, he seeks to construct 'the Supreme Fiction', the synthesis of reality and imagination in one great symbolic narrative. Never to be completed, and important mainly for its celebration of the very world we inhabit, this speculative myth challenges dead doctrines and rigid hierarchies, clearing a space for culture and nature to meet. For 'the great poems of heaven and hell have been written and the great poem of the earth remains to be written' (Stevens 1984: 142).

But though 'rage for order' may describe Eliot's own poetic effort, his 'mythical method' is meant to be a programme as far as possible from that of 'the visionary company' (to use Hart Crane's phrase). It seems to involve little trust in that ultimate accord of the world and the soul which Coleridge believed possible through the 'shaping spirit of imagination' (Coleridge 1971: 106). This dialectic of imagination and reality is not Eliot's business at this stage of his development. His 'ideal order' invokes the classical tradition, or at least one austere version of it, rather than the Romantic. In his 'neo-classicism', nature is to be revered only in so far as it is formalized, and no harmony is to be anticipated such as Coleridge desired. This order underpins his distinct complex of conservatism, pronounced by himself on the occasion of his conversion to Christianity in 1928 in the following words: 'classicist in literature, royalist in politics, and anglo-catholic in religion' (Eliot 1970: 7). Here we see exemplified what Burke calls 'perfectionism': for Eliot, art and history alike demand fulfilment in hierarchy; words demand fulfilment in the Word.

2

CHAOS

THE COMIC VISION

Having identified the paradigm on which Eliot deliberately based his particular idea of perfection, and indicated how he moved from the story of the dying god to the formulation of an aesthetic, political and religious doctrine, we will perhaps be entitled to some scepticism about his claim to represent universal order. We might feel entitled to replace his phrase, '*the* mythical method', with the more accurate one, '*a* mythical method'. Modernism did not produce just one distinct brand of mythopoeia. Here I will contrast Eliot's tragic vision with the comic vision of a poet and critic who consciously defined his own enterprise against that of Eliot – namely Edgell Rickword.

Perhaps we might situate this contrast by citing Kenneth Burke again. In his 'Definition of Man', he reminds us of Aristotle's designation of the human being as 'the laughing animal'. Burke goes further: 'mankind's only hope is a cult of comedy'. For: 'The cult of tragedy is too eager to help out with the holocaust. And in the last analysis, it is too pretentious to allow for the proper recognition of our animality' (Burke 1966: 20). Cryptic as these observations are, they may offer a clue as to why Rickword set himself the task of exposing what he saw as Eliot's reactionary elitism. Two kinds of modernism, and two understandings of myth, were involved.

When Eliot founded his long-running journal, *The Criterion* (1922–39), he did so – as his editorials constantly reminded his readers – to defend a classical ideal of 'reason'. In this endeavour, he was frequently challenged by a short-lived rival magazine, *The Calendar of Modern Letters* (1925–7), which persistently referred to Eliot's 'reason' as just another word for 'repression'. It accused him of adopting a defensive aesthetic position, which was the complement of a 'reactionary' political and theological position. The journal's main editor was the English poet and critic, Edgell Rickword. He was also the author of *Rimbaud: The Boy and the Poet* (1924), which was the first critical biography of the rebellious Symbolist published in English.

Two years after '*Ulysses*, Order and Myth' appeared, *The Calendar* printed Rickword's own essay 'The Returning Hero'. There would seem to have been a connection, in that the project advocated by Rickword almost wilfully contradicts that of Eliot. 'A Hero would seem to be due', he declares, an 'exhaustively disillusioned' one 'who has yet so much vitality' as to create 'an unbiased but self-consistent, humorous universe':

> Possibly he will be preceded (I should say that he is being preceded) by some tumbling, flour-faced harbingers to the progress (for we cannot grow serious all at once) just as the death-defying wire-walker in the circus is led into the ring by clowns who mime his tragedy. Perhaps the Hero will be one of those loons himself, for the death-defying gesture is a demoded luxury in the modern State. So long as the social mind has no coherent expression like that given it by a supernatural explanation of the universe, the fantastic and the comic, disintegrating forces, will continue the most reputable of styles. They need by no means be inimical to heroic poetry, to which not dignity is essential, but a conception of power.
>
> (Rickword 1974: 118)

Rickword adds that the further this new kind of hero myth can be removed from 'conventional erotic, ethical, or other social values' the better, for then it will regain the strength of 'the old culture'. By this term he seems to refer to the repressed 'folk' imagination, the source of all mythic paradigms. Thus, where Eliot's 'mythical method' would impose a strict form on 'futility and anarchy', answering vulgar chaos with classical convention, Rickword's new hero would trust to a residual mythopoeic urge. In doing so, he would spontaneously move the age beyond defeat and depression.

The mythic paradigm that is the starting point for Eliot is that of fertility, and from there he proceeds to consider also the hero myth (in his review of *Ulysses*). The mythic paradigm that is the starting point for Rickword is the hero myth, which he takes to imply the cyclical model of fertility (with his very notion of a 'returning' hero). But perhaps the difference between the two could be stated starkly as follows: for Eliot, myth connotes tragic restraint; for Rickword, it connotes comic release.

After all, *The Golden Bough* depicts fertility magic as conducted between two poles: that of the dying god and that of the reviving god. *The Waste Land* may be said to keep quite close to the lower pole: while the fertility paradigm serves as the basis for a hierarchical vision, the poem itself is a lament for the spiritual emptiness of an age. The distance of words from Word is dramatized as a collective tragedy. History is viewed as 'an immense panorama of futility and anarchy'. This is a legitimate theme for poetry, and one representative of much modernist work. But Eliot errs when he seeks to enlist the author of *Ulysses* into his own cause – Joyce really belongs to that other modernist stratagem, the case for which is given by Rickword in 'The Returning Hero'.

For the possibility raised by that essay is not only that the god may revive, but that his revival may be 'comic' in terms of both structure and mood. That is, first, if his business is not 'dignity' but 'power', then the crucial issue is whether he revives, whether he moves from death to life: a matter of structure. And second, if 'power' is not what we normally mean, but is rather associated with the force of human laughter, then his new life will be the source not of a solemn order, but of infinite revelry: a matter of mood. Moreover, whereas Eliot thinks the important thing about *Ulysses* is the supposedly pure, abstract shape of hero myth underlying the *Odyssey*, Rickword's 'Hero' would seem to confound all paradigms. That is, he has the centrality of a reviving god, but he has the sense of absurdity of a laughing animal. For above all, his universe will be 'humorous'; and he himself will emerge from the ranks of 'clowns' or 'loons'. He is, then, a force for endlessly productive imperfection rather than for arid and static perfection.

Leopold Bloom, in so far as he is a mock-hero, anticipates this conception. But it is in *Finnegans Wake* (1939) that Joyce realizes the possibility most clearly. Unlike Eliot's vision, Joyce's is democratically undignified and droll. Thus H.C.E. is announced as 'our low hero': 'O! the lowness of him was beneath all up to that sunk to!' And yet he is Joyce's very device for comprehending 'All marryvoising moodmoulded cyclewheeling history'. *Finnegans Wake* is a 'gaiety pantheomime' ('pan-theo-mime', the dance of the gods, identified with the whole of nature). It takes the reader to 'The poignt of fun where I am crying to arrive you at': that is, the moment where tragedy is understood to be only an aspect of comedy (Joyce 1966: 171, 186). Thus, Norman O. Brown praises the principle of 'Finnegan Beginnagain', which takes us back beyond the tragic to 'something more elemental' (Brown 1973: 60). Even those who have not attempted to read Joyce's last novel may know that it is over 600 pages long, and that it begins halfway through the sentence which breaks off, requiring completion by the reader, on the last page. It is massively cyclical, comprehensively comic: in 'disintegrating' habitual discourse (as Rickword would have it), it thereby offers 'the social mind' a new sense of 'power' by demanding an effort of return and renewal. According to Umberto Eco, it is a profoundly paradoxical book in that it assumes both order and disorder simultaneously: it constitutes a 'Chaosmos', a mixture of cosmos and chaos, which might be said to facilitate a new mode of living for this and the next century (Eco 1989: 87).

The Calendar was unqualified in its praise of Joyce, and recognized him as an essentially comic writer. As for Rickword's own writing, we might see his comic vision at work by glancing over one of his volumes of poetry, namely *Invocations to Angels* (1928). In 'To the Sun and Another Dancer', he takes Weston's hypothesis that Christianity is a mystery cult deriving from fertility religion and, rewriting the Easter story in terms of the archaic pattern of the mating of male sun and female earth, produces his own mythically structured love poem. In doing so, he also explores the endless comic play between nature and humanity, and between reality and imagination:

> The sun that lightened the first Easter Day
> traced in the arc of his familiar way
> the choreography of Resurrection,
> which works on our world now, the true reflection
> whereby the sun-foot dancer draws the dead
> out of the sepulchre of formless dread;
> and as the sun still seems to our slow wit
> to attend on us when we derive from it
> all vital qualities, these verses show
> no revelation you did not bestow.
>
> (Rickword 1976: 56)

This is metaphysical verse, after the fashion of two of Rickword's favourite poets, John Donne and Andrew Marvell, also admired by Eliot; but it does not involve that negative stance towards the natural world which characterizes some of Eliot's early work ('April is the cruellest month . . .'). Rickword relishes the dance performed by the sun and the earth, placing human love, hope and inspiration within that comic context.

From here we might turn to Rickword's playful 'masque', which he entitles 'A Happy New Year'. Clearly derived from *The Golden Bough*, it yet manages to avoid the earnestness of Eliot's investment in that work. With dances performed by 'The Frazer Eight' and 'The Lebanon Girls', it suggests a scepticism about that source even while it acknowledges the validity of the fertility paradigm. 'A Happy New Year' is, then, both like and unlike *The Waste Land.* It is like it in that, as the 'Girls' mime the death of the god, his rebirth stands in the balance: their 'little pot-clay Edens, mimic groves / of fresh-plucked twigs that symbolise desire' are 'swift-withering on the edge of expectation' (Rickword 1976: 82–3). It is unlike *The Waste Land* in that Rickword does not translate the paradigm of fertility into the terms of a hierarchical order, but rather emphasizes human possibility. The god is seen as a 'heavenly Ploughman', whose task is 'to draw Time's toppling wain / to all-men's Harvest Home'. Thus, the masque concludes with the presenter having a vision of 'others who walk the earth tonight', secular 'pilgrims' passing through a desolate city, making their way 'to a lucid zone, whence fresh horizons blazed' (Rickword 1976: 86). Rickword demonstrates that there is a way out of the Waste Land, but it need not be Eliot's. Here it is the mood of sympathy, a sympathy that is yet 'exhaustively disillusioned' about the ways of the world, that conveys the sense of promise. The horizon of possibility replaces the hierarchy of perfection. Indeed, the 'others' who chart the way might well be those figures excluded or patronized by Eliot's ascetic 'mythical method'.

In another poem, 'Terminology', Rickword offers his vision of what Ricoeur calls an 'unprecedented' world. He imagines a moment, inconceivable in Eliot's context, when 'women grown / too docile under habits not their own' and 'all tense lives' which have been 'subdued to what they seem' will 'stand up unsullied' in 'Time's stream' (Rickword 1976: 41). One line from this last poem, in which Rickword compares the oppressed women to 'shirted angels nailed to bedroom walls', is reminiscent of the vivid, hallucinatory verse of Arthur Rimbaud. In his study of that poet, Rickword praises the 'visionary' for having 'rebelled against the gods of order and tradition':

> [If] his art could function only at the expense of some confusion or distortion, there must be some great difference between his art and what we call art. And there was, for with us art is the setting of limits where psychologically there are no limits. Rimbaud desired his art to disregard even this capital condition, even though chaos were the price.
>
> (Rickword 1974: 118, 157)

For Rickword, the paradox of Rimbaud's work is that, while offering us a glimpse into chaos, or *Season in Hell* (as one of his works is entitled), it is 'often more serenely classic than that of any other modern' (Rickword 1974: 112). In the next section, we will consider another poet who was prepared to forego any received discipline, and plunge headlong into chaos.

SINGER AS SHAMAN

On 15 May 1871, Rimbaud wrote a letter to his friend Paul Demeny, which Rickword translates in *Rimbaud: The Boy and the Poet*:

> The poet makes himself a *visionary* by a long immense and reasoned *derangement* of *all the senses*. . . . For he comes to the *unknown*! . . . Though he collapses in his leaping among things unheard-of and nameless, other horrific labourers will come; they will begin at the horizons where the other sank.
>
> (Rickword 1974: 126)

Wallace Fowlie has well documented the influence that the writer of those words had on the poet and lead singer of The Doors, Jim Morrison (Fowlie 1994: 121–30). Morrison clearly saw himself as a visionary, and was certainly prepared to undergo a derangement of the senses in acting out the role. More importantly for us, he followed Rimbaud in seeking both to write and to live mythically, in defiance of convention. Like Rickword's 'returning Hero', he did not mind appearing as a 'loon', nor summoning up 'disintegrating forces' and defying 'conventional erotic, ethical, or other social values', in order to forge a new 'conception of power'.

In his poem 'An American Prayer', Morrison seeks to realize this new mythic awareness and challenge the logic of modern rationality, which culminates in war. He calls for us to 'reinvent the gods, all the myths of the ages', in order to counter the 'fat slow generals' who are 'getting obscene on young blood' (Morrison 1991: 3). Figuring himself as lizard, reptile, snake, Morrison affects to have achieved the wisdom of the *ouroboros*, the symbolic snake that continually renews its own life by eating its own tail. As 'lizard king' he further affects to be provoking humanity out of its present state of torpor; but paradoxically this means he is really leading them backward, to the moment of origin, so that they may be cured of the disease of linear history – the story of 'the American night'. The paradigm here is fertility myth; but, as we shall see, for Morrison this structure overlaps with that of creation myth.

Describing the impact and import of The Doors in 1967, Jim Morrison invoked the power of ritual. He saw America in need of rebirth: that is, redemption from the narrow, bureaucratic rationality that led to Vietnam and to global pollution. The only way to counter this shallow logic of progress was to recover the wisdom of archaic ceremony:

> First you have to have the period of disorder, chaos, returning to a primeval disaster region. Out of that you purify the elements and find a new seed of life, which transforms all life and all matter and the personality until finally, hopefully, you emerge and marry all those dualisms and opposites. Then you're not talking about evil and good anymore but something unified and pure. Our music and personalities are still in a state of chaos and disorder with maybe an incipient element of purity kind of starting.
>
> (Hopkins and Sugerman 1980: 143)

Conceiving of his art as a 'purification ritual', taking himself and his followers, or fans, through disorder and chaos to 'some cleaner, freer realm', Morrison here identifies with the medieval alchemist. But more usually, his authority is referred to the archaic role of the 'shaman': that is, 'priest or witch-doctor of class claiming to have sole contact with gods etc.' (*OED*). This is perhaps the most productive analogy by which to characterize his poetic performance, which he grandly refers to as 'the ceremony'.

Frazer explicitly linked the shaman with the King of the Wood, in turn identified with the all-powerful magician. Morrison himself explicitly aligns himself with this power in the internal commentary of 'The Lords'. But in doing so he shows his dissatisfaction, not so much with the fertility paradigm as with Frazer's rational domestication of it. The shaman achieved 'a sensuous panic, deliberately evoked through drugs, chants, dancing. . . . They mediated between man and spirit-world. Their mental travels formed the crux of the religious life of the tribe' (Morrison 1985: 24). Taking Morrison's point, we may add that the ecstatic shaman predates the conventional priest in the prehistory of religion: there is evidence of his presence long before the rise of the priestly class, associated as it is with religious institution and social hierarchy. For the important thing about the shaman is that, in contrast to the priest, he is not instructed in a body of doctrine; rather, he acquires his own powers. There is no *logos*, no fixed scheme or formula, for him to hold onto: he has to trust to the *mythos*, the narrative process of spiritual exploration. Only by transcending all definitions, whether of god or of self, can transformation take place. Orthodox beliefs and systems have to be left behind, and one must proceed by the sheer force of imagination. Only thus may the profane be transformed into the sacred, and time into eternity.

Though *The Golden Bough* may be a reference point for Morrison, his enthusiasm for the role of shaman must be radically distinguished from the rationalistic calm of Frazer's documentation. Situating the singer, we have to forget modernity, with its myth of mythlessness, represented by Frazer's conviction that humanity could and should progress beyond magic and religion. As we shall see, we have also to distinguish the impulse described above from that of modernism, as represented by Eliot's poetic appropriation of Frazer's material. Morrison is best understood as representing what Hans Bertens calls the 'postmodernism of immediacy and presence', expressed most effectively in 'performance art' (Bertens 1995: 74). Interestingly, the authority Bertens cites for this concept is an expert on shamanism. Suzi Gablik describes a process in which 'the artist as shaman' becomes 'a conductor of forces', who is able 'to bring art back in touch with its sacred sources'. That is, 'through his own personal self-transformation, he develops not only new forms of art, but new forms of living'. For Gablik, the new shaman is a 'mystical, priestly, and political figure' who has become a 'visionary and a healer' (Bertens 1995: 74–5).

Morrison's art may fairly be described, then, as postmodernist, pop neo-shamanism. But if we ignore the second epithet, then we miss the point. Rock 'n' roll, with its amplified music and universal appeal, has mythic potential in its own right, if we are to believe the late Marshall McLuhan:

> Electric circuitry confers a mythic dimension on our ordinary individual and group actions. Our technology forces us to live mythically, but we continue to think fragmentarily, and on single, separate planes
> (McLuhan 1967: 114)

In *The Medium is the Message,* we learn that the electronic age in general, and pop music in particular, enables us to prove anew the immediacy and simultaneity of experience apparently enjoyed by our pre-literate ancestors. According to the anthropologist Lévy-Bruhl (1857–1939), the archaic mind enjoyed a capacity for 'mystical participation', of individual with group and of group with cosmos. This capacity was lost with the advance of civilization and literacy. But McLuhan's account of popular culture suggests that the new oral-electronic age allows humans to integrate and intensify their lives again.

As a poet seeking to render his poetry accessible to the new pop audience of the postwar years, Jim Morrison might be seen as embodying the major shift in sensibility discerned by McLuhan. He would certainly count as one of those who restores the vitality of pre-literate culture by making poetry radically popular once more. In his hands the poem becomes an inclusive performance rather than an exclusive artefact. In McLuhan's perspective, to listen to a Doors record or attend a Doors concert is to participate in a new collectivity. The only ones excluded from this are those still living in 'the Gutenberg galaxy', where a poem is not a song, an overwhelming experience, but an arid series of words on a page. And, if we are to take the full force of the statements quoted above, Morrison may be envisaged as a myth-maker in the sense of offering a means to Lévy-Bruhl's 'mystical participation'; or, in McLuhan's formulation, giving 'young people' the very 'formula for putting on the universe' that they are looking for (McLuhan 1967: 114).

McLuhan's echo of Lévy-Bruhl's hypothesis of a pre-modern, anti-rational, non-positivist mentality raises the question of what model of myth is at work here. Lévy-Bruhl set himself against Frazer, whom he took to be unsympathetic to primitive thinking and fearful of the excesses of the mythopoeic imagination. Moreover, Frazer's seasonal pattern of death and revival failed to do justice to the intuition of cosmic forces that Lévy-Bruhl saw as crucial to myth. As Brian Morris points out, the significance of this kind of mythography was that, rejecting the Frazerian notion of myth as an intellectual error to be exposed by objective means, it fostered an interest in myth as a symbolic and subjective expression (Morris 1987: 182). But, though it obviously helps us situate Morrison, we have yet to clarify his choice of paradigm.

Here we should acknowledge briefly his undoubted debt to the Romantic poet William Blake, who will be discussed further in Part II. He is the source of the name of Morrison's band: 'If the doors of perception were cleansed, everything would appear to man as it is, infinite' (Blake 1971: 154). Certainly, Morrison's lyrics are all about seeing beyond the obsessively normative rationality of the contemporary American mind, beyond what Blake called 'single vision': 'Break on through to the other side' (The Doors 1992: 10). But what, mythically, do these words mean? Here we need to spell out the influence of the German philosopher, Friedrich Nietzsche (1844–1900), who developed the complementary myths of 'eternal recurrence' and 'the superman'.

Put simply, the former is the story by which the protagonist of the latter saves himself. In affirming his own existence to the point where he happily wills that his whole life might be repeated again and again forever, the superman becomes divine:

> What if a demon crept after you one day or night in your loneliest solitude and said to you: 'This life, as you live it now and have lived it, you will have to live again and again, times without number; and there will be nothing new in it, but every pain and every joy and every thought and sigh and all the unspeakably small and great in your life must return to you, and everything in the same sequence – and in the same way this spider and this moonlight among the trees, and in the same way this moment and I myself. The eternal hour-glass of existence will be turned again and again – and you with it, you dust of dust!' – Would you not throw yourself down and gnash your

> teeth and curse the demon who thus spoke? Or have you experienced a tremendous moment in which you would have answered him: 'You are a god and never did I hear anything more divine!'
>
> (Nietzsche 1977: 249–50)

What we have here, then, is the fertility paradigm translated simultaneously into the terms of the creation and hero paradigms. The fertility paradigm gives us the idea of human life as cyclical. The creation paradigm gives us the idea of facing up to primordial chaos, manifest in the absurdity of repetition, and so beginning life anew, as if from the very moment in which the universe began. The hero paradigm gives us the possibility of a human protagonist acting with a superhuman power: in this case, the power to live without regret. Indeed, if we are prepared to say 'yes' to life in this context of absurd, cyclical repetition, we are no longer living as mere human beings but have ourselves become gods. Or rather, the gods have ceased to dwell in the heights of Olympus; they have been rendered thoroughly material, thoroughly human. If for the shaman time becomes eternity, for the superman eternity becomes time.

So, deification consists in our being able to will that whatever is, shall be: it is the love of fate. Dionysus, dismembered by the Titans, to be born again from Zeus' thigh, and subsequently glorified as the god of ecstasy and transformation, replaces the figure of Christendom, 'the Crucified'. The latter is a curse *on* life, pointing to a redemption *from* life. The former, though torn to pieces, is a promise *of* life, teaching us how to live *in* life – eternally reborn without any ascetic doctrine, whether metaphysical or moral. Morrison too rejects the Christian way, understood as life-negation: 'Cancel my subscription to the resurrection', he declares in 'When the Music's Over' (The Doors 1992: 32). A contemporary Dionysus, Morrison is also Rimbaud's 'visionary': the life is as mythic as the art, and the truly heroic narrative is the rejection of the given paradigm, hierarchy and perfection. Hence, 'We Could Be So Good Together' (*Waiting for the Sun*, 1968) foretells a world 'without lament', one of endless, recurrent 'invitation and invention' (The Doors 1992: 40). The hero myth overlaps with the creation myth, and a new cosmos is envisaged as thanks to a new kind of hero-poet who is prepared to pay the price of chaos.

The principle of 'Chaosmos' is evident in Morrison's most famous work, the song which Coppola uses for the soundtrack of *Apocalypse Now*, 'The End'. Richard Goldstein, in his review of The Doors' first album, proclaims this work as 'Joycean pop'. That is right, and it would have been wrong had he said 'Eliotean'. However, to appreciate this last point, we have first to acknowledge the main similarity between 'The End' and *The Waste Land.* As with Eliot's poem, the primitive and the sophisticated, the simple and the complex, the antique and the new, are apprehended together, and are allowed to comment one on the other. Thus we are 'Lost in a *Roman* wilderness of pain' (my emphasis): this takes us back to the curious custom of Nemi, noted by Frazer as having survived into classical civilization, standing even then as a reminder of the Roman empire's 'savage' past. It also reminds us of what happened to Rome: how it declined into barbarism through its decades of 'pain' – of persecution, torture and sadism. Are the United States by implication identified with this decadence? We do not need to be told, perhaps, and we move on, or rather back, to the source of Frazer's primitive fertility religion. In their 'desperate land', the Waste Land, the people are 'Waiting for the summer rain', and are 'desperately in need of some stranger's hand'. The old King of the Wood is dead, but has not been replaced by the new, because we cannot remember the ritual significance of renewal. Meanwhile, we are spiritually desolate, as connoted by 'All the children are insane'. What is the answer? It is twofold: 'Ride the king's highway' (follow the way of the god) and 'Ride the snake' to 'The ancient lake' (trust to fertility, mystery, sexuality). But the song ends in uncertainty: inviting us 'to picture what will be, / So limitless and free', yet concluding with the refrain, 'This is the end'. Whether the end leads to a new beginning is left unclear. The call of the shaman is not easy to follow, especially not in unpropitious times.

Accompanying this narrative of collective trauma, there is in 'The End' another story, and another trauma: that of the re-enactment of the Oedipus myth. In this the son announces to the father: 'I want to kill you' (The Doors 1992: 19). We must defer discussion of the Oedipal complex, but here we may note Morrison's perceptiveness in seeing the hidden link between Freud and Frazer. The child who fantasizes about killing his father and marrying his mother, and so repeating the offence of Oedipus, is here economically aligned with the runaway slave who wishes to replace the reigning King of the Wood at Nemi. By juxtaposing the two stories, he intensifies the sexual content of Frazer's material and the mythic content of Freud's psychoanalysis. After all, the 'snake' of the earlier part of the song is an ambiguous image, at once phallus and seasonal cycle, sexuality and cosmic wisdom. Moreover, the injunction, 'Ride the snake', is as much playful as it is portentous.

Having acknowledged that irony and ambiguity characterize both *The Waste Land* and 'The End', we should stress that the latter works by way of the ritual urgency of rock 'n' roll rather than the elitist allusion of modernism. Not so much a 'rage for order' as a rage for purifying disorder, Morrison's mythopoeia is that of Rickword's and Joyce's carnivalesque heroes, rather than Eliot's austere persona (partially identified in his own notes to the poem as Tiresias, the old, blind seer of Greek legend). More generally, the summons to 'break on through to the other side', which recurs in various forms throughout Morrison's oeuvre, is opposed to high modernism in two respects. First, it is subversive in so far as it impels and organizes alternative forms of solidarity ('the other side' as the counterculture). Second, and more importantly for Morrison himself, it signifies the possibility of a spiritual renewal (access to 'the other side') which does not deny, but rather transforms, the life of the body. Eliot in 'Tradition and the Individual Talent' defined poetry as an 'escape from emotion' (Eliot 1975: 43). The Doors explore and expand emotion to the point of Dionysian affirmation.

THE SACRED AND THE PROFANE

Morrison, we have said, saw himself as able to reach 'the other side' because he had assumed the role of neo-shaman. A world authority on shamanism was Mircea Eliade, a Romanian scholar who became, and remained until his death, chairman of the department of history of religion at the University of Chicago. His expertise was the 'phenomenology' of religious experience: that is, what it feels like to be *homo religiosus* or 'the religious human'. He affirmed shamanism to be the practice providing the key to primitive humanity's attempt to live *in illo tempore* – 'in those times' or 'once upon a time'. By association, he saw all myth and ritual as an attempt to start the world again, as it was in the beginning, before the fall into mundane experience:

> In this respect, the mystical experience of primitives is equivalent to a *journey back to the origins*, a regression into the mythical time of the Paradise lost. For the shaman in ecstasy, this present world, our fallen world – which, according to modern terminology, is under the laws of Time and History – is done away with.
>
> (Eliade 1968: 64)

Morrison would seem to have gained his understanding of shamanism from Frazer. But it is perhaps Eliade who has the better grasp of the subject, and who provides the more relevant theoretical context for understanding The Doors' achievement. There again we have to be clear from the start that Eliade, as a general mythographer, weighs his evidence as deliberately as Frazer in order to favour his chosen paradigm. For Frazer, it is fertility which is the key to myth; for Eliade, it is creation.

Eliade has an advantage in this respect, if we consider the prehistoric evidence. To assume that a fertility ritual associated with cultivated crops is the source of myth and religion is to ignore the fact that such a ritual could not have started until the invention of agriculture in the Neolithic period, or New Stone Age, in about 10,000 BC. Eliade infers that there must have been myth and ritual before then, in the later stages of the Palaeolithic period, or Old Stone Age – perhaps as early as about 40,000 BC. (There is indeed evidence of religious ceremony and art from about this time, as Eliot himself indicated by his allusion to 'the rock drawing of the Magdalenian draughtsmen' in 'Tradition and the Individual Talent'.) This early, pre-agricultural culture could hardly have been concerned with the seasonal cycle of the crops, since its economy was that of hunter–gathering. True, it may have already begun to envisage the earth as a 'mother', but if there was a religious sense associated with her worship, that would have been the preserve of the shaman. Eliade's assumption is that the most important philosophical question to be asked by early humanity was: how did this world come to be? Thus, the first myth must have been creation myth, and this must have been recounted in primitive form long before the elaborate versions which developed in antiquity – most notably in Babylon, with the story of Marduk and Tiamat. The archaic mind knew that, for the world to be lived in, it had first to be founded: hence the essential narrative would have been one of origin and not of the fate of the crops.

This may seem a matter of anthropological rather than literary debate, but poets such as Eliot and Morrison need to be understood in this context. Eliade is saying that the primary mythic logic worked as follows. First, there must have been the moment of creation, which took place in 'sacred time'. Second, given that humanity knew that event to have taken place in the distant past, it felt itself to have fallen into 'profane time'. Whatever ceremonies archaic (that is, Palaeolithic) humans performed, whatever stories they told, they were attempting to turn 'profane time' back into 'sacred time'. On the one hand, the very distinction reminds us of Eliot's opposition between myth and history, between 'order' and 'futility and anarchy'. On the other hand, there is an implicit justification for Morrison's belief that paradise may be regained by pushing the fallen imagination to the point where it may 'break on through to the other side'. For Eliade is keen to demonstrate what he calls 'the dialectic of the sacred': 'The sacred is qualitatively different from the profane, yet it may manifest itself no matter how or where in the profane world because of its power of turning any natural object into a paradox by means of a hierophany [i.e., manifestation of the sacred]' (Eliade 1958: 30).

To gain the full benefits of this approach to myth, however, we need to push it further, and to explore the potential of the phrase, 'dialectic of the sacred', by expanding it to include its implicit term: 'the dialectic of the sacred and the profane'.

That is, the ideal of the sacred presupposes the reality of the profane. Without the feeling of having fallen, the desire for paradise would not make sense. Without the experience of profane time there could be no conception of sacred time. Ultimately, the very dialectic of sacred and profane produces the discovery of a 'coincidence of opposites', by which the sacred and profane are understood to be one. It is as though the same reality had two different dimensions: the profane-as-merely-profane and the profane-as-sacred. One is reminded of Blake's dictum, quoted earlier: 'If the doors of perception were cleansed, everything would appear to man as it is, infinite.' For Eliade, myth is the language within which archaic humanity narrates its awareness of the discrepancy between sacred time and profane time, and in which it projects their reconciliation. Ritual is the means by which it seeks to translate profane space into sacred space. Moreover, the mythic/ritual sense is that which knows the merely individual as the archetypal, and ordinary things as 'hierophanies'. One tree becomes 'the Tree of the World', one pool or lake becomes 'the Primordial Waters': a transcendent space is discovered within the fallen world of experience, just as eternity is discovered within time.

Another way of putting the latter process is that renewal *in* time turns out to be renewal *of* time. Primitive humanity 'lives in a continual present'. For 'the life of archaic man', though it takes place in time, 'does not bear the burden of time' (Eliade 1971: 86). 'Myth' is, then, synonymous with 'eternal return', with the desire to be at one with a cosmic beginning in an eternal 'now'. Having referred briefly above to the Babylonian creation myth, we might mention here that in the Babylonian new year festival, or *akitu*, the moment when chaos had originally become cosmos was lived through again, as if it were actually happening there and then. The combat between the young warrior god Marduk and the primal sea-monster Tiamat was re-enacted by two groups of actors, struggling against one another; the myth of creation, known as *Enuma Elish* (from its opening phrase, 'When on high . . .') was recited. 'The mythical event was present: "May he continue to conquer Tiamat and shorten her days!" the celebrant exclaimed. The combat, the victory, and the Creation took place *at that very moment*' (Eliade 1971: 56).

Eliade's celebration of creation myth and ritual as the reaffirmation of order and as the achievement of presence may suggest an affinity with Eliot's use of Frazer's account of fertility myth and ritual. Apart from the obvious difference in choice of paradigm, the affinity is striking. It must, then, be recognized, but it needs qualifying. Both Eliot and Eliade are interested in the question of 'form'; and both see this as a foundational and universal pattern, which humanity needs to regain. However, the 'mythical method', while it seems to involve treating antique narrative paradigms as if active in the present, is really a means of opposing sacred order to profane experience; whereas implicit in the notion of 'hierophany' is the necessity, indeed primacy, of the latter. After all, there can be no 'Tree of the World' until the archaic mind singles out this or that actual tree as especially symbolic. Moreover, Eliot associates form with the higher discipline of Western art or Eastern philosophy; for Eliade it is an aboriginal impulse, which has all too often been obscured by sophisticated speculation:

> Any form whatever, by the mere fact that it exists as such and endures, necessarily loses vigour and becomes worn; to recover vigour, it must be reabsorbed into the formless if only for an instant; it must be restored to the primordial unity from which it issued; in other words, it must return to 'chaos' (on the cosmic plane) to 'orgy' (on the social plane), to 'darkness' (for seed), to 'water' (baptism on the human plane, Atlantis on the plane of history, and so on).
>
> (Eliade 1971: 88)

It is by reaffirming form, that is the 'archetype' or primordially creative image, through the very act of returning to chaos, that archaic humanity is cured of the fall from paradise. It is in this respect that Eliade helps us appreciate Morrison's art and conduct, extravagant and indulgent as they may seem. For neo-shamanism is an attempt to push the experience of the profane to its limits, until a new sense of the sacred becomes possible. The only way is to 'break on through to the other side'.

That said, it would be misleading to conclude our account of Eliade by leaving the impression that his mythography is designed to condone counter-cultural rock music. For his acknowledgement of archaic humanity's need periodically to return to chaos, if necessary by means of orgy, should not distract us from his ultimate aim, which is the defence of an absolutist model of mythology. That is, his choice of the creation paradigm to the exclusion of all others allows him to promote a pure ideal of sacred origin, which he takes to be essentially and eternally valid. For we must be clear that Eliade, no less than Eliot, is advocating his own model of transcendence. Thus: 'The fact that a hierophany is always a historical event (that is to say, always occurs in some definite situation) does not lessen its universal quality' (Eliade 1958: 3). Indeed, the historical manifestation, subject as it is to variation and deterioration, cannot alter that quality. Once the archaic mind has constructed myths and rituals which suggest the existence of a primal time and place, these acquire total independence. As the years pass, and people forget their purpose, they continue to exist regardless of whether they elicit any human response:

> For a symbolism does not depend upon being understood; it remains consistent in spite of every corruption and preserves its structure even when it has long been forgotten, as witness those pre-historic symbols whose meaning is lost for thousands of years to be 'rediscovered' later
>
> (Eliade 1958: 450)

As Robert Segal has argued, in such pronouncements Eliade is effectively affirming religion as something opposed to, or at best indifferent to, the human act of belief. If Eliade is saying that a sacred entity retains its meaning even when nobody recognizes it, whether consciously or unconsciously, which it appears he does, then he effectively 'separates religion from believers' (Segal 1992: 147). This position is Burke's 'perfectionism' taken to the absolute limit. Eliade's documentation of myth and ritual indicates that they are the means by which human beings construct a sense of cosmic harmony, persuading themselves that they live *in illo tempore*; but simultaneously Eliade wants to argue that myth and ritual are 'completed' or 'perfected' only by acquiring a hierarchical status independent of human endeavour. In short, myth and ritual not only help humans transcend history, but themselves transcend history. Thus the concession that the sacred and the profane exist dialectically, that sacred time is only conceivable given the experience of having fallen into profane time, would seem to be incidental to Eliade's main aim, which is to reserve a large stock of the sacred free from human and historical taint. In that respect, Eliade is an ally of Eliot rather than Morrison.

THE HEART-OF-DARKNESS TRIP

If, despite our doubts about Eliade, we can still take away from our preceding discussion a sense of the complementary relationship of chaos and cosmos, we might briefly consider in that light another text which has associations with *Apocalypse Now*. Michael Herr, the scriptwriter for Willard's narration in Coppola's film, is also the author of an account of his own reporting of the Vietnam war for *Rolling Stone* magazine, grimly entitled *Dispatches*. This work is particularly interesting because its very subject is the challenge to make sense out of apparently senseless experience. As such it might be read as a postmodernist hero myth, in which the hero's task is not to slay a dragon but to face the full horror and absurdity of postmodern warfare without surrendering entirely the notion of some hypothetical order.

Early in the book, a GI offers to tell Herr a 'story': 'Patrol went up the mountain. One man came back. He died before he could tell us what happened.' Herr waits for the rest, 'but it seemed not to be that kind of story' (Herr 1978: 14). The subject of *Dispatches* itself might be described as the attempt to decide what kind of story one may tell about Vietnam, given its horrific chaos. The disorder is enacted by the prose:

> your vision blurring, images jumping and falling as though they were being received by a dropped camera, hearing a hundred horrible sounds at once – screams, sobs, hysterical shouting, a throbbing inside your head that threatened to take over, quavering voices trying to get the orders out, the dulls and sharps of weapons going off.
>
> (Herr 1978: 170)

But there is perhaps an implicit order, in the book's first and last chapter titles: 'Breathing In' and 'Breathing Out'. The paradigm suggested is the hero's descent into the abyss and his projected return. Again, Herr, recalling the impact his fellow war correspondents made on him, describes Sean Flynn, photojournalist and son of the film-star Errol Flynn, as looking as if he was 'coming out of some heavy heart-of-darkness trip' (Herr 1978: 15). The implicit structure, then, is that of the journey into chaos, the initiation into absurdity. Reminiscent of Conrad's novella, *Dispatches* is much more explicitly mythic.

Noting that Vietnam is the meeting place, at first sight arbitrary, of various, seemingly random and fragmentary narratives, Herr surmises that 'somehow, all the mythic tracks intersected' (Herr 1978: 24). The ultimate challenge is to decide whether there is one essential story underlying all the rest. The abortive tale of the GI is exceptional, in that it is at least directly told. Mainly the sources are the media, and in particular the cinema. The implication is that, even as Herr seems to be experiencing the war immediately, it will assume the shape of a favoured paradigm. Hence, he frequently ponders on the significance of the Western film genre – a modern, democratic variation on hero myth. John Ford's *Fort Apache,* the first in that director's cavalry trilogy, has Henry Fonda as Colonel Thursday, the new commander. A strict disciplinarian, he shows as little respect for his own men as for the neighbouring Indians. Captain York, 'the old hand' played by John Wayne, knows and respects both the soldiers and the native Americans, and tries to advise the colonel to alter his belligerent attitude. But Thursday will have none of it, and eventually leads his forces into a massacre. Significantly, Herr refers pointedly to the climax of the film, in which 'he and his command get wiped out', as a great 'mythopathic moment'. Vietnam would seem inevitably to suggest a narrative paradigm, no matter how inconclusively and absurdly.

If 'all the mythic tracks intersected', then there is always the possibility of one underlying structure. *Dispatches* does not confirm that it exists, only suggests that it might. John Hellmann has no doubts: 'Herr's narrative form – seemingly a chaotic assemblage of episodes and vignettes – actually represents a "howling" mental wilderness through which a heroic narrator journeys towards the grail of self-knowledge.' Not only that, but the 'grail' is ultimately to be found, and the tracks only intersect, in the larger terrain of American culture itself: 'The excitement of *Dispatches* for the post-Vietnam American is that it suggests Vietnam may yet be transformed into a frontier landscape affording a meaningful errand for the culture, an errand of self-examination' (Hellman 1986: 159–60). Taking Hellmann's point, and acknowledging Herr's elision of history (Vietnam) and myth (the Western), we may yet demur at having *Dispatches* recuperated for tradition by being thus neatly incorporated into what is sometimes called the American pioneer myth, of which Vietnam would form yet another episode. Here we would go no further than to affirm that Herr's work, as a postmodernist hero myth, demonstrates the potential of the 'heart-of-darkness trip', that of intuiting cosmos in the extremes of chaos, without ever finding it. Or, to put this another way, if *The Waste Land* was informed by a 'rage for order', in *Dispatches* we have 'rage' and we have 'order' but we have no guaranteed connection between them.

3

ENDINGS

THE CIRCUITOUS QUEST

We have found Eliade's creation paradigm to be useful in comparing and contrasting the poetry of Eliot and that of Morrison. The key is the phrase, 'the dialectic of the sacred and the profane'. However, we should bear in mind that Eliade, despite allowing for a vision of the 'coincidence of opposites', in which the sacred and the profane might be realized as aspects of each other, does not explore in any detail the historicity of this process. While he concedes that profane time is the only time in which sacred time becomes meaningful – since without the former there would be no point in imagining the latter – he pays little attention to the process of profane time itself. That is, he is content to identify the sacred with the past, with the moment of origin, and myth with that 'eternal return' by which history recovers the dimension of cosmos. In this chapter, we consider the mythic potential of profane time more carefully.

What we have said about the creation paradigm could be applied also to the fertility paradigm. The vegetation cycle is not the most historically promising of models for myth. Of course, we have had to distinguish between the 'tragic' interpretation of the paradigm, evident in Eliot's *The Waste Land* and '*Ulysses*, Order and Myth', and the 'comic', evident in Rickword's 'The Happy New Year' and 'The Returning Hero'. But both of those authors came to a point in their careers where the initial model began to seem inadequate. Both sought to go beyond the cycle. Eliot adopted the Christian myth of deliverance and Rickword adopted the Marxist variation upon it. Both opted for a narrative which emphasized the future rather than the past.

We will consider Rickword's development first. In or around 1930 he became a member of the Communist Party of Great Britain, and went on to found another journal, *Left Review* (1934–8). It is worth comparing the passion of his editorial of April 1937, 'The Cultural Meaning of May Day', with the playfulness of 'The Returning Hero'. But if we are expecting a complete break with the cyclical model we will be surprised:

> What is the deepest concept in all art, the form on which all our dramas and lyrics depend? It is the concept of struggle forged by men at work, by men and women joined in harmony in the struggle against Nature. It is the story of the death and the re-birth of the Year. That was the basic theme of all the mythologies of human life. For the Year was not something apart from man, it was the living shape of the earth which man had to contend with and master.
>
> Man the Worker symbolised his productive struggle in the changes of Nature. His enemy was the Old Year, the Greybeard of hate, all that became socially resistant to advance. And he, the undaunted, was the New Year, the youth of strong thews, who fought the Old Man for the bride of spring and the childing earth of his toil. And yet both death and life were in him. He, individually, must die, though the struggle went on. And so arose our tragedy, blessing life.
>
> But, when the bright season came, after the fight against the plots and menaces of winter, the bride was won, the field of work was cleared; and so our comedy arose, blessing life.
>
> Out of Man Working came all these concepts. . . .
>
> So now we gather again on May Day, in a world where force and greed have stolen the earth away from the happy feet. This is the

> right day for our gathering, chosen by an insight that went to the heart of things.
>
> (Rickword 1937: 130–1)

It is important to note that Rickword's case for communism gains its resonance from Frazer's 'myth and ritual' researches; he is, after all, talking about a workers' holiday which has its roots in the Celtic spring festival of Beltain. Thus the cyclical model of 'The Returning Hero' has survived his political conversion. But now 'comedy' denotes a structural principle only, which is held quite distinct from the earlier 'comic' mood. The author of this earnest manifesto is no longer refusing to 'grow serious all at once' or 'put up with another new creed'. As with Eliot, we may trace a move through narrative to commitment. Eliot will be seen to move from *mythos* to the *Logos*, to explicit faith in a distinctively Christian Word. Rickword is here seen to have rewritten *mythos* as *logos,* as the doctrine of Marxism. We may still call his position mythic, but we must recognize that the myth has been severely adapted in the service of a new kind of thinking. The crucial factor is the choice of the symbolic figure of 'Man the Worker'.

Interestingly, since there is no evidence that Rickword was acquainted with his work, Kenneth Burke put his mind to the same sort of phrasing in his address to the predominantly Communist body, the American Writers' Congress, two years before Rickword's editorial. Himself a fellow traveller rather than a party activist, he wrote his speech, 'Revolutionary Symbolism in America', to prevent Marxism becoming too arid. There are two important arguments in the address that are relevant to our discussion. First, Marxism cannot ignore its mythic dimension:

> 'Myths' may be wrong, or they may be used to bad ends – but they cannot be dispensed with. In the last analysis, they are our basic psychological tools for working together. A hammer is a carpenter's tool; a wrench is a mechanic's tool; and a 'myth' is a social tool for welding the sense of interrelationship by which the carpenter and the mechanic, though differently occupied, can work together for common

> social ends. In this sense a myth that works well is as real as food, tools, and shelter are.
>
> (Burke 1989a: 267)

So far Rickword and Burke might be in agreement. But Burke's second argument is this:

> The symbol I should plead for, as more basic, more of an ideal incentive, than that of the worker, is that of 'the people'. . . . The symbol of 'the people', as distinct from the proletarian symbol, also has the tactical advantage of pointing more definitely in the direction of unity (which in itself is a sound psychological tendency, for all that it is now misused by nationalists to mask the conditions of disunity). It contains the *ideal*, the ultimate *classless* feature which the revolution would bring about – and for this reason seems richer as a symbol of allegiance.
>
> (Burke 1989a: 270)

Burke, then, is suggesting how to keep Marxism alive as a myth, as a symbolic story that offers hope to as many people as possible. Rickword, probably under pressure from the Stalinist CPGB, with its obsession with the Five-Year Plan and other totalitarian projects, feels obliged to narrow the symbolism to 'Man the Worker'. Hence, 'The Cultural Meaning of May Day' is not as inclusive an exercise in mythopoeia as it might be.

Another problem with Rickword's editorial is that the Marxist vision is more usually seen as following another trajectory altogether. Like Christianity, the pattern traced by Marx's myth is meant to be essentially progressive. It treats history as an advance, proceeding stage by stage to the goal of a classless society. Where the Christian story begins with Eden and ends with Jerusalem, the Marxist begins with the primitive communism of tribal society and ends with the advanced communism of post-capitalist society. In between, in both cases, comes a series of conflicts and crises without which the historical goal cannot be reached. Adapting a useful diagram constructed by Trevor Blackwell and Jeremy Seabrook, we can outline the full story as follows:

1. Eden/primitive communism
2. the fall/the development of private property
3. the wilderness/class society
4. the crucifixion/the oppression of the proletariat
5. the resurrection/the rise of class consciousness
6. the day of judgement/the revolution
7. Jerusalem/classless society.

(After Blackwell and Seabrook 1988: 111)

Looked at this way, both Christianity and Marxism are myths of deliverance: both are progressive, both involve crucial choice and commitment, and both promise absolute redemption. They are 'comic' in the strict sense that they are oriented towards a new life ahead of us in time.

In this light we might say that the rhetoric of 'The Cultural Meaning of May Day' succeeds only in so far as it forgets the orthodox interpretation of Marxism. While 'the story of the death and rebirth of the year' is a suitable context for making 'Man the Worker' our new mythic hero, it might be objected that it cannot do complete justice to that final battle in which the proletariat gains mastery of the means of production. The cyclical model would not be ultimately appropriate. And yet Rickword's prose has its power, without our having to suspend our disbelief. Marx and Frazer are an unlikely alliance, but their simultaneous use does support the main aim of the *Left Review* editor at a time of severe class oppression: to express his trust in the victory of the proletariat by appeal to natural justice, or seasonal legitimacy. The spirit of revolution is evoked, even if the letter of orthodox Marxism has been revised. The 'event' of May Day, originally a fertility festival, is 'perfected', to use Burke's term, by being placed within a suitably mythic frame.

After all, as with the Christian quest, there is something unsatisfactory about figuring it as a starkly progressive pattern, with the implication that the earth and its rhythms are somehow to be superseded in a perfect state. More appealing is the idea that culture and nature would somehow be reconciled. Indeed, that does seem to be what the young, visionary Marx, as opposed to the later, 'orthodox' Marx, with his ideology of industrialism and his pretence of scientific exactitude, was anticipating. The literary historian M. H. Abrams, in his account of 'Tradition and Revolution in Romantic Literature' (the subtitle of his book, *Natural Supernaturalism*), quotes the young Marx's own description, in *The Economic and Philosophical Manuscripts* (1844), of his ideal communist state:

> It is the *definitive* resolution of the antagonism between man and nature, and between man and man. . . . The *natural* existence of man has here become his *human* existence and nature itself has become human for him. Thus society is the accomplished union of man with nature, the veritable resurrection of nature, the realized naturalism of man and the realized humanism of nature.
>
> (Marx, cited in Abrams 1971: 315)

The model which is at work here, Abrams suggests, is that of 'the circuitous quest'. For the conception is of the end as 'a "return" to the beginning, but at a higher level'. Thus, 'each man' will not only be 'rejoined with other men', but also 'reunited to a nature which is no longer dead and alien but has been resurrected and has assumed a companionable, because a human form' (Abrams 1971: 315–16). Marxism, or at least the doctrine of the early Marx, would then best be identified with the historical project of Romanticism. Poets such as Wordsworth and Coleridge, Blake and Shelley, seeing themselves as 'poet-prophets', in various ways announced 'the certainty, or at least the possibility, of a rebirth in which mankind will inhabit a renovated earth where he will find himself thoroughly at home' (Abrams 1971: 12). Given what we have already noted, we might even agree with Abrams that this Romantic-Marxist ideal is a secular variant on the Christian myth, itself a 'circuitous quest'. The paradigm of deliverance is informed by the paradigm of fertility ('rebirth'), which is in turn informed by the paradigm of creation ('renovated earth'), and that informing process is mutual. Jerusalem is Eden both regained and transformed.

The problem that Rickword faced was that the Communist Party of the 1930s, concerned to espouse what it saw as Marxist orthodoxy, was hostile to mythic thinking. So he was constrained from the start. It is all the more remarkable, then, that he managed to smuggle his visionary editorial into the pages of the party-controlled journal. In positing the victory of 'Man the Worker', a victory at once recurrent and progressive, he was being true to a Marx not recognized by most Marxists. However, if we admit Burke's contention that Marxism is a myth of universal deliverance, then Rickword's failure – inevitable, given the circumstances – is the narrowing of focus and the exclusion of possibilities entailed in his choice of symbol.

If Rickword was constrained by his chosen orthodoxy, Eliot found his to be exactly appropriate. As we may infer from our previous discussion of *The Waste Land,* his move to Christianity was not the dramatic break with his earlier mythic interests it might otherwise seem. It is likely that Frazer suspected he had undermined Christianity by demonstrating its roots in primitive fertility worship. But Eliot went on to conclude, perhaps with Weston's help, that Jesus' affinities with Osiris and Adonis only gave him 'roots', those absent from the 'stony rubbish' of the modern wilderness. 'He who was living is now dead': that this might refer either to the god or to the son of God was an ambiguity which increased the power of Eliot's poem, and which anticipated the poet's own spiritual transition. Moreover, in so far as Jesus recalled Attis, he might be situated in terms of mystery religion, itself based on fertility religion: that only enhanced his appeal, and did not reduce his spiritual credibility.

Eliot's transition was not inevitable, however: it is one thing to note affinities between nature/mystery cults and Christianity, in the spirit of the comparative method, and it is another to embrace the latter without reservation. The Eliot who declared himself 'classicist', 'royalist' and 'anglo-catholic' had – officially, as it were – abandoned the fertility and mystery paradigms for that of deliverance. Only, he interpreted 'deliverance' in such a way as to defuse its radical potential.

Thus we can see Rickword and Eliot as engaged in two different attempts to relate myth and history. The one runs the risk of distorting the progressive ideal by privileging the circular over the progressive metaphor. But he achieves his rhetorical effect, in keeping with the early, Romantic Marx, despite representing social transformation in exclusive not inclusive terms ('Man the Worker'). The other risks imbalance by using Christian myth as a retreat from history, thus depriving the deliverance paradigm of its temporal trajectory. Eliot's model of spiritual salvation looks more like a version of Weston's 'Mystery Cult' than a promise of universal liberation.

THE RHETORIC OF REVELATION

We may now consider the myth of deliverance at more leisure. There are two reasons for this, one general and one specific. First, we should be aware of how the narrative which still informs Western culture and literature came to be articulated, as itself a cultural and literary expression. Myth does not arise from nowhere, and in the case of the Biblical myth we can watch the myth-making at work. Second, if the Book of Exodus is the earliest version of the myth of deliverance, then the one that is much more explicitly and consciously mythical is the Book of Revelation. In studying its apocalyptic myth, we can provide a context for subsequent visions of the end – notably, of course, *Apocalypse Now*.

The myth of deliverance is oriented forwards. Though, in its original religious form, it assumes a hierarchy, in the form of a heaven above, it also assumes a horizon, in the form of a promised land, or Messianic kingdom. It offers hope that God's chosen people will be liberated from oppression; in doing so, it assumes that history is not only purposeful but also redemptive. That is why it is known in theological terms as 'salvation history'. The phrase can, of course, be applied equally to secular variants on the structure, such as Marxism, with its anticipation of the moment of revolution, when inequality and exploitation will be done away with and a classless society issued in. There is always the danger, however, that tyrannical regimes, whether religious or secular, might justify themselves as the fulfilment of the promise that the narrative makes, as the desired state projected by the myth. We might think of the 'papal inquisition' initiated by Pope Gregory IX in the 13th century, by which an ecclesiastical hierarchy violently imposed itself on supposed 'heretics'; or again, we might think of Stalin's soviet dictatorship, with its purges, show trials and gulags. So it should be borne in mind that the deliverance paradigm is authentically invoked in the midst of struggle rather than at the supposed point of actualization. Its power lies in its promise.

Martin Luther King understood this when he represented the struggle for civil rights in the United States in terms of Biblical narrative, inspiring his followers in explicitly visionary rhetoric. His sermons and public speeches consistently echoed the language of the Book of Exodus, culminating in the address he gave the night before he was assassinated, in April 1968, in which he famously declared: 'I just want to do God's will. And He's allowed me to go up to the mountaintop . . . and I've seen the Promised Land' (King 2001: 223). Nor should we forget the famous speech in August 1963 to the massive civil rights gathering at the Lincoln Memorial in Washington DC: 'I have a dream that one day on the red hills of Georgia, the sons of former slaves and the sons of former slave owners will be able to sit down together at the table of brotherhood' (King 2001: 85). The dream is not an empty one, nor is the language deceptive; rather, the speech assumes the validity of the myth of deliverance, and gains its power by invoking the Bible in defiance of the white racists who, in their ignorance, believe that bigotry and segregation are sanctioned by that very same book. Thus he goes on: 'I have a dream that one day even the state of Mississippi, a state sweltering with the heat of injustice, sweltering with the heat of oppression, will be transformed into an oasis of freedom and justice' (King 2001: 85). Such language makes the oppressed see the relevance and resonance of the language of Exodus in a radically new light.

Now let us turn to the apocalyptic version of the myth of deliverance. Implying a movement of time towards a decisive culmination, the trajectory of deliverance is called 'eschatological' (Greek *eskhatos*, 'last'). However, only those eschatological myths which envisage a dramatic break between the present order and a new existence, and a total transformation of the world, are called 'apocalyptic'. The word 'apocalypse' comes from the Greek word for 'revelation': hence such myths give the impression of revealing the future. Historical existence as previously understood will, we learn, be over; and then we will know a state in which eternity and history, sacred time and profane time, are reconciled once and for all. The ending is decisive: at once a closure to one kind of life and a transition to another, 'unprecedented' mode of existence. Out of catastrophe comes a new cosmos. The Judaeo-Christian Bible culminates in a major apocalyptic work, the Book of Revelation.

Incongruous as it may sound, Jim Morrison, in the song which features on the soundtrack of *Apocalypse Now*, is invoking the Biblical tradition, as must any Western writer who announces an absolute ending. Though Coppola uses the lyric to accompany the sequence in which Willard kills Kurtz, and in so doing evokes the fertility paradigm, it certainly suits the title of his film. 'This is the end,' it declares: the end of 'all our elaborate plans'; the end of 'ev'rything that stands' (The Doors 1992: 18–19). Coppola's film itself draws its power, however indirectly, from Revelation. The Vietnam war was a catastrophe that merits the epithet 'apocalyptic'; and the epithet has its scriptural connotations. However, there is an attendant question which we have to ask: what can it mean to speak of *Apocalypse* as *Now*? The film may be mythic in its scale, stretching from the sacred grove of Nemi to the napalm-scarred landscape of Vietnam, but how can it actually be about the last days? The short answer is that it cannot, but that it need not be. In what follows we may come to accept that that is an enigma intrinsic to the apocalyptic genre itself. We will first consider the Book of Revelation; and then, by way of another glimpse at *The Waste Land*, we will reconsider *Apocalypse Now* in the light of Revelation.

The Book of Revelation was written in about AD 90. Nero had ruled the Roman empire in AD 54–68, and had been succeeded by Domitian. Both were savage persecutors of the followers of Jesus of Nazareth, who had been executed by the Romans earlier in the century. These Jewish followers, whose ranks were being swelled by Gentiles, were derisively known as 'Christians', because they believed their leader to have been 'the Christ', the anointed one, the Messiah. In order to test their loyalty to the empire, Christians were required to worship the emperor himself as a god and Rome itself as a goddess ('Roma'). John the Divine, as he came to be known (to distinguish him from John the Evangelist), wrote

Revelation in order to encourage the persecuted communities of Christians – in particular, the seven churches of Asia Minor. He claimed to have had a vision on the island of Patmos (off the coast of present-day Turkey): this would, he hoped, inspire the faithful to withstand persecution. Above all, they were to hold fast to the promise of Christ's second coming, when he was expected to return again to earth, after his crucifixion, resurrection and ascension to heaven, in order to judge the living and the dead.

In brief, the story Revelation tells is that the Messiah, figured simultaneously as 'Lamb' and as 'Lion of the tribe of Judah', defeats the dragon that is Satan, and establishes his thousand-year reign or millennium. There are other key figures in this drama of salvation. There are, for instance, the four horsemen of the apocalypse: conquest, blood, famine and death. There is 'the woman clothed with the sun', giving birth to a son, probably the Messiah, whom the archangel Michael has to rescue from the clutches of the dragon. There is the beast whose number is 'six hundred threescore and six' (in later Christian tradition to be known as the 'Antichrist'), whose mark the people are forced to wear; probably, if the logic of numerology is applied to the Greek alphabet, his name spells out 'Emperor Nero'. There is the 'whore of Babylon', who lives in luxury by oppressing the mass of the people; she is probably Rome itself, the author using the code name of a previous oppressor of God's people. The key episodes of the drama include the collapse of the empire of this 'whore': when the early Christians heard that 'Babylon the great is fallen', they would understand that the fall of Rome was being foretold (Revelation 18: 2). Even more crucial is the subjugation of Satan by Jesus in his capacity as Messianic warrior, appearing on a white horse; 'and he that sat upon him was called Faithful and True, and in righteousness he doth judge and make war' (Revelation 19: 11). Nor should we forget the penultimate moment of the battle between the forces of good and evil at Armageddon. And then there is the final vision of 'a new heaven and a new earth', centred on a 'heavenly city' called Jerusalem; there will be no more tears and no more death; in the middle of the city will be a tree – the 'tree of life', which Adam and Eve were denied after the fall.

That last-mentioned symbol is especially significant. Beneath and beyond all the particular correspondences, the essential pattern is clear. Revelation, the last book of the Judaeo-Christian Bible, is a retelling of Genesis, the first book. We move from the creation of the earth to its re-creation; we move from the 'fall' from Eden in the beginning to the final redemption of humanity and its entry into Jerusalem at the end. Despite its forward trajectory, Eliade would read the Biblical structure as circular in implication. That is, sacred time is recovered, and we experience a moment of regeneration, by which cosmos re-emerges out of chaos; only, it is placed at the end of profane time and not at the beginning. But we have already indicated that the myth of deliverance does not depict Jerusalem as a simple repetition of Eden, the primordial paradise. Though the tree of life is restored, it is now placed in a celestial city ruled by the son of God. According to the 'circuitous quest' paradigm, the end is the beginning transformed, on a higher level. It takes on a whole new significance because it is informed by the long struggle through the wilderness of sin and death, during which God's people endures a sequence of oppression (slavery in Egypt, exile to Babylon, persecution by Rome).

However we envisage the implicit structure of the grand narrative which the Bible as a whole recounts, the point to remember is that the recounting always takes place in a specific book (Exodus, Isaiah, Daniel, Revelation), and that book is primarily a response to its own day. John the Divine addresses his contemporaries; he may be talking about the future, but his primary concern is how he and they may endure persecution in the here and now. Indeed, the very promise of Christ's second coming is always a present promise. What matters chiefly is the act of waiting for the end. As we read in the Gospels: 'when ye shall hear of wars and rumours of wars, be ye not troubled: for such things must needs be; but the end shall not be yet' (Mark 13: 7). The readers of Revelation exist in a moment of eschatological tension: they believe that Jesus has indeed saved them, has fulfilled the promise of the exodus, by virtue of his resurrection; but meanwhile they must await the signs of the final victory over Satan. They exist between the 'already' and the 'not yet', between 'realized' and 'future' eschatology (Moltmann

1967: 16–17). Both past promise and future possibility exist in the here and now.

The Book of Revelation, then, is an intervention in history rather than a transcendent overview of the meaning of history, but its claim to visionary status is essential to its appeal and its effect. However, while the proclamation that the end is nigh is a useful tactic for inspiring and consolidating the faithful, it must be recognized to be primarily a matter of language (it is written in the form of a letter to the church communities) and of projection (it is written at a particular moment of crisis). The issue of whether the text is revealed truth must remain an open question. What we can say is that Revelation is a highly concentrated form of visionary rhetoric. It is an extraordinary example of what Kenneth Burke calls 'symbolic action': a linguistic 'strategy' designed to meet a given 'situation'. Without the latter, the intense historical constraint, there would be no need to try and extend language to the limit. But given that ambition, the symbolic act becomes also 'the dancing of an attitude', an imaginative exploration (Burke 1989b: 79). From the particular moment of persecution, then, Revelation takes the promise of deliverance, and pushes it 'to the end of the line', as Burke would have it. Once its author has recognized the dilemma – that Christians suffer and that Rome flourishes, that the poor and the good are oppressed by the rich and the evil – then the whole saving myth may be generated, so to speak. In so far as there is a conflict, there must also be a narrative. There must be a Christ and an Antichrist, a bride and a whore, a warrior on a white horse and a devouring dragon; and so there must be a final and absolutely decisive battle.

Moreover, because the focus of the rhetoric must be the audience, we have to ask ourselves how Revelation works on its reader, how it fulfils its strategic function. Elisabeth Fiorenza considers John's text in the light of Burke's thinking about the relation between verbal arrangement and vital effect. She agrees with him that the 'mythic' structure is also a 'ritual' structure: not in Frazer's sense, but rather because it 'follows the form of a cathartic journey'. This crucial inner voyage 'moves the audience from alienation through purification to redemption'. Experiencing an emotional 'separating out', it sees its own 'passion (persecution and suffering) . . . transformed into an assertion'. That is: 'In taking his audience on the dramatic-cathartic journey of Revelation, John seeks to "move" them to control their fear and to sustain their vision' (Fiorenza 1985: 198).

This is not, then, 'myth and ritual' according to either Frazer's fertility or Eliade's creation paradigm. It is not that a whole society is focusing attention on a god who dies and revives. Nor, although there is a cosmic battle between divine warrior and dragon, are we to think in terms of eternal return. Rather, an oppressed minority is purging itself of fear by attending to a language that creatively turns the world upside down, transforming defeat into victory. Here myth, as rhetoric, becomes a verbal ritual. It effects an identification – of the individual with her faith, and of the individual with her fellow Christians. This it does by persuading her of a transformation: that is, the historical time of suffering (*chronos*) becomes the crucial time in which a new cosmos comes out of catastrophe (*kairos*).

If we can accept that Revelation is rhetorical, and that apocalypse is always effectively now, we will not be surprised to find secular writers putting John's paradigm to their own contemporary use. In the first book of Edmund Spenser's *The Fairie Queene* (1590), the Red Cross Knight is commissioned by Gloriana, Queen of Fairy Land, to accompany a young woman called Una to the kingdom of her parents and deliver them from a dragon that is laying waste their land. This poem, written in honour of Elizabeth I, is what we might call a Tudor apocalypse: its rhetorical purpose is to celebrate her reign as a variation upon the model of the millennium. It is no coincidence that in the first canto, we read of the knight, 'Right faithfull true he was in deede and word'; and of the lady, that 'by her in line a milke white lambe she had' (Spenser 1966: 4). The echoes from Revelation are deliberate: the knight's quest is meant to remind us of Christ's apocalyptic battle; and so Una's parents may be identified with Adam and Eve, their land with Eden and the dragon with Satan. All this allusion is put to pragmatic, political use by Spenser: 'Una' signifies the one true Protestant faith of England, and the dragon signifies all the various threats to the

Reformation. The specific threat of Catholic idolatry is represented by Duessa, the witch of falsehood, who tries to lead the knight astray, and who is reminiscent of the 'whore of Babylon'. And so the knight's quest is also that of ensuring that Gloriana's (Queen Elizabeth's) land remains true to the spirit of her Tudor predecessor Henry VIII. Her court in London can then approximate to Jerusalem, the heavenly city. And appropriately enough, no sooner is his quest completed and the battle against the dragon won, than the Red Cross Knight is revealed to be none other than St George, patron saint of England. Strictly speaking, then, *The Fairie Queene* may be characterized as a reactionary use of Revelation's rhetoric, in that its aim is to confirm the established hierarchy, not to offer a horizon of hope to the oppressed. The authoritarianism of Christendom thus replaces the revolutionary impetus of primitive Christianity.

This becomes obvious when we contrast Spenser's poem with the political prose of Gerrard Winstanley, the leader of 'the Diggers or True Levellers' during the English Revolution of the seventeenth century. For him, it was not only Anglicanism and monarchy which embodied the status quo, but also Cromwell and the leaders of the republic – none of whom represented the interests of the poor artisans or the peasants. They still adhered to a world of power and property because they had not acknowledged the radical and apocalyptic spirit of Christ. Thus, *Fire in the Bush* (1650) alludes on its title page to 'The great Battle of God Almighty, between Michael the Seed of Life, and the great red Dragon, the curse, fought within the Spirit of Man'. Winstanley identifies 'the power of darkness' with the 'dragon' in the human soul, 'which causes all wars and sorrows' and is 'the son of bondage, which must not abide in the heart for ever but must be cast out'. For 'Christ the anointing spirit doth not enslave any, but comes to set all free', to dispense with 'all mourning weeds' and to 'wipe away all tears' (Winstanley 1973: 211–17). That last phrase, a direct quotation from Revelation, is taken as a political programme as well as a religious promise. Winstanley's Christ guarantees an end to the unnecessary suffering which results from an unjust society.

Both *The Fairie Queene* and *Fire in the Bush*, then, are variations on the myth of deliverance, as dramatized by the Book of Revelation. The former emphasises the 'already'; the latter emphasises the 'not yet'. But both are responses to the present: the former wants to justify it; the latter wants to repudiate it. The former assumes the given hierarchy to be divinely ordained; the latter wishes to topple it in the name of Christ. Both are 'symbolic acts', but the former works hard to equate the symbolism of apocalypse with stasis, while the latter takes from John the Divine's text the understanding that all symbols are promises, figures of possibility. The rhetoric of Revelation is rich enough to sustain both alternatives, and perhaps many others. For example, in the modern age we find D. H. Lawrence, whose own work culminates in a study of John the Divine's text, propounding an eschatology of sexual resurrection. *Lady Chatterley's Lover* (1928), in which the female hero is initiated into the mysteries of carnal love (including anal sex) by her gamekeeper, is an ostensibly realistic novel which may be easily translated into visionary terms: 'Mellors, in the England of Lloyd George, is the Saint George who kills the dragon (the serpent of corruption, of shame at defecation) and sets the lady free; an act as apocalyptic as that of Spenser's St George' (Kermode 1973: 131). Deliverance and fertility here are made to coincide; the 'not yet' of a nation's transformation is shown to be realized in the 'already' of the sexual act. Needless to say, Spenser would not have approved, despite the above analogy; nor, for that matter, would Winstanley.

APOCALYPSE WITHOUT APOCALYPSE

Study of the Book of Revelation reminds us forcibly of the way myth may work on history, and vice versa. However, as we have already seen, the modernism of Eliot is based on the premise that myth and history are opposed, the one offering transcendence of the other. Here we want to consider *Apocalypse Now*, which might be described as a postmodernist film, as a work in which the intimate relation between myth and history becomes of interest once more. The 'apocalypse' of its title has something to do with this, of course, and so perhaps we need to situate the film in relation to both Eliot and John the Divine.

Frank Kermode has suggested that *The Waste Land* might be related to Revelation in so far as it depicts a demonic metropolis, ripe for destruction. He quotes from John the Divine's account of the fall of Babylon, that city personified by a 'whore': 'And the merchants of the earth shall weep and mourn over her . . . saying, Alas, the great city, that was clothed in fine linen, and purple, and scarlet, and decked with gold, and precious stones, and pearls! For in one hour so great riches is come to nought' (Revelation 18: 11–17). He comments: 'This is the London of *The Waste Land*, the City by the sea with its remaining flashes of inexplicable imperial splendour: the Unreal City, the *urbs aeterna* declined into *l'immonde cité*' (Kermode 1990: 308–9). But there is an ambiguity underlying Eliot's use of Revelation, expressive as that book is of contempt for all worldly empires, and in particular Rome. For the 'eternal' city of the classical Latin poet Virgil (author of the *Aeneid*, which celebrates the founding of Rome) remains the yardstick by which to measure the modern decadence of Baudelaire's 'unclean' or 'impure' city. Committed to the ideal civilization of Virgil, to the true, everlasting essence of Rome underlying its manifest corruption, Eliot wishes to identify squalor and spiritual poverty only with the contemporary city. In doing so, he finds the rhetoric of Revelation congenial, but 'behind the temporal disaster of Babylon he knows that the timeless pattern of the eternal city must survive' (Kermode 1990: 309). The imagery of disaster and that of continuity coexist. Myth remains aloof from history, and Revelation is read as somehow transcending the sense of crisis and catastrophe which occasioned its desperate rhetoric.

With *Apocalypse Now* the sense of crisis and catastrophe predominates, as is appropriate in a film about Vietnam. Atrocity follows atrocity, in this postmodern war, to no apparent purpose. Thus we find Colonel Kilgore leading a bombing raid on a Vietnamese village to the sound of Wagner, in order to clear the beach area for a surfing display. Again, we find the Do Lung bridge being manned by leaderless, drug-hallucinating soldiers, shelling an invisible enemy, merely so the generals can say that the bridge is open. If out of these symptoms of chaos we infer a narrative pattern, we are hard put to name it. Kilgore's massacre and the Do Lung fiasco become eschatological signs of an ending which is immanent rather than imminent, chronically pervasive rather than critically forthcoming. This is a postmodernist film – the appropriate response to a postmodern war. Eliot's hierarchy, his identification of myth with transcendent truth, is not available. But nor is any other position, apparently. Myth here is scattered amidst the fragments of profane time.

That is, where Eliot's myth was a means of controlling 'the futility and anarchy which is contemporary history', Coppola makes no distinction between myth and history, order and chaos, the grove of Nemi and the war zone of Vietnam. Ultimately, perhaps, there is not even any distinction between Eliot's poetry and Colonel Kurtz's recitation of it in the depths of his Cambodian temple. What matters is the image. Any narrative we discern in *Apocalypse Now* is built up by the juxtaposition of images: the tribespeople slaying the buffalo (primitivist motif); the bombing of the temple (apocalyptic motif); Kurtz's reading matter, lingered over by the camera (modernist motif); and so on, right back to the assignment of Willard to the mission, as in the Grail legend (romance motif) and the opening sequence in which he confronts his demonic double in the mirror (Gothic and/or psychoanalytic motif). The effect is that of cultural tourism, moving through both space and time. Though Eliot spoke of the 'presence' of the past, the effect intended was quite different. *The Waste Land* was preoccupied with 'roots'; *Apocalypse Now* is preoccupied with 'routes'. What William Carlos Williams predicted has happened: the 'pure products of culture' have gone 'crazy', and all one can do is make one's way through the bewildering array without ever expecting to find a position of final fixity (Clifford 1986: 1–17). Chaos is certain; cosmos is hypothetical.

The import of this discovery is that we must not speak of 'myth', but rather of 'myths'. Eliot could shape a whole modernist epic poem around Frazer's dying god, as refigured in Weston's Grail monarch, confident that he had found a universal and eternal order transcending the disorder of his day. Coppola offers us imagery from the same sources, but hesitates to grant it any further status. Such visual allusions are on a par with all the others in the film; and all of them may be illusions as well as allusions. Here are icons whose sacred significance is in question. Where Eliot worked on the assumption that beneath or beyond all his words there resided the Word, waiting to be recovered, Coppola addresses the possibility that beyond the image there need be nothing at all; beneath the signifier there need be no signified; outside the sign there need be no referent. Hence, even if several scenes from *Apocalypse Now* are reminiscent of John the Divine's vision of the end, that vision has now been cast adrift from the grand narrative of deliverance which originally gave it meaning, and we are left with floating intimations of a cosmic transformation that will never happen.

Thus we reach the paradox of Coppola's vision. This turns out not to centre on the film's title since, as I have demonstrated, all *Apocalypse* is *Now*: the revelation of the end of history always takes place in history, and for good rhetorical purposes. The tension we are interested in is not that between present and future, but that between present and present. It is between the present of the 'already' and the present of the 'not yet'.

Perhaps we could illuminate this tension in the context of the postmodern era by briefly tracing the way the philosopher Jacques Derrida changed his mind in the space of little more than a decade. Here we will juxtapose two statements, one from 1981 (translated the following year) and the other from 1994. Writing two years after the release of *Apocalypse Now*, Derrida reflects on the fact that virtually the last main sentence of the Book of Revelation is the exhortation, 'Even so, come, Lord Jesus.' He sees that one word 'come' as the clue to our postmodern apocalypse, since the more it is looked at the more it resists definition. It addresses us from that elsewhere which is always just the other side of where we are:

> Now here, precisely, is announced – as promise or threat – an apocalypse without apocalypse . . . without last judgment, without any other eschatology than the tone of the 'Come' itself, its very difference, an apocalypse beyond good and evil. 'Come' does not announce this or that apocalypse: already it resounds with a certain tone; it is in

> itself the apocalypse of the apocalypse; 'Come' is apocalyptic. Our *apocalypse now* . . .
>
> (Derrida 1982: 94)

The rhetoric of Revelation still fulfils a function, in that it unsettles, disturbs, 'deconstructs' the present. The narrative promise of the 'not yet' survives the loss of doctrinal belief; the challenge of apocalypse may be felt without the religious meaning of apocalypse. It is the permanent power of possibility possessed by the myth of deliverance that speaks to us, not the doctrines of a particular religious system. Or we might say, in a reversal of Bultmann, *mythos* is what matters, not *Logos* (sacred Word) or *kerygma* (scriptural message).

Between this first statement of Derrida's and the second comes Francis Fukuyama's *The End of History and the Last Man* (1992), which proclaims 'apocalypse now' in a different sense. In effect, Fukuyama is declaring that the Messianic kingdom has been realized, and it has taken the form of Western, liberal democracy. Capitalism has won; Marxism and other modes of resistance are dead. The historical project advocated by Marx is now defunct, and the symbol of the free market entrepreneur has permanently replaced that of the militant proletariat. Derrida's response is caustic. He begins by invoking Marx's declaration at the beginning of *The Communist Manifesto* (1848): 'A spectre is haunting Europe – the spectre of communism.' He insists that 'the inheritance of Marxism' is still alive, because inheritance 'is never a given, it is always a task'. Far from assuming democracy to have been established, it is necessary 'to speak of a democracy *to come*'. He now addresses the theme of global justice, neglected by Fukuyama:

> Instead of singing the advent of the ideal of liberal democracy and the capitalist market in the euphoria of the end of history, instead of celebrating the 'end of all ideologies' and the end of the great emancipatory discourses, let us never neglect this obvious macroscopic fact, made up of innumerable singular sites of suffering: no degree of progress allows one to ignore that never before, in absolute figures, never have so many men, women, and children been subjugated, starved, or exterminated on the Earth.
>
> (Derrida 1994: 53)

Given Fukuyama's apocalyptic pronouncement, which has destroyed the creative tension between the 'already' and the 'not yet', Derrida feels obliged to disassociate himself completely from the rhetoric of Revelation. It has become tainted. So, in posing again the question of justice, he endorses (without committing himself to Marxism) the fundamental concerns of Marx. That is, he invokes (despite his own hostility to 'mythology', a word synonymous for him with Western thinking and the illusions of origin, presence and Word) the myth of deliverance. He invokes it, though, not in its apocalyptic but in its historical aspect. He refuses to accept 'the end of history' if that means also the end of the struggle on behalf of the oppressed.

Coppola's apocalypse, I would suggest, is not best understood in terms of Fukuyama's scenario. Its 'already' is the 'now' of crisis and catastrophe, not of smooth settlement. Thoroughly mythic and anti-doctrinal, it forces the viewer to inhabit a moment of endless, traumatic transition, in which Babylon is continually about to fall and Armageddon about to be fought. Justice is absent, but the viewer is forced to confront that absence. Far from setting aside the issues of power and oppression, the film articulates them through images that remain mythic even as their supporting narrative is put into question. If these 'fragments' are not 'shored' against 'ruin', as Eliot has it in *The Waste Land*, they demand that we sketch some structure for ourselves, fragile as it might be. Where Fukuyama cuts short the promise of apocalypse, neutralizing the very historical anxiety which gives it its power, Coppola asks us to see the vision through to the point where it almost might end.

Here we come back, finally, to the relation between myth and paradigm. We have said before that the modernist 'rage for order' has different manifestations, ranging from Eliot's 'mythical method' to Stevens' own 'Supreme Fiction'. We have also said that with postmodernism, there is an exploratory interaction between 'rage' and 'order', chaos and cosmos, as with Morrison's neo-shamanism. It would be naive to contrast modernist mythopoeia and postmodernist mythopoeia as simply synonymous with order and chaos, as if these were mutually exclusive principles. Myth, after all, is inseparable from the idea of totality; yet myth has only ever been a gesture towards it. It may posit a perfect beginning, or paradise, or it may posit a perfect ending, a Messianic kingdom, but the point is that it always does so 'in the midst', between the two (Kermode 1967: 7). Myth, then, is the exemplary form of Aristotle's 'plot': it follows the rhythm of temporal experience (chronology) and yet, by virtue of its organization, it approximates to a timeless paradigm which can never quite be realized (eternity). Kenneth Burke thinks of myth as 'the temporizing of essence', for where it speaks of origins and 'firsts' (the first day of creation, the first man and woman, the first sacrificial offering) it is always speaking simultaneously of the nature of things as understood here and now. 'Principals' are also 'principles' (Burke 1966: 381). The same goes for 'ends', which are as 'essential' as origins. Language and humanity alike are 'rotten with perfection', which certainly has its positive aspect. For unless we were 'goaded by the spirit of hierarchy', we would not stir ourselves to make narrative sense of the world (Burke 1966: 16). Words about planting and reaping, living and dying, inevitably produce words about gods and goddesses, creation and apocalypse – eventually leading all the way up to God, the one Word. And it is here that the positive aspect meets the negative. For Burke, while suggesting that 'perfectionism' is inevitable, also suggests that, knowing this, we still have a choice as to where we start from.

We can see what he means when we apply his principle to Eliot and Coppola. Eliot starts from the point of view of perfection and hierarchy, and then works downwards: he views time from the aspect of eternity. Coppola starts from the fallen world, in its most barbaric manifestation, and proceeds from there. As motif follows motif, and allusion follows allusion, we begin to form a narrative, which in turn implies a pattern. That pattern is endlessly implicit, and will never be attained. But both the director and the audience of the film cannot help but infer it – which amounts to improvising it. Thus, just as John the Divine produced, out of the most challenging historical circumstances, a text that is still regarded as the perfect apocalyptic myth, in which cosmos is reaffirmed out of chaos, so does Coppola produce a film that, we might say, is exactly appropriate as an apocalyptic myth for our age. It is appropriate, not because it reimposes order on disorder, which Eliot does, for we can no longer believe in that kind of victory. It is appropriate because it starts from the appropriate place, in an age that knows more about chaos than it does about cosmos, and more about imperfection than perfection. If myth is ultimately about possibility, that place – 'in the midst' – will always be appropriate.

PART II

Mythic reading

INTRODUCTION TO PART II

> Your vocabulary shapes your world for you and enables you to get a grip on it. Conversely, the limits of your language are the limits of your world. All this, people know already. We add a further consideration: the end of the philosophers' dream, that the human mind could altogether outsoar the limits of language and history and lay hold of absolute speculative knowledge, is a great event. In religious thought it means giving up the attempt to transcend our myths and symbols, and returning into language.
>
> (Cupitt 1990: ix)

Taking his cue from the philosopher Ludwig Wittgenstein's claim that 'The limits of my language are the limits of my world', Don Cupitt here declares that human beings make sense of the world through their words. But more importantly for our purposes, he wants to say something else. That is, whether we talk of one God or of many gods, we are talking, and so thinking, mythically. No matter what absolute reality we imagine to exist, it is through language that we conjure it up. As Kenneth Burke would put it, insofar as we are human, linguistic creatures, there can be for us no notion of an ultimate Word without the words with which we speak of that Word (see Burke 1970: 7ff.). Cupitt's declaration is particularly appropriate here, since what we have been discovering in Part I is the primacy of myth – a story that can, of course, only be narrated, received and understood in temporal terms – over abstract ideas of eternal truth. *Mythos* produces *logos.*

In Part II, I will be spelling out the consequences of this discovery. Though Eliot, Coppola and Morrison will from now only be passing references, we should find that inferences made from their work begin to acquire some coherence. We will be taking an overview of the history of mythography, roughly from Plato to the present. But we will simultaneously be indicating the development of literary mythopoeia, roughly from Homer to the present. And as we proceed, it should become apparent that reading myth (mythography) and making myth (mythopoeia) are complementary activities. Indeed, they both involve mythic reading.

Chapter 4 will establish our two main kinds of mythic reading: allegory, which we will be identifying as 'realist'; and typology, which we will be identifying, at least in its radical form, as 'non-realist'. Homer and Plato will be our reference points for the former; Joachim of Fiore and Dante for the latter. From Chapter 5 onwards, things will become slightly more complicated, as we move from theory past to theory present. Rather than simply 'tick off' key theorists as exclusively expressive of either 'allegory' or 'radical typology', it will be more productive to consider their work as existing within the tension between two tendencies. Among those featured will be: Sigmund Freud, Carl Jung and Claude Lévi-Strauss (Chapter 5); Roland Barthes, Northrop Frye, Fredric Jameson and Marina Warner (Chapter 6); Gary Snyder, James Lovelock, Theodore Roszak and Michel Serres (Chapter 7). Texts discussed in Part II will range from *The Divine Comedy* to *The Matrix.*

4

TRUTH

REALISM AND NON-REALISM

Perhaps, in the light of the argument so far, the following statement by a contemporary mythographer will not seem particularly eccentric:

> [M]yth is neither true nor false *in a theoretical sense* but viable or not viable for the tasks (both theoretical and other wise) which confront us. This viability is not determined in intellectual terms but in the very process of living, by whether or not one is energized, whether or not problems are being solved, whether or not life is integrated at a variety of levels, whether or not it is endowed with a significance that pulls one toward the future in hope. Viability is not determined in advance of inhabiting a myth . . .
>
> (Scarborough 1994: 110)

This is a useful way of reaffirming what we have said about the primacy of narrative over doctrine, and about the danger of asserting belief in *logos* while forgetting its origin in *mythos*.

Alert to this danger, Don Cupitt has preferred to scandalise many of his fellow Christians by arguing that it is not only *logos* but also the *Logos* that needs a radical rethinking. We now live 'after God', he has declared; the future of religion will involve 'the end of dogmatic metaphysics' and the flowering of a 'poetic theology' (see Cupitt 1997: 57–62, 110–120). As I have hinted, this position is close to Kenneth Burke's, who takes the Judaeo-Christian Bible to be a work of art rather than a handbook of doctrine: a work in which the divine Word is constantly and miraculously begotten by human words in the form of metaphors and myths. Given the resurgence of religious fundamentalism in recent years, with its accompanying bigotry and violence, we can benefit from the insights of Burke and Cupitt: they agree that the desire for literal certainty beyond language, the urge towards a complete system of explanation, is the problem rather than the solution. Burke is especially shrewd on the nature of hierarchy: while he sees it as inevitable, given the human impulse to move from words to Word, he reminds us of the human responsibility to guard against the 'hierarchical psychosis', by which those with power and/or wealth impose their wills on those without (Burke 1984b: 374).

The best way to challenge any given hierarchy is, according to Ricoeur, myth itself, in its capacity of opening up a 'possible world'. We have already seen that the myth of deliverance suggests a final end of history, an eschatological moment of completion (*eskhatos*, 'last'); but we have also seen that apocalypse cannot help but be a present projection, a response to historical crisis. The 'already' and the 'not yet' both exist in the 'here and now'. The myth of the future (deliverance), like that of the past (creation), is always about the present. Ricoeur, while insisting on 'the principle of hope', denies the notion of a future totality. The point about his 'possible worlds' is that they are always 'possible'. One of the main reasons we need 'the *eschatological* sense' of some final 'unity of truth' is in order to counter the received wisdom of our own times; the story and symbolism of the 'Last Day' offer a necessary refusal of a life that has become oppressive (Ricoeur 1965: 190–1).

Myth for Ricoeur is a 'social imagination' which functions by virtue of a dialectic between 'ideology' and 'utopia'. The former – which is a necessary condition of 'integration' – need not become oppressive so long as the latter is kept alive. 'On the one hand, imagination may function to preserve an order. . . . On the other hand, though, imagination may have a disruptive function; it may work as a breakthrough.' Ideology represents the first kind of imagination: 'it has the function of preservation, of conservation.' Utopia represents the second kind of imagination: 'it is always the glance from nowhere' (Ricoeur 1986: 266). Without the first kind, we would have no sense of society or tradition; without the second kind, we would simply equate the given society and tradition with eternal truth, never challenging or reforming them. Utopia prevents ideology becoming a claustrophobic system; ideology prevents utopia becoming an empty fantasy. Myth, or the social imagination, involves both. As such, it necessitates a temporal engagement, not a gesture of transcendence. Commenting on the sociologist Karl Mannheim's 'paradox' that we are always caught between the two poles, Ricoeur expresses his own dialectical conviction:

> There is no answer . . . except to say that we must try to cure the illness of utopia by what is wholesome in ideology – by its element of identity, which is once more a fundamental function of life – and try to cure the rigidity, the petrification, of ideologies by the utopian element. . . . My more ultimate answer is that we must let ourselves be drawn into the circle and then must try to make the circle a spiral. We cannot eliminate from a social ethics the element of risk. We wager on a certain set of values and then try to be consistent with them; verification is therefore a question of our whole life. No one can escape this.
>
> (Ricoeur 1986: 312)

Put simply, the present exists as a tension between the way things seem to have always been and the way things might be.

The notion that myth traverses past, present and future has an important implication for Ricoeur. We do an injustice to a myth if we read it as an *explanation* of the world: it can then be assessed as being once true but no longer true, and so dismissed in the present as a false remnant of the past. We should rather read the myth as an *exploration* of the world: it is constantly offering a new sense of potential, pointing from the present into the future. But even then, the danger of literalism still lingers, in the sense of expecting that the utopian dimension of the myth will one day be actually and finally realized; that way lies the madness of modern totalitarianism. The dialectical nature of mythology and the imaginative nature of mythology must be borne in mind simultaneously.

Thus, Burke, Ricoeur and Cupitt agree that to recognize the primacy of language is to recognize that we are always involved in history. Moreover, it is through language and it is in history that we make our myths. In doing so, we suppress neither the past nor the future, but remain open to the potential of both. The only error is to posit an independent and self-validating truth that might be accessed beyond the temporal process of myth-making. As Ricoeur puts it: 'the claim of the *logos* to rule over *mythos* is itself a mythical claim' (Ricoeur 1991: 486).

At stake here are two philosophies which Cupitt calls 'realism' and 'non-realism', and it is his use of these terms which we must now consider. Cupitt's overall aim is to repudiate 'realism' and affirm 'non-realism'; but what do we mean by 'realism'? Sometimes Cupitt uses the word to indicate the assumption that there is a real world outside of language. For example, in the very same paragraph as that quoted at the beginning of this chapter, Cupitt attempts to refute this position by declaring that 'language creates reality'. We need not follow him down that path, which leads to linguistic idealism (a risk he is aware of, for even in his most recent work he is still qualifying his position). We are on surer ground when he tells us: 'Your vocabulary shapes your world for you and enables you to get a grip on it' (Cupitt 1990: ix).

For our purposes, then, it would be less misleading to surmise that language creates our differing versions of reality. Here we may be reminded of that ancient strain of Indian wisdom known as Vedanta, in which the word 'maya' is used to describe the illusion of thinking that the way we view the world coincides with absolute reality ('Brahman', the godhead). Or, taking Cupitt's cue, we may think of Wittgenstein: 'The limits of my language are the limits of my world.' Whether it is Hindu metaphysics or modern linguistic philosophy which is more to our taste, we need not go on from here to deny existence to birds, for example, just because we apprehend and recognize them through words ('robin', 'chaffinch', 'skylark'). However, in the later twentieth century, it became fashionable in literary studies to assert blithely that reality is nothing more than a 'cultural construction'. Here, of course, we must make a distinction. To say that we 'construct' the world is true only insofar as we give it a human structure by means of human language; to suggest that we somehow create it out of nothing, as was often unthinkingly implied, is to border on nonsense. As the ecological philosopher Patrick Curry reminds us, one can assuredly have 'reality without realism' (Curry 2008: 60).

How, then, are we using the word 'realism' here? We are using it to mean belief in the possibility of unmediated, objective access to reality, the essence of which can be understood and which may be stated as universal truth. The attempt to make such a statement has a lengthy history, though we might generalize by referring to two main stages, premodern and modern.

With premodern realism, the typical metaphor of choice is the ladder or staircase: reality is thought to culminate in an ultimate and absolute essence, towards which the human soul seeks to ascend: for example, the Good, or God, or the Word. Strictly speaking, this would be called 'metaphysical realism', but Cupitt favours the more graphic term, 'ladder realism', which he defines as follows:

> A form of religious consciousness for which the reality of God consists in his being necessarily at the summit of a hierarchized ontology, or ladder of degrees of existence. In himself God is regarded as being at once supremely real and supremely intelligible; but because human beings are finite and caught up in a world of mere appearance that is far removed from him, he seems to us to be distant, mysterious and even unknowable.
>
> (Cupitt 1986: 219)

With modern realism, the typical metaphor of choice would seem to be the building, if we are to take Marxism as representative, with its talk of society as essentially an economic 'base', consisting of the means and relations of production – what he calls the 'real foundations' – upon which arises a cultural 'superstructure' of institutions and beliefs (Marx and Engels 1973: 503–4). It is this sense of realism which is implicit in the Marxist critic Georg Lukács's praise of nineteenth-century 'realist' fiction as a means of gaining access and insight into the nature of the capitalist mode of production, explicable only in terms of the Marxist model of history as a series of modes (for example, slavery, feudalism, capitalism, socialism).

Now, in what we call the postmodern era, attention has shifted to the paradox by which realism inevitably makes sense chiefly through metaphor, whether that of the ladder or that of the building. But even that insight is scarcely new. It was Nietzsche who declared in the latter half of the nineteenth century that 'truths are illusions which we have forgotten are illusions; they are metaphors that have become worn out and have been drained of sensuous force' (Nietzsche 1979: 84).

With this mention of Nietzsche, we have moved from 'realism' to 'non-realism'. The term would seem to have originated with him, and it has had an important influence on twentieth-century thought. According to Cupitt the basic idea is that of 'perspectivism': 'there are many perspectival viewpoints, but there is no absolute and perspectiveless vision of things' (Cupitt 1986: 223). For the non-realist, then, 'we are the only makers of meanings, truths and values, and our theoretical postulates, such as God, gravity and justice, have no being apart from the language in which we speak of them and the practical uses to which we put it' (Cupitt 1995: 148). If we forget this, and claim to be able to treat metaphor as fact, so that we think we can state once and for all the principles of existence, we are deceiving ourselves.

The philosopher most frequently invoked when the question of the relationship between language and reality is discussed is probably Jacques Derrida. In particular, his pronouncement in *Of Grammatology*, translated as 'There is nothing outside of the text' (Derrida 1976: 158), has been quoted repeatedly. Granted, it does sound very much like linguistic or, more accurately, textual idealism. But a reading of the relevant essay, 'The End of the Book and the Beginning of Writing', does not necessarily support that conclusion. It is important to bear in mind that by 'text' Derrida means 'writing' generally, not just literary works, and that the statement is translatable as 'There is no outside-text'. In this light, we can see that his aim is to 'deconstruct' the discourse of philosophy, showing that it can never get to the point of making referential sense. Every text has other texts as its context, and this accumulation of 'con-texts' is not contained by an ultimate 'Text of texts', so to speak, which would articulate 'the Truth'. That is, there is no Word which can explain the meaning of the world once and for all.

Derrida is a notoriously evasive thinker, and his very evasiveness has encouraged his followers to espouse variations on the 'cultural construction' argument; but in the light of the above, he may just as easily be enlisted to the cause of 'non-realism', in the sense in which we are using it here. Rather than declaring that there is no reality, he is putting the question of the referent in parenthesis, and warning his readers against the dangers of 'realism'. The absence of the referent from the text does not necessarily mean reality is an invention: his point is about the limits of language, the impossibility of ever reaching 'the transcendental signified', or the final meaning.

Those who prefer their non-realism stated more accessibly may turn to Burke, for whom language is 'symbolic action', that is, a way of addressing a situation rather than stating the way things actually are. He put this point succinctly early in his career, in his book *Permanence and Change* (1935): 'A way of seeing is also a way of not seeing' (Burke 1984a: 49). Having done so, he went on in later years to outline his idea that each one of us sees reality through a 'terministic screen' which defines and limits it, filtering out other possible ways of seeing. In an essay on this subject he states: 'Even if any given terminology is a *reflection* of reality, by its very nature as a terminology it must be a *selection* of reality; and to this extent it must function as a *deflection* of reality' (Burke 1966: 45). In short, if realism is the illusion of truth, then non-realism is the truth of illusion.

But even here an objection might arise: does the adoption of non-realism mean resigning oneself to a bland, evasive relativism? Burke suggests not: he recommends that we each of us should be on our guard, prepared to query our own 'way of seeing' in the interests of a 'collective revelation'. Taking the idea that language is a form of 'symbolic action', he speculates that the basis of this revelation might be found in the congruity of words from antiquity used to describe the workings of the universe, such as *tao*, *karma*, *energeia* and *hodos*, each of which suggest action – specifically, the act of following a 'path' or 'way' – rather than mere motion (Burke 1966: 53–4). Humanity, Burke implies, would do well to picture nature as a dynamic, creative process rather than as an inert, alien realm. It is not a question of an idea being abstractly true or false; it is a question of an idea making imaginative sense in that it helps us step outside our limited, 'common-sense' way of seeing.

Thus, non-realism in the Burkean sense tells us that, while we need not expect absolute knowledge, we can learn to think in a way that promotes a sympathetic attitude to the rest of creation. For Burke, this involves the 'comic frame', which 'should enable people to be *observers of themselves, while acting.* Its ultimate would not be passiveness, but *maximum consciousness.* One would "transcend" himself by noting his own foibles' (Burke 1984b: 171). More generally, it should alert us to the dangers of dismissing the ideas of the distant past as wrong-headed and irrelevant. For example, even though Frazer himself treated the myths and rituals of antiquity as evidence of a benighted state of mind, Burke praises *The Golden Bough* precisely because it 'gives us the necessary cues for the detection of similar processes in even the most practical and nonpriestly of contemporary acts'. For the 'comic frame . . . does not *waste* the world's rich store of error, as those parochial-minded persons waste it who dismiss all thought before a certain date as "ignorance" and "superstition". Instead, it cherishes the lore of so-called "error" as a *genuine aspect of the truth*' (Burke 1984b: 172).

In the light of the above definitions, differentiations and deconstructions, we may offer a tentative generalization about myth. Traditionally, there have been two opposed theories of the interpretation of myth, equally influential, one of which is broadly realist, in the sense differentiated and emphasized above, and one of which is broadly non-realist. One assumes the perspective of perfection, translating narrative into the terms of truth, *mythos* into *logos*. The other sees myth as a matter of permanent possibility, trusting in the ongoing power of *mythos* itself. One is bound to a hierarchy; the other is open to a horizon. Moreover, while both are examples of what we are calling 'mythic reading', it is the latter which is the more conscious of itself as a mythopoeic activity. The two mythic readings are 'allegory' and what I call 'radical typology'. The latter is in turn to be distinguished from 'orthodox typology', which is halfway between the two. It is only 'radical typology' which has a perpetual sense of horizon, involving an ongoing dialectic of the sacred and the profane.

ALLEGORY: THE PERSPECTIVE OF PERFECTION

Whoever Homer was, he would probably have been surprised had he encountered an allegorical reading of his own poetry. Allegory did not spring spontaneously from anything we might call 'the Greek mind'. But the fact that one particular interpretive practice did emerge in Hellenic culture should not be ignored. Here I will indicate how and why it developed, and what it involved.

We may infer that the poems known as the *Iliad* and the *Odyssey* – which reached their final form in the eighth century BC – offered to the Greeks of their time a useful summary of received myths, as well as recounting the history of their glorious past, focused on the Trojan War. But perhaps the most important thing about them is that they were, and are, sophisticated works of literary invention, involving impressive use of received formulas. These could be set phrases, such as 'rosy-fingered dawn'. They could be typical scenes, such as the arming of a warrior prior to battle. They could even be recurrent plot structures, such as the withdrawal of the greatest warrior from combat (in the case of the *Iliad*, Achilles), with all its dire consequences for his comrades in arms, followed by his triumphant re-engagement. It was this material which was embellished orally over the years, until it attained the written form which we know.

That form is usually known as epic. Though the word 'epic' (from the Greek, *epos*) may be defined as an oral narrative, which suggests an affinity to myth, we normally distinguish it from myth proper because its subject matter is historical humanity rather than divinity or superhuman heroism – though at many points it does have strong suggestions of the paradigm of hero myth. The main protagonist of the *Iliad* is Achilles, the warrior of formula who withdraws from combat only to return just in time to ensure victory. The protagonist of the *Odyssey* is, of course, Odysseus: having fought in the war, he returns home to his kingdom – encountering, again according to formula, various monsters and mishaps on the way. Achilles is characterized by his devastating wrath; Odysseus, a more subtle figure, is characterized by the ingenuity with which he escapes from perils. Either way the focus is on the human world, albeit a noble or regal one. Or, to put this the other way round, though the protagonists are mythic in the simplest sense (Achilles and Odysseus did not exist), they are presented as if historical, and so of intense human interest.

The hero of epic is a noble warrior or king, and his business is the founding and destroying of cities – for instance, 'Ilium' (Troy) – and the affirmation of his own excellence in the face of imminent death. By virtue of his heroism he stands halfway between divinity and mere humanity; yet if he errs or offends against the higher, cosmic law, he must suffer, more terribly than any ordinary mortal. The protagonist of Homeric epic stands poised between the gods and ourselves. But unlike the protagonist of hero myth, he is always convincingly human. Thus, we are usually more interested in his exploits than in the activities on Mount Olympus, which provide a fanciful setting for the war or adventure on which we are invited to concentrate. The deities of Homer are, significantly, presented as vividly, sometimes ridiculously, anthropomorphic: they exhibit all the lust and greed, pettiness and spite, of which humans are capable. They shift their allegiances in the war according to whim, or decide to hinder the hero's progress because of some nurtured grievance. Such figures are hard to imagine as the object of reverence. They are primarily literary devices, which help to get the tale told.

The contrast here is with the *Theogony*, which is attributed to Homer's contemporary Hesiod. It is primarily an exposition of divine order, besides which human aspiration is made to seem a negligible matter. A literary elaboration on primitive creation myth, it celebrates the rise and triumph of Zeus, the sky father. Though the poem shows his authority being challenged – as by Prometheus, the Titan who steals fire from heaven on behalf of humanity – we also see it strongly reasserted. Providing the genealogy of cosmic rule, the *Theogony* effectively justifies the given social hierarchy. As Fritz Graf puts it, the story demonstrates that 'religious and cultural integration is what defines humanity' (Graf 1993: 86). Or, as Burke would say, in narrating 'principals' the poem consolidates 'principles'.

However, it was Homer's apparent irreverence, not Hesiod's attempt at authorization, which set the agenda for subsequent approaches to myth in Greece. If we take the evidence of fifth-century Athenian tragedy, we might say that myth was maintaining its hold on the popular mind, but that the authority of the Olympian cosmos was beginning to be eroded. For instance, the tragedies of Euripides (480–406 BC) explored the problem of making sense of an apparently unpredictable and unfair universe. Indeed, he so frequently put into the mouth of his characters a critique of the gods that we may well be entitled to infer a consistent authorial position. But then, Euripides' implicit enquiry was only echoing the explicit statement of the philosopher Xenophanes (570–475 BC) that Homer had 'attributed to the gods everything that is a shame and reproach among men, stealing and committing adultery and deceiving each other' (Kirk and Raven 1960: 168). This 'rational' approach to myth, as it is usually called, went further than any of Euripides' characters, in that it took the anthropomorphic nature of the gods to be a reason for rejecting myth itself. For the truth which Xenophanes sought was transcendent; myth, with its naive projection of human qualities onto supposedly higher beings, simply got in the way. The medium was obscuring the message. Xenophanes wanted a religious meaning beyond mere narrative.

This kind of thinking was significant as part of a general process of demythologization. Increasingly after the fifth century BC the power of Greek myth diminished in the face of Greek philosophical speculation. Even those sympathetic to the old gods, and even those engaged in writing narrative poems themselves, effectively undermined the aura of their mythic material. In about 300 BC, Euhemerus of Messene wrote his *Sacred Document*, recounting a voyage to an island where the secret of the gods' origins was waiting to be discovered. Zeus, it transpired, had originally been a human hero who was deified by the community in return for his ousting of tyrants from the vicinity. The term 'Euhemerism' is still used for any mythography which explains away myth as 'merely' historical. Despite the reverent intentions of the *Sacred Document*, its influence was negative: if Zeus had once existed in history, as a mortal, and was subsequently turned into a deity by human will, then the aura of the founding narratives had been effectively diminished.

The line running from the 'rational' to the 'Euhemeristic' constituted the negative aspect of Greek mythography, by which myth was thereby drained of its power. It is perhaps possible to allocate the philosopher Plato (428–348 BC) to this same process. When, in his most famous philosophical dialogue, *The Republic*, he had his mentor Socrates regretfully banish the poets from his ideal state, Homer and Hesiod were not exempted. Like Xenophanes before him, Plato subordinated narrative to reason, human-made myth to transcendent truth. If the citizens of the republic were to fall under the spell of 'the sweetened Muse', then 'pleasure and pain will be enthroned in your city instead of law and the principle which the community accepts as best in any given situation' (Russell and Winterbottom 1972: 74).

Yet it would misrepresent Plato to say that he simply rejected narrative *mythos* in favour of rational *logos*. Rather, he thought the one could be made to serve the other. To appreciate this, we must clarify his general philosophical position briefly. He posited a timeless world of what he called 'the Forms': that is, universal essences. They alone were real, so that to call someone good or something beautiful was to say that they reflected, in their own inferior fashion, that higher realm in which the Good and pure

Beauty resided. Plato opposed the eternal order of being (above) to the temporal chaos of becoming (below). Thus, his position was what Cupitt calls traditional or 'metaphysical realism' – or again, given its rigidly hierarchical thinking, 'ladder realism' (Cupitt 1986: 43). However, gestures could be made from the lower realm to the higher. Or rather, truth could be made palatable by being embellished in the inferior mode of narrative; designed as it was to please the senses, it could yet serve the intellect. Thus, Plato's dialogues themselves are most vividly remembered for Plato's own fables. *The Republic* itself contains the story of the cave, a curious variation on hero myth. It depicts the world of sensual experience as a dark underground cavern, the inhabitants of which take flickering fire-lit images to be reality. Eventually one of their number – the hero of the story, in effect – escapes and sees the sun for the first time. In other words, the hero is the philosopher, who is able to transcend our illusory world by the power of contemplation and reason.

Essentially, what we have in this tale is an allegory. That is what happened to Greek myth once it had been demythologized, as Xenophanes had already done by the time Plato recounted the myth of the cave and as Euhemerus would do a century or so later. Allegory was the positive aspect of the same demythologizing process. Where they explained away the power of myth, reducing it to anthropomorphism and 'mere' history, Plato allowed it its place in the larger scheme of rational understanding. For him the philosophical meaning preceded the myth, and the myth's interest resided in its capacity to illustrate that meaning. The word 'allegory' comes from the Greek, *allos*, or 'other'. Allegorical tales are those which in effect announce, or are made to announce, their own intention: to say *this* in terms of *that*. The 'other' is always subsumed under the 'same'. The narrative is not allowed to exceed the argument; the medium is not allowed to exceed the message. Allegory is domesticated myth.

Thus, Homer himself was rendered safe, so to speak, in the centuries following Plato. The text was translated into the manageable terms of a presupposed meaning. This could be philosophical, but also theological. Indeed, Christianity was particularly interested in taming Homer. While the early church fathers found the negative Euhemeristic approach to Greek myth useful, since it exposed the Greek deities as glorified mortals, it also made the most of allegory, since it positively demonstrated that even benighted pagans could appreciate the necessity for moral instruction. Homer had not been able to benefit from Christ's redemption, but his narratives had glimmerings of Christian truth – obscured, of course, by all the absurd, or even demonic, antics of the Olympian gods and goddesses. Beyond the narrative lay the theological and moral essence, the transcendent truth, the allegorical meaning. This mode of mythography survived the Middle Ages, despite the disappearance of the primary Homeric texts, to be revived with enthusiasm in the Renaissance. Searching through Graeco-Roman myths for Christian truths became something of an obsession. The Italian mythographer Natale Conti was perhaps typical when, in his *Mythologia* (1616), he read Odysseus' return to Ithaca as demonstrating that a wise Christian, patiently enduring hardships and avoiding temptation, would eventually live 'in his true fatherland, sharing with other men in the councils of God' (Allen 1970: 95). Myth had been tamed once and for all – or so it seemed.

RADICAL TYPOLOGY: PERMANENT POSSIBILITY

Allegory was only one aspect of early Christianity. The other was typology, which might be illustrated by reference to the New Testament itself. Here the role of such crucial figures from early Biblical myth as Adam and Moses is reaffirmed and yet also rewritten. To St Paul, Jesus is the 'second' Adam, restoring the paradisal bliss lost in the original fall from the Garden of Eden. For 'as in Adam all died, so in Christ all shall be made alive' (I Corinthians 15: 22). Moses, hero of the earliest myth of deliverance, anticipates Jesus more positively, and in at least three ways. John Ferguson explains:

> First, because he was the instrument of the first great act of liberation; the Messiah would re-enact the act of liberation. Second, because he was associated with the Old Covenant, as Jesus with the New, in

> which Law found its fulfilment in love. Third because Moses striking the rock so that water gushed out formed the living emblem of Jesus giving the Living Water (John 4.7–13).
>
> (Ferguson 1980: 99)

In each case, the former person or event provides the 'type', which carries with it its special promise; the latter provides the 'anti-type', which does not constitute the opposite of the type, despite the unusual prefix, but rather its realization. The type is the prefigurement; the anti-type is the fulfilment. The whole of the Bible is taken to point forward to the triumph of Jesus Christ over death. Typology is the myth of deliverance turned into a foolproof mode of mythography.

The first, correct impression of this kind of mythic reading is that it is an arrogant act of appropriation. A whole body of scripture and belief, such as the Judaic, which already comprehends the Israelite and the Hebrew, is translated at a stroke into a mere prologue to an upstart religion. It becomes an 'Old' Testament, foil to the 'New'. (The resonance of this hegemonic act is still with us in our very dating system, BC and AD, which is in itself evidence that the modern mind continues to think mythically.) But just as with apocalyptic myth, there is a dynamic tension between the 'already' and the 'not yet', so with the mythic reading known as typology we must distinguish between the orthodox and radical aspects.

Orthodox typology, which is implicit in the Epistles and Gospels, and which is explicit in the works of early church fathers such as Origen and Augustine, sees all promises as now fulfilled, with the Word having been incarnated into the darkness of this world and then having returned to heaven, its mission complete. Now it speaks to us through the hierarchy and authority of the church. In this sense typology is only a variation upon allegory, and is committed to traditional realism. Orthodox typology is wary of admitting the fantastic or legendary nature of the story of Jesus, or *mythos*, and wants to translate it into doctrine, or *logos/Logos*. For if the promises of the Old Testament have been finally and absolutely fulfilled in the New, then narrative is no more. That is, orthodox typology is a kind of demythologization.

But it is possible to extract the pattern of promise and fulfilment from that of scriptural completion, and see it working through and beyond the Bible. Peter Munz has suggested that typology is a valid mythic principle in its own right, and needs appreciating as such. 'Every myth we know', he declares, 'has both a past and a future' (Munz 1973: ix). The elements of myth that are called 'type' and 'anti-type' could, if rescued from orthodoxy, be taken as explicit indices of the way mythology works anyway. This is 'the phenomenon of historical seriality' (Munz 1973: xii). In other words, all myths presuppose a previous narrative, and in turn form the model for future narratives. Strictly speaking, the pattern of promise and fulfilment need never end; no sooner has one narrative promise been fulfilled than the fulfilment becomes in turn the promise of further myth-making. Thus, myths remake other myths, and there is no reason why they should not continue to do so, the mythopoeic urge being infinite. This understanding is what I call radical typology. Where orthodox typology works in terms of closure, radical typology works in terms of disclosure.

Accepting the idea that typology can occur both within and without the Bible, we can see the Bible itself as a body of mythology which does two things. On the one hand, it develops in response to other mythologies; on the other hand, it reworks its own myths as it expands, providing further material for post-Biblical mythology. But to do so, we have to see how earlier, pre-Biblical mythology was developing. Here let us briefly compare Mesopotamian creation myth with the Hebrew/Israelite creation myth that opens the Judaeo-Christian Bible.

The earliest known creation myth of the region that lies between the rivers Tigris and Euphrates dates back to at least the middle of the third millennium BC, during the occupation of the Sumerians. It tells us that Nammu, the primeval sea, is the source of all life: she is the divine matrix, and from her proceed all the other deities, and so in turn the universe, the earth and humanity. With the rise of the highly aggressive Babylonian state within the Mesopotamian region early in the second millennium BC, it seemed appropriate to narrate a new version of the creation myth, in which the power of the Babylonian state god, Marduk, could be demonstrated. *Enuma Elish*, the Babylonian creation myth, so called because of its opening phrase ('When on high . . .') tells us that in the beginning there are two beings, one male and one female, both identified with water: Apsu, the sweet water; and Tiamat, the salt water. They produce the other deities, notably the sky god Anu and the earth god Ea (who, curiously, replaces the Sumerian earth goddess Ki). But now the younger gods rebel against the existing order, and Ea puts Apsu into a deep sleep so that he can slay him. Tiamat is furious and decides to do away with the younger gods. Marduk, who is the son of Ea and Damkina, wishes to prove himself as a warrior and so he goes to battle against Tiamat and her offspring, Kingu. Triumphant, he cuts the body of Tiamat into two, setting the heaven above and, resting on the ocean, the earth below. So it is that the cosmos is formed from the corpse of a primeval deity. Then, from the blood of Tiamat's firstborn, Kingu, he creates human beings, as an afterthought, for the sole purpose of serving the gods. This myth, recited annually at the Babylonian new year festival, or *akitu*, confirms the status of Marduk as state god and of the current Babylonian king as the representative of Marduk. It presupposes the earlier, Sumerian myth, but rewrites it in such a way as to glorify patriarchal power and male violence: the maternal source of being has become raw material for the state god's display of authority. However, we should not overlook a residual Sumerian detail: humanity is created out of nature, in the form of the primeval mother's son, even if the event involves his murder.

Now we turn again to the Bible, and specifically to the first book, Genesis, which was 'redacted' (put together by editing earlier Hebrew myths) during the late sixth to early fifth century BC after the Israelites had returned from exile in Babylon. We may infer that the Israelites, determined to celebrate their independence, wanted to produce a creation narrative which would outdo the Babylonians'. Bear in mind that 'Enuma elish' is expressive of polytheism: though Marduk becomes leader of the gods, he is not regarded as one unique God. By contrast, Genesis 1 seems to envisage creation as being performed by a single deity: in that case, polytheism would thereby be superseded, and an explicit monotheism would be asserted for the first time in history. Bear in mind also that *Enuma Elish* describes creation as coming about after a battle between a younger sky-god and an older sea-goddess. By contrast, Genesis 1 seems to describe creation as being performed all at once, out of nothing: in that case, the very idea of creation would thereby be transformed; the Israelites' deity seems to create by simply uttering his sacred Word ('Let there be light') amidst the darkness.

However, the persistence of the worldview of the Babylonian myth becomes evident when we consider two factors. First, though by the time Genesis 1 came to be written, the name of 'Yahweh' was current, the text uses another, older name, 'Elohim'; and, while the word 'Elohim' can be used in the singular to mean 'God', it is just as often used in the plural to mean 'gods'. Thus, the divine creator may be envisaged as the leader of a divine assembly just as much as the supreme deity: monotheism is not asserted decisively. Second, the idea of creation out of nothing is very difficult to articulate and maintain. The very language of Genesis 1 suggests that Yahweh/Elohim is intervening in a pre-existent mode of being, characterized by words such as 'void' and 'darkness'. Moreover, *tehom*, the Hebrew name for 'the deep', over which the spirit of Yahweh/Elohim is said to move, is etymologically related to the Babylonian name of 'Tiamat'. The old cosmology lingers between the lines of the new narrative; myth is hidden within myth. Yet there has indeed been an advance made upon the original source; Genesis is no mere footnote to 'Enuma elish'. Creation is envisaged as a much more subtle process: God creates the world by language rather than by violence; and he does so by differentiation rather than defeat. Again, it is a much more compassionate process: humanity is made in God's own image and with God's blessing, rather than as a servile afterthought. Thus, when we look at the whole process by which myth reworks myth, we can say that there is a tension in typology: the anti-type is impossible without the type; yet the anti-type manages to go beyond the type.

So much is similarly evident when we consider the internal dynamic within the Judaeo-Christian Bible itself. The last, Christian book totally rewrites the first, Judaic book. Genesis forms the type; Revelation forms the anti-type. Genesis gives us the creation, the Garden of Eden, Adam and Eve, and the tempting serpent (itself obviously owing something to the chaos dragon Tiamat). Revelation gives us 'a new heaven and a new earth', the garden-city of Jerusalem, the Messiah and his bride, and the lamb who overthrows both dragon and beast. The latter text makes no sense without the former, since re-creation presupposes creation, just as salvation presupposes the fall. But the former text has been, in effect, rewritten as a prologue to the apocalypse. There again, if this internal dynamic is inseparable from the wider project of making and remaking myth, we need not take the achievement of Revelation as final. Indeed, as we have seen, the rhetoric of that work speaks out of a sense of crisis, transition and instability; informed by a past promise, it projects, from a present of oppression, a future of liberation. The apocalypse is always now, but that now is always involved in an ongoing dialectic. Thus, the apocalyptic myth, while available for orthodox recuperation, as in Spenser's *The Fairie Queene*, can never finally be domesticated, but will always invite radical reaffirmation, as in Winstanley's *Fire in the Bush*.

According to Erich Auerbach, typology, or 'figural interpretation', of its very nature 'differs from most of the allegorical forms known to us by the historicity both of the sign and what it signifies' (Auerbach 1984: 54). But this assessment may be misleading unless we recall the distinction, made above, between orthodox and radical typology. Indeed, we should be aware that many 'figural' interpreters have tried to tame Biblical myth, constraining its 'historicity'. Hence, we need to rescue typology from its orthodox proponents, and affirm its radical potential. Myths work according to the imperative of narrative dynamism and will always evade the stasis of doctrine. Thus, the premature finality of realism is the death of myth; the 'not yet' of apocalypse becomes, then, the key to mythic life.

One mythic thinker who resisted finality was Joachim, twelfth-century abbot of Fiore. He projected a global history based on the Holy Trinity, inspired by his reading of Revelation. Constructing his own post-Biblical myth, inspired by the apocalypse, he envisaged a sequence of three ages: the first *status* (Latin, 'state', 'situation', 'stance') was that of the Father; the second was that of the Son; the third, which was to come, was that of the Spirit. Joachim's visionary, threefold scheme is summed up by Marjorie Reeves as follows:

> [T]he first *status* was under the law, the second *status* under grace, the third *status*, which we expect soon, will be under a more ample grace; . . . the first was lived in the servitude of slaves, the second in the servitude of sons, but the third will be in liberty; . . . the first was lived in fear, the second in faith, the third will be in love; the first was the *status* of slaves, the second of sons, but the third will be that of friends; the first of old men, the second of young men, the third of children; the first was lived in starlight, the second in the dawn, the third will be the perfect day.
>
> (Reeves 1976: 14)

It should be stressed that it was essential to Joachim's belief in 'the fruition of history' that the agencies to bring the church through the transition period to the third age must be human, albeit divinely inspired (Reeves 1976: 29). Indeed, the 'everlasting gospel' announced in Revelation 16:6 was going to express the freedom of a new 'Spiritual Intelligence' possessed by men and women.

Thus, Joachim's triadic scheme of the three ages, of Father, Son and Holy Ghost, is both a valid, post-Biblical myth in its own right and a good example of what we are calling radical typology. For, taking his cue from Revelation, he refuses to accept the closure of fulfilment: that is, he follows the logic of type and anti-type to the point where both are subsumed in a dialectic of infinite potential: 'the reign of love on this earth, love from the heart, can dispense with the law of both Testaments; Judgement Day is indefinitely postponed and its awesome sting is removed by the transitional third stage of the Holy Ghost. The great expectation for which Joachim prepares the faithful is not the end of the world and a transcendent resolution in Heaven, but . . . the appearance . . . of the Holy Ghost on earth' (Manuel 1965: 38–9). This third age of the spirit will be expressed by a 'Third Testament'. The product of the profane imagination, it will supersede even the proclamations of Christ.

One author who may be seen as having attempted to draw up his own 'Third Testament' is the Italian poet Dante Alighieri (1265–1321). Here we will consider the text which became known as *The Divine Comedy*, but which was known by its author simply as the *Comedy*. We will take it to be a secular 'anti-type' to the whole of the Bible, and we will take it to be a major mythopoeic work. In order to do that, we must bear in mind what was said above about the dynamic context of the Biblical myth. If orthodox typology involves a thorough rewriting of scripture, radical typology involves a shift of emphasis from the sacred to the profane. While it may appear to be arrogant appropriation, similar to that by which one set of scriptures becomes a foil to another, its effect is to liberate the imagination. Its business is not dogmatic assertion, but narrative exploration. Dante's *Divine Comedy* (1314–21) may be taken to exemplify it. It is not only an extension of Biblical myth, it is a unique mythopoeic achievement. It creates not one but three 'unprecedented worlds': those of the *Inferno*, the *Purgatorio* and the *Paradiso*. Though derived from scriptural hints, in detail they are uniquely Dante's invention. Here we will briefly summarize the plot which contains them.

Midway through his life, the narrator dreams that he has lost his way in a dark wood. The Roman classical poet Virgil appears, offering to escort him through hell and purgatory, from where he can proceed to heaven itself. Hell is conceived as a conical tunnel, reaching to the centre of the earth. Various categories of sinners are assigned to the nine infernal circles, where they receive appropriate punishments. At the very bottom is Satan himself. Passing him by, Dante and Virgil find their descent becoming an ascent, and they eventually reach the opposite surface of the earth. Here is located the foot of the mountain of purgatory: this is the place where the souls of the dead are purged of their sins before admittance to heaven. The two pilgrims encounter various groups of repentant sinners on the seven circular ledges of the mountain. On its summit lies the earthly paradise, or the Garden of Eden, where Dante meets none other than Beatrice, the woman he admires more than any other. As she approaches, a hundred angels sing '*Benedictus qui venis!*': that is, 'Blessed are thou that comest', which is only a slightly modified version of Matthew 21:9: 'Blessed is He who cometh' (Dante 1995: 364–5). Virtually the same words are applicable to both Christ and Beatrice. Her importance could not be greater. Indeed, Dante stands trembling in adoration before her. Virgil, as a pre-Christian pagan, can serve as guide no longer, and it is Beatrice who conducts Dante through heaven. As hell was divided into circles, so heaven is divided into spheres: those of the moon, of Mercury, Venus, the sun, Mars, Jupiter, Saturn, the fixed stars, and the '*primum mobile*' or first mover. The spheres are in ascending order of merit, and he is conducted through them by Beatrice. The journey culminates in a vision of the divine light itself, which is the primary expression of 'the Love that moves the sun and the other stars' (Dante 1995: 585).

This ambitious work, culminating in a sacred vision of perfection, while obviously indebted to Christian doctrine, is original and powerful enough to be recognized as a myth in its own right. Over the centuries, however, the myth has been systematically tamed by orthodox interpretation. Again and again, it has been defined and read as an allegory. After all, it depicts the progress of the human soul from error and ignorance to the contemplation of God. It comprises a journey through three eternal realms: hell, purgatory and heaven. The poet's guide through the first two, Virgil, might allegorically stand for classical reason. Regarding Beatrice, we might say that reason, while valid, can only take us so far, and that she represents the ultimate power of Christian grace. Read in this way, the poem becomes a monumental justification of medieval order. Its vertical journey, in which the protagonist-poet acquires the wisdom of humility as he ascends nearer and nearer to God, articulates the need for submission to hierarchical authority. However, the *Comedy* is such a richly imaginative work that when reading it we always sense the narrative power exceeding any neatly paraphraseable meaning. Certainly, more recent commentary on the poem has dwelt on the enigma of the *mythos* rather than seeking out directly the certainty of the *logos*.

Thomas Altizer, following the logic of Dante's narrative, celebrates his 'heresy'. For him the presence of Joachim is vital, and he sees Dante as dramatically influenced by the abbot's secularization of sacred revelation and his affirmation, against St Augustine, of the 'City of Man' as equal to the 'City of God'. Thus, the *Comedy* is 'the first Christian and apocalyptic epic', fusing history and heaven. It effects 'the transcendence of eternity in time itself, as time once again becomes an eschatological time, a time in which eternity is here and now'. Altizer explains:

> Now time itself is simultaneously an earthly and chronological time and a sacred and eternal time, a simultaneity revealed in the very chronology of the *Commedia*. For its epic action occurs during Eastertide in the year 1300 and lasts just a week, from the night of Maundy Thursday when Dante finds himself astray in the Dark Wood, until noon on the Wednesday after Easter, when Dante is transfigured in Heaven. The period of Dante's descent into Hell repeats and renews the time of Christ's death and burial, just as his journey through Purgatory renews and repeats the time of Christ's entombment, and his entrance into Paradise coincides with the dawn of Easter Sunday.
> (Altizer 1985: 123)

Thus, Altizer confirms that Dante's vast, visionary work constitutes an approximation to Joachim's 'Third Testament'. It rewrites Christian myth in secular terms, and opens up a whole new world of promise. The 'coincidence of opposites', where the sacred and the profane meet, is not a distant goal but a present possibility. We might concur with Erich Auerbach in calling the form in which Dante achieves this dialectical vision 'figural realism', but only if we understand 'realism' as the realization of the sacred in the profane, and forget all notions of a truth external to language, history and myth (Auerbach 1968: 196).

The poem's positive focus is the figure of Beatrice, who is not merely an aspect of Mary, mother of God, but ultimately 'the one and only avenue of salvation' for the poet (Altizer 1985: 127). Pushing this argument further, and recalling the benediction in the earthly paradise, we might conclude that Beatrice is as important to the poem as Christ himself – perhaps more so. Heretical as this sounds, it is not entirely misleading. Dante's audacious glorification of this female figure is consistent with

Joachim's radical typology, and what we have said about the temporal dynamic of Biblical myth. We recall that in 'Enuma elish' creation was only achieved through the violent suppression of a she-monster. In Genesis, at the beginning of the Old Testament, this battle remained implicit in the creation story, but became explicit in the subsequent story of the fall, in which the first human female was associated with a serpent that would in time be identified as Satan. In Revelation, at the end of the New Testament, the defeat was announced of another demonic female, the 'whore of Babylon', whose power derived from that same serpent or dragon. Now, in this 'Third Testament', not only is the balance redressed by giving Mary her due as the agent by which the Messiah comes into the world, but the bounds of dogma are overleaped entirely by making a female figure who is of no theological significance, except to Dante, the main focus of redemption. If allegory presupposes an act of demythologization, radical typology proposes an act of remythologization. The sacred may be realized in the profane. The apocalypse may inform every moment of history.

ENLIGHTENMENT AND COUNTER-ENLIGHTENMENT

In the ancient and medieval eras, the hierarchy of allegory was tempered by the historicity of typology; beyond both stretched the infinite horizon of radical typology, which still persists. Less dramatically, but still significantly, in early modernity the Enlightenment, which glorified reason and truth, was met by the counter-Enlightenment, which reaffirmed the power of imagination and myth. Here I give the broad outline of this antithesis, in preparation for assessing the mythic readings of our own era. Radical typology will not be forgotten, but reaffirmed in a variety of settings.

In situating allegory, we had to consider two other kinds of mythography: the 'rational', which explained away myth as an inferior way of representing transcendent truth; and the 'Euhemeristic', which explained away myth as the deifying of historical figures. Together these comprised the negative aspect of allegory itself. Where they broke down the mythic material, allegory put it together again, but by now that material had effectively been deprived of its power. Similarly, when we come to the European Enlightenment, we find the same double-bind at work. Again, I will take one stage at a time.

The 'rational' approach may be represented by Pierre Bayle (1647–1706), who in his *Historical and Critical Dictionary* equated 'myth' with 'absurdity' (Graf 1993: 14). The context of this usage should not be overlooked. For if it was in or around 1700 that modern mythography began, then it did so in a spirit of hostility to the very material it sought to explain. In particular, we might note that exploratory voyages to Africa and North America in the sixteenth and seventeenth centuries had suggested embarrassing parallels between contemporary 'savage' customs and the very myths that Renaissance scholars had been gleaning for signs of moral wisdom. Thus, the distinction was introduced between archaic Greek myth (any narrative which was uncomfortably obscene or violent) and classical Greek literature (any narrative which pleased the enlightened mind). Reinforcing this rational approach was an equally modern version of Euhemerism. In *The Natural History of Religion*, the philosopher David Hume (1711–76) argued that myth was the origin of religion, and that both were founded in primitive humanity's fear of its environment. Terrified by any unfamiliar object in its surroundings, it had converted it into a sacred being – a god or goddess. Thus had the worship of natural objects begun. Thereafter, it had seemed only fitting to deify extraordinary men and women, just as Euhemerus argued.

Though the scholar of Greek mythology, Fritz Graf, argues that the Enlightenment was averse to the allegorization of myth, it is possible to discover something like allegory complementing the negative views of Bayle and Hume. For example, though Christian Gottlob Heyne (1729–1812), who had formed his ideas about myth by about 1760, agreed with Hume that it expressed a primitive terror, he thought the very nature of the expression might repay serious study. For the concrete, sensuous language of myth, though crude, had led to the subtle delights of poetry. Myth was a product of the childhood of humanity, but as such it could afford insights into our origins. Myth was the primary content; poetry was the secondary form. The method required to discover the content underlying the form was philology, the historical and comparative science of language. In the case of Greece, the myths had come down to us in complex and sometimes contradictory ways: for example, Homeric epic and Athenian tragedy. The task was to work one's way back beyond both to discover the original material. In that way, we could begin to understand the essential Greek mind in its linguistic context. It is possible, then, to see Heyne's approach as allegorical, working upon the narrative or *mythos* in two retrospective stages (first form, then content) until it delivered the hidden meaning he sought.

It is through Heyne that we can intuit the positive mythographic interest of the Enlightenment, such as it was. Thus, though archaic myth-making was understood to be immature compared to modern rationality, it could not simply be left behind. Moreover, though ancient Greek literature had derived from archaic Greek myth, it was clearly of interest as an example of emergent clarity. The Enlightenment in the main celebrated classical Greece without reservation, withholding approval only from the dark centuries preceding it. This darkness was considered to have been interrupted only by the light of the occasional poet such as Homer, provided he had been suitably allegorized first.

As with Plato, the allegorical principle of the late seventeenth and early eighteenth centuries was reason – *logos* set out to explain *mythos*. But now it went much further. As Thomas Docherty explains: 'The Enlightenment aimed at human emancipation from myth, superstition and enthralled enchantment to mysterious powers and forces of nature through the progressive operations of critical reason.' This solution, however, turned out to create its own problems. 'In the desire to contest any form of animistic enchantment by nature, Enlightenment set out to think the natural world in an abstract form.' Thus, it could only 'think' that which could be systematized. 'In a word, reason has been reduced to . . . a specific *form* of reason. More importantly, this specific inflection of reason is also now presented as if it were reason-as-such, as if it were the only valid or legitimate form of rational thinking.' What offered itself as emancipation turned out to be suppression. Docherty quotes from Theodor Adorno and Max Horkheimer's *Dialectic of Enlightenment* (1944): 'Enlightenment behaves toward things as a dictator toward men. He knows them in so far as he can manipulate them.' Reason, that is, became power; and power could only function by having an 'other' to suppress, whether nature, human beings (as 'savages') or myths (Docherty 1993: 7–8).

However, in the very act of demystifying traditional myths, the Enlightenment was engaged in its own mythic enterprise. We have already referred to the 'myth of mythlessness'. Now we can go further, and take into account Jean-François Lyotard's proposition that the Enlightenment invented two modern 'metanarratives', which have held good up to the present era. The first, particularly strong in France and finding dramatic expression in the French Revolution, is that of 'the liberation of humanity'. The second, particularly strong in Germany and finding more refined but no less ambitious expression in the writings of Georg Wilhelm Friedrich Hegel (1770–1831), is that of 'the speculative unity of all knowledge'. Each of these grand narratives of modernity has its own ideal protagonist: the 'hero of liberty', or activist, and the 'hero of knowledge', or philosopher (Lyotard 1984: 31). The paradox of both narratives is that, though dedicated to *logos* – aiming to transcend error, whether perceived as injustice or as ignorance, in the name of reason – they by definition exemplify the need for *mythos.* Unfortunately, Lyotard has since confused the issue by suggesting that, though the 'metanarratives' of modernity clearly derive from Christianity, they are not myths as such since 'they look for legitimacy not in an original founding act but in a future to be accomplished' (Lyotard 1992: 29). This is to ignore the very dynamic of the Biblical myth of deliverance, which comprehends both creation (founding) and apocalypse (future). That said, his overall case remains valid, that these 'metanarratives' only work provided they are taken as non-narrative truth, the conviction being that the Enlightenment is an end which justifies the means. That is, it remains valid as the expression of a universal law, whatever or whoever is suppressed in the name of its progress.

It was this facile assumption of non-narrative truth that provoked what Isaiah Berlin calls the counter-Enlightenment. If there was such a movement, and if it had a founder, then that title must go to Giambattista Vico (1688–1744). An inspiration to a writer we have already considered, James Joyce, he refused to see myth as error, and insisted that it was an early, necessary and wholly admirable phase in the development of civilization. In his *The New Science*, he argued that the only 'science' of humanity which could be of use was one that comprehended what lay behind *logos*. Not reason but imagination was the key to myth. Myth was not a failed attempt to articulate rational truth, but was the creative impulse underlying human history. Primitive mythopoeia was the source of all experience and all expression. If it represented the childhood of humanity, that was no reason to treat it with condescension. Far from patronizing it, the modern age should be trying to understand how it had informed its own character and ideas. Vico, according to Joseph Mali, achieved the 'rehabilitation of myth':

> [He] saw that in our (and any other) civilization the fictions of mythology illuminate the 'real world' by constituting or 'prefiguring' all its human actions and institutions: unlike natural occurrences which display law-like, repetitive regularities which are unknowable to us because they are totally alien to our form of life, human occurrences throughout history display forms of action which are knowable to us insofar as we can recognize in them the coherent narrative patterns of the mythical stories with their well-made characters and plots.
>
> (Mali 1992: 3–4)

That is, myth shapes history, and therefore it shapes culture. The religious beliefs, social customs and linguistic commonplaces of each age are reaffirmations of, and elaborations upon, primitive mythic patterns.

We may say, then, that what characterizes the counter-Enlightenment, as represented by Vico, is not the allegory of reason but the typology of imagination. As Peter Munz explains:

> In Platonic thought and in every philosophy that was derived from it, there had been an unbridgeable gulf between time and Idea, the particular and the universal, becoming and being. The gulf remained unbridgeable even when modern evolutionist thinking reversed Plato's evaluation of it. Plato had believed that truth was on the side of the Idea and that becoming was a form of illusion. Modern evolutionism stood Plato on his head; but the dichotomy remained. Vico's explanation eliminated the gulf. The Truth of Idea depended on the temporal extension of the typological series.
>
> (Munz 1973: 120–3)

That is, *mythos* precedes and informs *logos*. Without Homer there can be no Plato. The profane imagination expresses itself initially through mythic narrative; the principles of philosophy, far from being eternal, are the result of a long process of reflection on, reaction to and rewriting of that initial imaginative expression. They form the anti-type to its type. Time produces the 'Idea', imagination produces 'Truth', the profane produces the sacred.

The typology of imagination was, it might be said, the inspiration of the Romantic poet William Blake (1757–1827). Putting all his effort into revitalizing the Christian myth, it was he who in 1820 called the Bible 'the Great Code'. But far from seeing that book of books as a constraining presence, he felt able to rewrite it totally, in the belief that 'Eternity is in love with the productions of time' (Blake 1971: 151). Instead of setting out from the idea of an omniscient and omnipotent God who had created the cosmos and then created humanity, he saw humanity as the source of both cosmos and creator. That is, long before Hegel proposed, and Nietzsche confirmed, the 'death of God', Blake had comprehended that very principle within a new, radical Christianity. The God of the Old Testament, whom he also identified with the abstract, inhuman deity of the Enlightenment, he called 'Urizen' (the product of 'your reason'). Moreover, according to his dramatic rewriting of the New Testament, that God – who had never existed in the first place, except as a human projection – could be said to have died once and for all with the birth of Jesus. The God of the New Testament had freed us from the obligation to worship a deity distinct from ourselves.

Moreover, if 'Empire' – the tyranny of Urizen – was 'against Art', then Jesus was the greatest of 'Artists': 'The Old & New Testaments are the Great Code of Art. Art is the Tree of Life. God is Jesus' (Blake 1971: 777). In other words, false religion was the dogma that enslaved; true religion was the story that liberated. But meanwhile, Christianity went on clinging to its arid and abstract sky-father and asserting sacred truth against the challenge of profane imagination.

Blake, then, has his own myth to recount: a rewriting and fusion of the creation and deliverance paradigms. But his particular genius is to remain faithful to the form of his 'Great Code' while turning its world, as far as the orthodox are concerned, upside down. *Songs of Innocence* (1789), with its comforting, apparently stable imagery of shepherd and lamb, father and child, forms the conventional prologue to this radical myth, which begins with *The Marriage of Heaven and Hell* (1793). Here he demonstrates that ostensibly stark opposites such as heaven and hell, good and evil, reason and desire, always turn out to be dialectical 'contraries', without which 'there is no progression'. In order to redress the balance against orthodoxy, the *Marriage* commends the wisdom of the 'devils': 'Energy is eternal delight. . . . The road of excess leads to the palace of wisdom. . . . What is now proved was once only imagined. . . . Exuberance is Beauty. . . .' Humanity has repressed this wisdom because it has forgotten that 'All deities reside in the human breast'. It is as if 'man has closed himself up, till he sees all things thro' narrow chinks of his cavern'. He has come to regard the very limits he has set himself as eternal and immutable. The alternative, which we have already encountered in our discussion of Jim Morrison, is clear: 'If the doors of perception were cleansed every thing would appear to man as it is, infinite' (Blake 1971: 150–4).

Hence, in the poem 'London' from *Songs of Experience* (1794) we learn that it is 'the mind-forg'd manacles' which keep humanity subject to state and church hierarchy (Blake 1971: 216). If 'all deities reside in the human breast', then so do all oppressive doctrines. In *The First Book of Urizen*, published the same year as *Experience*, the Book of Genesis is rewritten so that the creation of our cosmos turns out to have been simultaneous with the fall.

For if the world we know is the result of Urizen's having separated himself out from a primal harmony known as eternity, and if Urizen, like all deities, is human in origin, an aspect of our own minds, then to find ourselves in this world of false laws and limits is effectively to have restricted our own vision. Letting reason take over from our other faculties, we have become alienated – or 'fallen'. We have constructed a false ideal, have come to believe in a tyrannous perfection: 'One King, one God, one Law' (Blake 1971: 224).

We move beyond this fallen world, with its sterile antithesis of innocence and experience, in Blake's notes to *Vala, or The Four Zoas* (1795–1804): 'Unorganiz'd Innocence' is, we are told, 'An Impossibility' (Blake 1971: 380). There is, we understand, a third realm beyond the two worlds of the *Songs*: an innocence that is 'organized', that synthesizes what are now recognized as contraries. Again, he elaborates upon his 'Great Code'. In the Bible, the 'innocence' of the Garden of Eden is lost, to be replaced by the 'experience' of the demonic city. Only then may Jerusalem, the heavenly city which is also a garden containing the lost tree of life, be attained and appreciated. Blake infers from his reading of the Bible that the unfallen and the fallen worlds, as inner dispositions, presuppose one another. Thus, the task of the imagination is to forge – out of the contraries – that third realm of 'organized innocence'. In the 'Preface' to *Milton* (1810), the poet, as bard, declares that he 'will not cease from Mental Fight' until 'we have built Jerusalem / In England's green and pleasant Land' (Blake 1971: 481). If we were ever in any doubt, we now see that Blake is a visionary in the tradition of Joachim:

> Rouse up, O young Men of the New Age! Set your foreheads against the ignorant Hirelings! For we have Hirelings in the Camp, the Court & the University, who would, if they could, for ever depress Mental & prolong Corporeal War. . . . We do not want either Greek or Roman Models if we are but just & true to our own Imaginations, those Worlds of Eternity in which we shall live for ever and ever in Jesus our Lord.
>
> (Blake 1971: 480)

Blake's radical Christian myth is typological, since it draws on the Bible in order to rewrite it; and it is apocalyptic, since it foresees the overthrow of those who have served Babylon. It invites the reader to abandon the Hellenic, allegorical distinction between eternity and time, and through the power of imagination end the state of alienation. That state, manifest in 'Corporeal War', has its source in mental oppression. Only by 'Mental Fight' may the heavenly city be built on earth.

The imaginative potential of humanity is represented in his last major work, *Jerusalem* (1804–20), by the figure of Albion, who is simultaneously England and the primal, universal man. He is woken from his long and heavy slumbers by Los, the artist, 'the Prophet of Eternity'. Albion realizes that he has been living a life of illusion rather than vision, and that he has failed to see both the sacred dimension of earthly life and his own divinity. Having been roused from his slumbers, he is able to meet Jesus as an equal and as a friend. The latter appears – appropriately, since he too is an 'Artist' – in the likeness of Los. Jesus is, ultimately, Albion's waking self, and his resurrected body may therefore be identified with the body of a newly risen humanity, open to imagination and love.

Blake's mythopoeic urge is firmly centred on the human imagination, but it is this capacity that in turn allows us to see reality for the first time. Myth is reaffirmed in an exploratory rather than an explanatory spirit. Indeed, we might say that with Blake it becomes possible to believe that the imagination and nature are two halves of the same whole. Blake states his understanding of the complementary relationship of these forces in his famous letter of 1799 to Dr Trusler:

> I feel that a Man may be happy in This World. And I know that This World Is a World of Imagination & Vision. I see Everything I paint In This World, but Every body does not see alike. To the Eyes of a Miser a Guinea is far more beautiful than the Sun, & a bag worn with the use of Money has more beautiful proportions than a Vine filled with Grapes. The tree which moves some to tears of joy is in the Eyes of others only a Green thing which stands in the way. Some see Nature all Ridicule & Deformity, & by these I shall not regulate my

> proportions; & some scarce see Nature at all. But to the Eyes of the Man of Imagination, Nature is Imagination itself.
>
> (Blake 1971: 793)

By stressing the creative nature of perception, Blake is in effect reminding us of the dangers of what we have called realism. He tells us that each of us has a choice: to dismiss the profane world as 'all Ridicule & Deformity' or to celebrate its sacred dimension. To choose the latter is simultaneously to choose liberation, to let 'Vision' flourish. The answer is within the human mind as much as without. It is perhaps no coincidence that it was Blake's contemporary poet, Samuel Taylor Coleridge, who invented the word 'psychology'. For there is a deep continuity between Romanticism and modern movements such as psychoanalysis. Nor is it a coincidence that their focus is on myth. We now turn, therefore, to the relationship between myth and the psyche.

5

PSYCHE

THE PRIMAL CRIME

The word 'psyche' comes from a Greek word meaning 'breath' or 'life', and by extension 'soul'. The myth of Cupid and Psyche, originally Greek, features prominently in *The Golden Ass* by Apuleius, a Roman writer of the late second century BC. The story is as follows. Psyche is a beautiful maiden enamoured of Cupid, the god of love (the equivalent of the Greek Eros). He visits her every night but departs before sunrise, not having let her see him. But curiosity gets the better of her, and one night she lifts up her lamp to catch a glimpse of her lover; a drop of hot oil falls on his shoulder, and he awakes and flees. The abandoned Psyche wanders far and wide in search of Cupid. She becomes the slave of Venus (the Roman equivalent of Aphrodite, whom we have already met in our discussion of Frazer); the goddess imposes impossible tasks on her and treats her cruelly. Eventually, however, she is reunited with her lover and becomes immortal.

What fascinated Sigmund Freud (1865–1939) about this story was the implicit identification of the soul with sexuality, and the implicit identification of sexuality with conflict. Indeed, it might be said that the founder of psychoanalysis, drawing on what he had learnt about the human mind from the Romantics, made the implicit explicit, and in so doing radically revised the traditional understanding of the psyche. Marina Warner's entry on Freud, in her 'Short Dictionary of the Inner World', reads: 'Interpreter of dreams, story-teller, fantasist, hypnotist, mythographer, collector, reinvented the soul for C20' (Warner 1996: 41).

There are, however, two Freuds to contend with. There is first the heir of the Enlightenment, who equates religion with illusion and who confidently declares it possible to progress beyond the neurotic repetition compulsions which characterized primitive myth and ritual. This Freud is heavily influenced by Frazer. Like Frazer, he is a rationalist who sees myth as a kind of rudimentary error. For the one, its reliance on fertility magic means it is a false kind of science: killing the god was thought to effect a renewal of the crops, but the modern mind knows better. For the other, myth and religion are explained away once they have been recognized as neurotic. Like Frazer, he is an Euhemerist. For the one, the god was originally a king or magician, or at any rate a personage crucial to the well-being of the tribe. For the other, the god was the primal father deified. Again, like Frazer, he offers his own complementary allegory: where Frazer thinks the hidden meaning of myth lies in the cycle of vegetation, Freud thinks it lies in sex. This first Freud holds psychoanalysis to be a science, offering the one and only key to the mysteries of the unconscious. As our capacity for rational explanation of psychic drives expands, he tells us, so it will be possible to cure people of their neuroses. In other words, the Enlightenment metanarrative of emancipation holds good.

The second Freud, by contrast, is the heir of the counter-Enlightenment; it is he who answers to Warner's description. This Freud, while still thinking sex is the key to myth, is fully aware that his own ideas are provisional, narrative explorations of the soul rather than scientific truths. This is the man who, in conversation with Einstein towards the end of his life, goes so far as to question the very existence of objective veracity: 'It may perhaps seem to you as though our theories are a kind of mythology. . . . But does not every science come in the end to a kind of mythology?' (Freud 1950: 283). This is also the man who chooses as the epigraph for his *Interpretation of Dreams* (1900) a quotation from Virgil: 'If I cannot move heaven, I will stir up the underworld.' Rational order can never, it seems, finally transcend the darkness of the unconscious.

It is this second, counter-Enlightenment Freud on which we will be concentrating. This is a figure who takes risks of interpretation, who radically rewrites the material he studies: in short, one who knows his 'science' to be 'a kind of mythology'. His source is *Oedipus Rex*, but he turns Sophocles' fifth-century Athenian drama into an exploration of repressed desire. Here is the background to the play, as summarized by Freud in *The Interpretation of Dreams*:

> Oedipus, son of Laius, King of Thebes, and of Jocasta, was exposed as an infant because an oracle had warned Laius that the still unborn child would be his father's murderer. The child was rescued, and grew up as a prince in an alien court, until, in doubts as to his origin, he too questioned the oracle and was warned to avoid his home since he was destined to murder his father and take his mother in marriage. On the road leading away from what he believed was his home, he met King Laius and slew him in a quarrel. He came next to Thebes and solved the riddle set him by the Sphinx who barred his way. Out of gratitude the Thebans made him their king and gave him Jocasta's hand in marriage. He reigned long in peace and honour, and she who, unknown to him, was his mother bore him two sons and two daughters. Then at last a plague broke out and the Thebans made enquiry once more of the oracle. It is at this point that Sophocles' tragedy opens.
>
> (Freud 1974: 261)

And it is from this point that Sophocles begins his painstaking analysis of the conflict between reason and unacknowledged error. Not knowing himself to be the cause of the plague of Thebes, Oedipus is shown to be zealous in his efforts to discover the guilty one. It is only at the end that he realizes that figure to be himself. Paul Ricoeur calls Sophocles' version of the myth a 'tragedy of truth', over which Freud has in turn transcribed a 'tragedy of sex' (Rée 1992: 39). The one is primarily interested in the dramatic convention of recognition, by which the protagonist is forced to face the consequences of his own actions, regardless of intention. The other is primarily interested in analysing repressed desires, hidden motives. He takes Sophocles' narrative as evidence that all male children experience a sexual trauma by which they desire the mother and detest the father, secretly wishing to commit incest and patricide. Thanks to Freud's radical rereading, it is now impossible to read the Athenian play about Oedipus (type) without thinking of the psychoanalytic theory of the Oedipus complex (anti-type).

The paradox and originality of Freud's typology, and what distinguishes him most from the Enlightenment, is that it looks backwards. Thus, contradicting the rational advocacy of emancipation from neurosis is the mythic fascination with what neurosis involves, namely the need to remember, return and repeat. Of course, this also distinguishes him from the radical visionaries so far discussed. In the typology of Joachim, Dante and Blake, the present, while informed by past paradigms, is permanently open to the possibilities of the future. The apocalyptic moment is always just ahead, ready to suffuse the present with its power. It promises a new cosmos out of catastrophe. This very moment is the *kairos*, the moment in which *chronos* is transformed. Freud believes in something like a *kairos*; but he places it in the past. 'The kairotic event has already happened' (Rieff 1951: 117). It is the time of sexual trauma, of the Oedipal complex. The present points not to a serene, rational future, as the Freud of the Enlightenment would believe, but rather backwards to a disturbing, irrational past. However, his *kairos* has its positive side. The story he tells of 'the primal crime' destabilizes the present by throwing it into the long perspective of guilt, and so challenges us to reconsider our civilization and our own lives. It has, perhaps, the same power, the same provocative effect, as Nietzsche's myth of eternal recurrence.

It is in *Totem and Taboo* (1913) that Freud develops his own myth. There we read that the founding event, decisive and irrevocable, was the Oedipal crime of the killing of the father.

That is, the neurosis of the modern individual is a re-enactment of the collective guilt of 'the primal horde'. According to Freud, the first groups of human beings, existing in the latter part of the Old Stone Age, were patriarchal. The tribal patriarch appropriated all the women for himself. 'One day', as Freud puts it, in suitably fictional fashion, the other males, who were effectively his sons, 'came together, killed and devoured their father and so made an end of the patriarchal horde'. Now they had access to the females of the horde, their sisters. He goes on:

> Cannibal savages as they were, it goes without saying that they devoured their victim as well as killing him. The violent primal father had doubtless been the feared and envied model of each one of the company of brothers: and in the act of devouring him they accomplished their identification with him, and each one of them acquired a portion of his strength. The totem meal, which is perhaps mankind's earliest festival, would thus be a repetition and a commemoration of this memorable and criminal deed, which was the beginning of so many things – of social organization, of moral restrictions and of religion.
>
> (Freud 1985: 203)

Of course, this is not wholly original: the influence of Frazer is evident here. For one thing, father is to son as dying god is to reviving god. For another, the community is presented as gaining access to the patriarch's energy by means of magic. However, Freud's radical contribution is to introduce the psychological factor. The murder of the primal father induces such strong remorse that the group makes the patriarch its totem, associating him with a particular animal, here unspecified, to which it feels a special bond. The totemic meal, the eating of the animal in ritual fashion as if it were the father, has become the focus of the totemic clan, which replaces the primal horde. With the totem comes the taboo: a prohibition, for obvious reasons, against both patricide and incest. The logic of remorse leads to the revered totem-father becoming a god, and the totemic meal becoming a full-scale ritual. Human culture has begun, and with it, simultaneously, guilt, repression and religion.

Freud looks backwards from the neurosis of the modern individual to the Oedipus myth; and then he looks further back, to 'the primal crime'. In order to understand the urge to remember, return and repeat, he does exactly what he sees his own patients doing. Thus, his account of mythic thinking is itself mythic. Moreover, his myth is one that obliterates reassuring distinctions, most notably that between history and prehistory, and that between civilization and savagery, as he orients all his evidence back to a founding sexual trauma. This runs the risk of being reductive, but the effect is more likely to be creatively disorienting. Sacred memory and sexual drive are played off against each other dialectically. There is always a further surprise in store.

Thus, in his last major work, *Moses and Monotheism: Three Essays* (1934–8), we find him going so far as to rewrite the Biblical myth of deliverance in terms of a repeated Oedipal struggle. The followers of Moses had, Freud conjectures, murdered him after the departure from Egypt. They had then decided to subscribe to monotheism, his favoured religious form, as a sign of remorse. They adopted Yahweh, a local god, promoting him to the status of the one, universal God, and it was in this way that the Hebrew-Judaic faith became the religion of the father. But then, with the emergence of Christianity, for many Jews the crucified Jesus took the place of God the father, to whom St Paul believed him to have been sacrificed. The Christian faith centred on the son, not the father. Thus, it was a reaffirmation, paradoxically, of the primal crime itself: though the starting point was the need to atone for humanity to God the father, it ended up glorifying the one who did the atoning. Later than Judaism, Christianity was effectively more retrogressive: it was more primal, more Oedipal, than the religion from which it had developed.

Situated in the perspective of both archaic past and living present, a more audacious rewriting of Biblical myth could not be envisaged – except perhaps Joachim's and Blake's. However, it has to be acknowledged that the Oedipal interest does not always lead Freud to produce illuminating literary criticism. His reading of *Hamlet* in *The Interpretation of Dreams*, for example, is notoriously crude and reductive. It may begin promisingly by presenting Shakespeare as reworking Sophocles' themes in an age when 'the secular advance of repression in the emotional life of mankind' leads to a greater 'indirectness' in treatment. But this awareness does not prevent Freud from going straight on to explain away the protagonist's actions – or, rather, failure to act. Hamlet's hesitation in killing the murderer of his father is, we are told, entirely due to a repressed desire to have done exactly the same thing. For Hamlet cannot bring himself to punish Claudius, because he feels himself to be no better than the sinner whom he is supposed to condemn. Not content with thus dispelling the enigma of the play, Freud goes on to attribute its protagonist's complex to its author:

> [I]t can of course only be the poet's mind which confronts us in *Hamlet*. I observe in a book on Shakespeare by Georg Brandes (1896) a statement that *Hamlet* was written immediately after the death of Shakespeare's father (in 1601), that is, under the immediate impact of his bereavement and, as we may well assume, while his childhood feelings about his father had been freshly revived.
>
> (Freud 1974: 265)

It is important to recognize the paucity of this, Freud's first attempt at interpreting Shakespeare's most famous work. First, it reminds us how fine is the line which divides the two Freuds that we distinguished earlier. Indeed, in the course of the same volume, *The Interpretation of Dreams*, we find both the counter-Enlightenment myth-maker, who reads *Oedipus Rex* in the spirit of radical typology, and the Enlightenment rationalist, who explains away and reduces *Hamlet* in a perspective that is reminiscent of allegory. Second, it demonstrates that a mode of interpretation which may be daring and provocative in one instance may become dull and ponderous in another, if the sense of dynamism is lacking. For the whole point of radical typology is that making and reading myth should be part of an ongoing, narrative process and should not be nullified by mechanical and formulaic repetition. Once the Oedipal complex becomes a contrivance for slotting texts into place, then literary mythopoeia is effectively denied. Third, the use of biographical information enforces the realist principle that the meaning of fictions are external to the workings of narrative. The fact of Shakespeare's father's death is used to rationalize, and so negate, the enigmatic power of the text.

A much more promising reading of *Hamlet*, which conveys his residual distrust of the Enlightenment cult of rationality, is given in his essay 'Psychopathic characters on the stage' (1906). Commenting on this, Jacqueline Rose reflects on the significance of Freud's use of a quotation from Lessing in connection with the play: 'A person who does not lose his reason under certain conditions can have no reason to lose':

> Freud includes *Hamlet* in that group of plays which rely for their effect on the neurotic in the spectator, inducing in her or him the neurosis watched on stage, crossing over the boundaries between onstage and offstage and breaking down the habitual barriers of the mind. A particular *type* of drama, this form is none the less effective only through its capacity to implicate us *all*.
>
> (Rose 1986: 43)

That is, 'instead of safely diagnosing Hamlet, his Oedipal drama, his disturbance, and subjecting them to its mastery and control', this radical interpretation 'turns back on to spectator and critic, implicating the observer in . . . irrationality and excess' (Rose 1986: 43). Radical typology, the notion that we are all of us continually in the making, and that the certainty and stability of *logos* must always be put into doubt, here replaces the comfortably reductive allegory of the earlier reading.

It is ironic to note that Franz Kafka (1883–1924), another Jewish myth-maker, another visionary concerned to rewrite the legacy of father-centred religion, has suffered more than most writers from that kind of heavy-handed psychoanalysis which Freud intermittently practised and inadvertently encouraged. It is as if his challenge and his mythopoeic power were so great that they needed defusing. Biographical explanation, crudely supported by Freudian concepts, thus saves us from having to acknowledge our own implication in his narratives:

> His tortured relationship with his father appears to have been a dominating influence on his work . . . His father – authoritarian, self-confident, bullying, philistine. Kafka – timid, sensitive and literary. 'In front of you,' Kafka wrote, 'I lost my self-confidence, and exchanged it for an infinite sense of guilt.' Most of Kafka's stories and novels are about people who suffer, with no good reason, humiliation and chastisement.
>
> (Jones and Handley 1988: 22)

To balance this kind of approach, we might cite W. H. Auden's judgement: 'Had one to name the author who comes closest to bearing the same kind of relation to our age as Dante, Shakespeare and Goethe bore to theirs, Kafka is the first one would think of.' George Steiner, confirming this judgement, adds that the power of the novels and stories evades biographical speculations, and concludes that Kafka's significance is that of a 'prophet'. His art is not merely personal; nor is it realistic. It is best described as 'transrealism', hallucinatory and terrifying: 'The key fact about Kafka is that he was possessed of a fearful premonition', that he saw 'the horror gathering'. Thus, *The Trial* exhibits 'the classic model of the terror state'. It 'prefigures the furtive sadism, the hysteria which totalitarianism insinuates into private and sexual life, the faceless boredom of the killers' (Steiner 1969: 163).

Kafka criticism is perhaps the better for acknowledging this uncanny intuition of totalitarianism rather than attributing his creativity, in a reductive fashion, to an Oedipal trauma. For Kafka's fiction, while no doubt informed by anxiety concerning the author's father, is drastically diminished if we read it as primarily an expression of Oedipal trauma. It is how Kafka moves from this starting point to a full-scale interrogation of God the father and his project for humanity that should be the real focus of mythic interest. Again, though his recognition of sadism and sexual manipulation as necessary components of an oppressive regime is no doubt indebted to psychoanalysis, the latter cannot explain his power as 'prophet'. For ultimately, what marks him out as original is his radical relation to the legacy of the Law. Receiving it as a narrative which has hardened into a doctrine, Kafka sets out to remythologize it.

Moses was understood to have received the ten commandments, or decalogue, from Yahweh on Mount Sinai. These were, it transpired, designed to guide the Hebrews in their progress towards the promised land and the creation of the kingdom of Israel. With the division of the kingdom, and such catastrophes as the exile in Babylon, the need to observe the Law became more and more imperative, and it was hoped that if the people remained faithful to Yahweh's commandments, a divinely inspired ruler, or Messiah, would emerge to re-establish the kingdom once and for all. Waiting for this remained an essential part of traditional Judaic religion. Except for certain texts such as the Book of Daniel and certain immediately pre-Christian sects such as the Essenes, and unlike early Christianity, it expected a culmination of history rather than an apocalypse as such, with its radical disruption of chronological time. Kafka's genius was to take the act of waiting, now severed from its sacred dimension, as the clue to his own era.

The plot of his novel *The Trial* (1925) consists in the protagonist, Joseph K, being arrested without being accused of any specific crime. He keeps expecting to receive a proper charge and judgement. Finally, he is taken one evening by two nameless men to the edge of town and a knife held to his throat in a deserted stone quarry. At this moment, K looks across to the top window of a nearby house, from which a human figure leans out: 'Who was it? A friend? A good man? Someone who sympathized? Someone who wanted to help?' No help is at hand, however, and he dies, in his own last words, 'Like a dog!' (Kafka 1970: 250–1). The mythic power of the novel consists in the constant gestures it makes towards the idea of some ultimate Messianic moment, in which perspective all the bewilderment and agony of the protagonist might be situated and understood, only to deny us that possibility. All that is left is the individual, alone, alienated and afraid; and over and against him, an anonymous and destructive system.

Indeed, the heart of *The Trial* is itself a myth, but not one belonging to any distinct paradigm. This is the story of the doorway to the Law, which is told to K by a priest he meets in the cathedral. The story is simple enough in form. A man comes to the doorway of the Law, but the doorkeeper tells him he cannot admit him 'at this moment'. The man waits outside for days, for weeks, for months, for years. Finally, approaching death, he asks the doorkeeper why nobody else has ever come to the doorway, given that everybody 'strives to attain the Law'. The reply is: 'No one but you could gain admittance through this door, since this door was intended only for you. I am now going to shut it' (Kafka 1970: 236–7). We belittle the power of this myth if we label it, as many critics have done, as an allegory. For one thing, there is no code that can provide the answer to its mystery. It is not 'about' one particular theme or event. Rather, it is a terrifying parody of religious revelation, entirely appropriate to what Auden calls 'the age of anxiety'. For another thing, its effect is inseparable from radical typology. As with Freud, a legacy has been rewritten. In the Judaic scriptures, as in the Christian, there is an expectation of collective salvation: the kingdom will come. But here, the very promise of redemption has been both abstracted and atomized, and thereby negated. The Law is universal, indeed wholly impersonal, in its modern secular manifestation; but one lives, one is judged and one dies in isolation and absurdity. Kafka replaces the myth of deliverance with a myth of denial, and the hero myth with an anti-hero myth.

Further analysis of this central fable is not necessary here, but if one were to situate *The Trial* as a whole in literary terms, the obvious reference point would be Charles Dickens's *Bleak House* (1853). That novel traces the legal case of Jarndyce versus Jarndyce, which lasts so long that there is no estate left for the litigants once it is finished. Lives are wasted in the process, while the self-perpetuating bureaucracy of the Victorian legal system flourishes. We witness the oppression of the poor and the corruption of the rich. A massive work of great imaginative power, it comprises a denunciation of the workings of the demonic metropolis, the city ripe for destruction. Early in the novel, Miss Flite, a forlorn figure who keeps songbirds in a cage by her window, and who has been driven mad by her own chancery case, addresses Richard and Ada, the young wards of court in the case of Jarndyce versus Jarndyce: 'I expect a judgment. Shortly. On the Day of Judgment.' She adds that she has discovered that the sixth seal mentioned in the Book of Revelation is 'the Great Seal' of England (Dickens 1971: 81). The characters inhabit a London which seems identical with Babylon. And sure enough, this apocalyptic novel does place the demonic metropolis within the framework of the Biblical myth of deliverance. Chapter 1 begins with a vision of the city that parodies Genesis: 'As much mud in the streets, as if the waters had but newly retired from the face of the earth' (Dickens 1971: 49). At the end of Chapter 65, which is almost the last, the dying Richard tells Ada: 'I will begin the world!' And then comes the apocalyptic sign: 'at a late hour' the narrator Esther Summerson is visited by 'poor crazed Miss Flite', who tells her that she has 'given her birds their liberty' (Dickens 1971: 927).

Dickens's ending is, then, meant as a new beginning. A justice, which we might call divine but is probably better called poetic, is recognized and restored. The contrast with Kafka is extreme. For if *The Trial* rewrites the apocalyptic text of *Bleak House*, it does so by refusing its solace and so intensifying the depiction of the demonic world. This is no less an example of radical typology than is Kafka's revision of the Judaic legacy itself. That is why we may place Kafka with Freud as a myth-maker of the modern era, conscious that myth-making is inseparable from mythic reading. Where Freud confronts us with an intolerable past, Kafka confronts us with an intolerable future. But again, as with Freud, Kafka seems to close off possibilities only to reopen them: his enigmatic vision demands that the reader, aware that she is in the presence of myth, must return again and again to the text in search of its elusive power. Kafka's very deconstruction of the principle of hope is itself apocalyptic: it unsettles, challenges and reorients the present.

THE SEARCH FOR THE SELF

Freud had numerous disciples, the most famous being Carl Jung (1875–1961). Jung broke with him in and around the time of *Totem and Taboo*, disillusioned with his master's identification of the psyche with sexuality. Perhaps we might explain their differences more exactly by taking the Greek hero myth of Theseus' battle with the minotaur, and seeing how their interpretations might differ.

Theseus, the son of Aegeus, king of Attica, volunteers to become one of the victims provided as human food for the minotaur, a monster which is half-man and half-bull. Every year, due to a grievance held against Aegeus by Minos, king of Crete, seven young men and seven young women have to be shipped over to that island and forced to enter the labyrinth which was built for the creature by Daedalus the craftsman. There they will die. Theseus is determined to end this practice and, volunteering to lead the expedition, promises his father that when he returns to Athens he will indicate that he has succeeded in defeating the monster by displaying white sails; if not, he will display black. On arrival on Crete, he meets and seduces Ariadne, Minos's daughter and the minotaur's half-sister, and she offers to help him, on condition that he will marry her. After Theseus is shut up in the labyrinth, he does manage to slay the monster. He is only able to escape, however, with the aid of Ariadne, who provides him with a thread by which he finds his way out of the underground maze. On his way home, Theseus decides to abandon his new wife, and sails off without her when they break their journey at the island of Naxos. She curses him as he goes, but is soon rescued by the god Dionysus, who takes her as his mate. Meanwhile, Theseus and his companions sail on, but so excited is he by his own triumph that he forgets to change the sails. When Aegeus, standing on a cliff, sees the black sails approaching from afar, he throws himself into the sea (thereafter known as 'Aegean') and is drowned.

A Freudian reading of this myth would emphasize the repressed Oedipal desire of the hero, or ego, Theseus. Not intending to 'kill' his father, he unconsciously 'forgets' to change the sails, and so effectively provokes Aegeus to commit suicide. The myth, then, is about the inevitability of the son needing and wishing to replace the father. And sure enough, with Aegeus dead, Theseus does indeed assume the throne of Athens – his reign being suitably turbulent and his own end being violent.

A Jungian reading would focus not on the Oedipal conflict, but on the task itself. Theseus, the young male hero, is only able to negotiate the depths of the labyrinth, representing the unconscious, by trusting to the help of Ariadne, representing female intuition. His subsequent abandonment of Ariadne would, then, symbolize the reassertion of aggressive, male rationality, for which a price must be paid, symbolized by the violent end of both father and son. In Jung's own terminology, which only partially derives from Freud's, we would say that the 'ego' (Theseus) is able to encounter and assimilate the power of the 'shadow' (minotaur) under the inspiration of the 'anima' (Ariadne). If, having done so, he chooses to ignore the further direction indicated by the 'anima', he will not be able to approach the wisdom of the 'self'.

These terms, which we will explain shortly, represent what Jung, and Eliade after him, calls 'archetypes'. Literally, an archetype is an original or founding image or figure. In *The Psychology of the Unconscious* (1913), later retitled *Symbols of Transformation*, Jung goes further: for him, archetypes are permanent, eternal patterns of understanding. Though unrepresentable in themselves, they are made manifest as 'archetypal images'. These are universal motifs that come from the 'collective unconscious' and are the basic content of religions and mythologies. They emerge in individuals through dreams and visions. The 'collective unconscious' is inherited not acquired. It is true that Freud refers in *Totem and Taboo* to 'the heritage of emotion' and in *Moses and Monotheism* to 'the archaic heritage' (Freud 1985: 221, 343), but his point is that certain symbols evolved as a result of the historic (or, more accurately, prehistoric) trauma of the primal crime. For Jung, the symbols are simply there, buried and waiting in the universal psyche: 'There is no difference in principle between organic and psychic growth. As a plant produces its flower, so the psyche creates its symbols' (Jung 1990: 64). The task of life is to come to terms with the contents of the individual unconscious through relating them to those of the collective.

Moreover, where Freud is mainly interested in myths as the expression of sexual anxiety and conflict, Jung looks for signs of the impulse towards sacred meaning. Where Freud sees neurosis as the compulsion to remember, return and repeat, Jung sees neurosis as a sign that the soul yearns for something beyond physical or material satisfactions. Where Freud sees dream as a distorted fulfilment of a sexual wish, Jung sees dream as a natural expression of the psyche, by which it tries to heal itself. Thus, though it is Jung who speaks of 'archetypes', it is Freud who is the true 'archaeologist' of the mind. Jung's interest is less in how the psyche evolved, and more in its spiritual goal or purpose. He offers, we might say, a 'teleology' of the spirit (Greek, *telos*, 'end'). Where Freud constantly looks back to childhood trauma, both in the individual and in the race, Jung looks forwards to mature adulthood. What is interesting for him is not how we learn to live, as sexual beings, but how we are going to face, as spiritual beings, our own deaths. He calls this process, this discovery of psychic harmony beyond the ego, 'individuation': the experience of the 'self' as the regulating centre of the psyche. Thus, when Jung considers 'archetypes' he is looking for clues to the religious nature of humanity. Religion for him is the expression not of acquired guilt, but of that urge which is natural to humans, to be at one with oneself and the cosmos. This urge is evident for him in all narratives, whether sacred or secular. It is just that one has to look harder for them in the latter.

In Jung's own mythic model, there are four main archetypes which tell us the story, as it were, of the psyche. Though collective, they have to be realized at the individual level. First, there is the 'ego', the conscious mind; this is one's sense of purpose and identity. Second, there is the 'shadow', the unconscious aspect of the psyche which the ego tends to reject or ignore, usually symbolized in dreams by a figure of the same sex as the ego. The ego, if it is to develop, must face and assimilate the power of the shadow. Third, there is the 'anima' (Latin, 'soul'), the unconscious, feminine side of a male personality; or the 'animus' (Latin, 'spirit'), the unconscious, masculine side of a woman's personality. In short, the one is the man's inner woman; the other is the woman's inner man. If these are positive images, they may inspire the ego to undertake the journey through and beyond the realm of the shadow. Fourth, there is the 'self': the central archetype, that of the fulfilment of potential and the integration of personality. Frequently symbolized by a mandala or magic circle, it is the psychic totality towards which all life moves. Indeed, we may infer that the very journey from ego to self is circular, involving descent into the darkness of shadow and ascent towards the light of self. There is obviously a rough parallel with Frazer's cycle of the dying and reviving god, or even Eliade's eternal return, by which cosmos emerges from chaos; but here the ultimate model is psychological integration.

As we have seen, in the Theseus myth, the hero is the ego, the minotaur is the shadow and Ariadne is the anima. The self is not represented, which means that this is merely a hero myth and not a 'wisdom' myth. The latter, which is for Jung the most important kind, would seem to be roughly parallel to what Weston means by a 'Mystery' narrative. The paradox of Theseus is that his material success is really a kind of spiritual failure. For a model of attainment of the self we might perhaps turn to the stories of Jesus Christ and of Orpheus. In both cases, material failure leads to spiritual success. Jesus is crucified as a common criminal, but is then resurrected as the Christ. Orpheus' story is less familiar, and may appear very different, but there is an underlying pattern in common. Orpheus, a musician and poet, allows his very concern for his wife Eurydice to prevent him bringing her back from the dead: forbidden to look back towards her on their way up from the underworld, he cannot help but do so in his anxiety for her safe release. But having lost his wife, and then having been dismembered by angry women for neglecting his arts in mourning, he becomes the object of an esoteric religious cult, his music and poetry symbolizing cosmic harmony. Both Jesus Christ and Orpheus, then, may be taken to be embodiments of the self.

There is some difficulty in applying Jung's sequence of archetypes to literature, since very few texts represent the completed process. The nearest equivalent might be Dante's *Divine Comedy*, in which the poet/ego has to descend into the world of the shadow, or hell, where he meets many demonic doubles of himself, and even sees that greatest shadow of all, Satan. Then, guided by Beatrice, his anima, he is able to ascend to heaven and attain a total vision of the cosmos and of his place within it, thus acquiring the harmony of the self. It is especially significant that his journey takes place in a dream; we are to infer, in the

Jungian perspective, that when he awakes and returns to temporal existence, he will have learnt how to balance the conscious and unconscious aspects of his psyche. Another, less obvious example might be *Faust*, Parts I and II (1808 and 1831), by Johann Wolfgang von Goethe. The protagonist is a middle-aged alchemist who sells his soul to Satan, in exchange for diabolical powers. Possessing these, and aided by Satan's servant Mephistopheles, he proceeds to seduce and abandon an innocent young woman, Margareta. Then, having gained the love of the legendary Helen of Troy, which ultimately proves insufficient, he achieves the full expression of his powers in, of all things, the project of reclaiming land from the sea. His material victory is complete, but the end of Part II shows him having to be redeemed by the intervention of Margareta and the healing powers of 'the eternal feminine'. Here, then, we have Faust as the ego, Mephistopheles as the shadow, Margareta as the positive anima, Helen of Troy as the negative anima, and the Mater Gloriosa, or queen of Heaven, as the self. (Faust, it is implied, will take some time to attain true selfhood.)

Recognizing the difference between Margareta and Helen is important, for we must not make the mistake of seeing Jung's archetypes as simple signposts on the route to spiritual realization. They are supposed to indicate the complexity of the psyche. Thus, the positive anima must not be confused with the negative anima. By the same token, the negative anima must not be blandly subsumed within the shadow. Indeed, we must avoid the temptation to see all demonic figures as examples of the latter. The shadow is the dark side of the ego, and usually of the same sex: the demonic, murdering brother (Cain to Abel in the Book of Genesis, or Set to Osiris in the Egyptian myth of fertility), or else the alter ego (Enkidu the wild man to Gilgamesh the great king in the Babylonian epic *Gilgamesh,* or Mr Hyde to Dr Jekyll in Stevenson's novel). Though he may be monstrous, as is the minotaur, all monsters are not shadows. In the medieval romance of St George and the dragon, the dragon might be seen as the 'terrible mother' who wants to drag him back to an infantile state; George must overcome this danger if he is to prove himself mature enough to save and marry the damsel, who is the positive anima of psychic development.

The Bible is full of both negative and positive animas: for example, Eve and (as young maiden) Mary; Delilah and Ruth; Babylon the whore and Jerusalem the bride. It is easy to see how the Hollywood film industry constructs approximations of positive animas, such as Marilyn Monroe, but Jung would see these as inadequate models. Cinema is much more convincing when it comes to the negative anima: typically demonic females include the manipulative, man-hating murderer Catherine Tramell (Sharon Stone) in *Basic Instinct*, and the violently jealous 'other woman' Alex Forrest (Glenn Close) in *Fatal Attraction*. Less controversially, the nineteenth-century English novel seems particularly inclined to the figure of the animus. Again, we have negative and positive: Wickham and Darcy in Jane Austen's *Pride and Prejudice*, Casaubon and Ladislaw in George Eliot's *Middlemarch*. Or, particularly in the fiction of the Brontë sisters, we have the negative turning into the positive as a result of the dedication of the female protagonist: Heathcliff in Emily's *Wuthering Heights*, Rochester in Charlotte's *Jane Eyre*.

As for the fourth main archetype: though it is rare to see the whole sequence of psychic growth depicted, we can find plenty of images of the self in fiction, film and song. Again, we have male and female aspects, which in effect are secondary, autonomous archetypes. There is the 'wise old man', such as Merlin in Arthurian romance, Gandalf in Tolkien's *The Lord of the Rings*, or Obi-Wan Kenobi in George Lucas's *Star Wars*. And there is the 'great mother', such as the fairy godmother in Cinderella, the Good Witch of the North in *The Wizard of Oz*, or 'Mother Mary' in the Beatles' 'Let It Be'.

Any dissatisfaction we feel with Jung's mythography may well focus on his concept of the archetype, which might be said to lend itself to an allegorical interpretation. Jung tells us:

> There are no inborn ideas, but there are inborn possibilities of ideas that set bounds to even the boldest fantasy and keep our fantasy activity within certain categories: *a priori* ideas, as it were, the existence of which cannot be ascertained except from their effects.
>
> (Jung 1966: 81)

Here we seem to locate a Jung who still clings to the universal and eternal forms of Plato. Eric Gould calls him an 'essentialist' and a 'fundamentalist': whatever scope he seems to offer for the secular imagination, he will always insist that beyond it lies the indispensable source of all images, the truth which exceeds all narratives (Gould 1981: 15–16). Again, G. S. Kirk suggests that Jung's ultimate aim is the 'stasis' of symbolism rather than the 'dynamism' of narrative (Kirk 1970: 278–80).

In assessing Jung's contribution to mythography, though, the positive seems to me to outweigh the negative. First, Jung provides a model of balance. Here he differs markedly from some of those who borrow his terminology, such as Joseph Campbell. Unlike Campbell, he is not advocating 'absorption in the unconscious', but rather a condition of equilibrium: 'neither rejection of the unconscious nor surrender to it' (Segal 1987: 133). Indeed he argues against the merger of the ego into the self, a condition which he calls 'inflation' and which he sees as leading to a form of psychosis. In his *Archetypes and the Collective Unconscious* (1959), Jung states: 'the great psychic danger which is always connected with individuation . . . lies in the identification of ego-consciousness with the self. This produces an inflation which threatens consciousness with dissolution.' Quoting and commenting on this, Robert Segal remarks: 'The Jungian aim is no more to reject ego consciousness for the unconscious than, like the modern aim, to reject the unconscious for ego consciousness. The aim is, rather, to balance the two' (Jung 1992: 23). Second, Jung challenges the Enlightenment faith in rational explanation and, trusting in the power of myth, demonstrates the possibilities of imaginative exploration. We might say, then, that he queries allegorical interpretation rather more than he represents it: indeed, his method seems to demonstrate an ability to adapt ideas rather than impose them. We might even go so far as to say, with Edward Casey, that the psyche he discovers is 'at once prepersonal and pluripersonal (or more exactly, omnipersonal)': he stresses creativity and improvization rather than stable identity (Barnaby and D'Acierno 1990: 322). He thus demonstrates that the mythic life is a matter of role-playing as much as authenticity: indeed, without 'image-ination', the willingness to live symbolically, there can be no 'individuation'.

It is this Jung of permanent possibility which I would like to end by emphasizing. Perhaps it would be best to cite the Jungian literary theorist, Susan Rowland, who has audaciously defended Jung's mode of writing by using my own terms in a way I had not thought applicable when working on the first edition of this very book. Her focus is on Jung's *Memories, Dreams, Reflections* (1963), a work in which he tried to fuse autobiography, mythography and psychology. Here are the main tenets of her summation:

> Jung composes his personal myth principally using the narrative method that Coupe defines as radical typology. It is a form that resists closure and makes no claims for universal transcendent significance. Its recapitulation of other mythical stories is potentially limitless: radical typology is *radical* in the notion of rewriting narratives without boundaries, so never producing an 'other' to become a scapegoat. . . . *Memories* is suspended between the desire to accept 'concepts' and the realization that such language is itself a barrier to Jung's understanding of the psyche. . . . The psyche is *mythos* in the infinite recreation of stories by which unconscious and conscious mesh. It can only be authentically represented by a radical typology endlessly re-reading the mythical models cast into life.
>
> (Rowland 2005: 37–39)

Generalizing about Jung's relevance for literary studies, she concludes:

> [By] bringing past forms of consciousness into the present, Jungian reading of literature might provide opportunities to reframe the conflicts of our age. Just as, it is my contention, literary approaches to Jung's own writings have lasting value. For within Jung as a writer we find epistemological and aesthetic tools for redesigning the ethical consciousness of the world not yet known, not yet brought into being.
>
> (Rowland 2005: 211)

That repeated phrase, 'not yet', is well-used: though Jung veered dangerously towards allegory in formulating his method of interpretation, his work as a whole conveys a sense of possibility and liberation, such as we would associate with radical typology.

THE GRAMMAR OF THE MIND

It might seem strange that Jung could ever be accused of preferring 'stasis' to narrative, when we consider that in the mid-twentieth century there was a whole movement devoted to that very principle: I refer, of course, to 'structuralism'. Its most celebrated application to myth is that of the anthropologist Claude Lévi-Strauss. He may be aligned with Freud and Jung in so far as his subject is the workings of the human mind, and it might be worth making an initial, broad comparison. Lévi-Strauss, sharing many of the assumptions of psychoanalysis, agrees with Freud that the meaning of myth is unconscious, and that human culture is always and everywhere characterized by the taboo against incest and patricide. But he rejects the biological model of instincts from which Freud starts. We may say that both Jung and Lévi-Strauss take a synchronic and spatial view of myth rather than a diachronic and temporal view; and both are concerned with the collective psyche. But the former sees his archetypes as having an eternal quality beyond their various manifestations, while the latter insists that the units of myth, or 'mythemes', make sense only in relation to other units. This in itself, however, implies abstraction, for if the key to myth is language, with the mythemes functioning like phonemes or words, then for Lévi-Strauss the key to both is grammar. In interpreting myth, we are not to attend to the single symbol, but to the overall structure; not to what it may or may not mean to the individual, but to the communal logic which is implicit. Hence: 'myths get thought in man unbeknownst to him'; mythography is 'the quest for the invariant, or for the invariant among superficial differences' (Lévi-Strauss 1978: 3, 8).

In reading Lévi-Strauss, then, we may have the curious impression of entering a 'brave new world' of confident clarity, while at the same time wondering if we have not been here before:

> To speak of rules and to speak of meaning is to speak of the same thing; and if we look at all the intellectual undertakings of mankind,

> as far as they have been recorded all over the world, the common denominator is always to introduce some kind of order. If this represents a basic need for order in the human mind and since, after all, the human mind is only part of the universe, the need probably exists because there is some order in the universe and the order is not a chaos.
>
> (Lévi-Strauss 1978: 12–13)

On the one hand, we are reminded of Eliot's 'mythical method' and so of a certain strain in modernism. On the other hand, we are reminded of the ambition of modernity, to abstract and rationalize everything. Either way, what is likely to suffer from this obsession with 'order' is the dynamism of the particular myth under consideration. Moreover, the claim to have inferred the absolute truth about the universe suggests that the mythic reading undertaken will be realist in principle rather than non-realist.

Lévi-Strauss's interpretation of the Oedipus myth has the advantage over Freud's that he does not confine himself to Sophocles' version. It has the disadvantage that he does not tell the whole story: the mythemes appear as if from nowhere in his own 'arrangement'. Hence, the reader finds herself confronted by four columns of narrative items, respectively containing such cryptic and non-chronological information as: (1) 'Cadmos seeks his sister, ravished by Zeus' (Cadmos being the founder of Thebes); (2) 'Eteocles kills his brother Polynices' (both being sons of Oedipus fighting for the right to rule in his place); (3) 'Cadmos kills the dragon' (sent by Zeus to hinder his pursuit of himself and Europa); (4) 'Oedipus=*swollen-foot*?' (due to his being tied down when abandoned as a baby). The key to these sets of mythemes is the opposition that Lévi-Strauss regards as the most fundamental of all, that of culture and nature. For him, all others follow from this: order and chaos, life and death, self and other, eternity and time. It is the task of myth to articulate such contradictions, and so resolve them. Moreover, whatever the contradictions of the particular myth, the resolution achieved will be, in essence, that of culture and nature. The manifest concern may be familial affection, expressed in extreme form by incest (column 1), as opposed to familial aggression, expressed in extreme form by patricide or fratricide (column 2). On the other hand, it may be our attempt to sever contact with the earth from which we originated, symbolized by killing monsters (column 3), as opposed to the fact that we cannot entirely leave our origins behind, as symbolized by lameness or difficulty in walking upright (column 4). But the latent concern will be the most fundamental of all: how culture relates to nature.

As Lévi-Strauss puts it: 'the overrating of blood relations is to the underrating of blood relations as the attempt to escape autochthony [earthly origin] is to the impossibility to succeed in it. Although experience contradicts theory, social life validates cosmology by its similarity of structure. Hence cosmology is true' (Lévi-Strauss 1968: 216). That is, culture (the familiar, or 'familial', world of columns 1 and 2, concerning our valuation of kinship) and nature (the unfamiliar world of columns 3 and 4, concerning our relation to the earth) have been mediated. Moreover, there has been a simultaneous resolution within culture: it is wrong to commit incest and patricide, and it is right to marry outside your clan. And that resolution involves a kind of compromise with nature: we admit that we originally sprang from earth, but reserve the right to go beyond it.

Though Lévi-Strauss is indebted to psychoanalysis, in that he assumes the above process of resolution to be unconscious and in that he takes the taboo against incest and patricide to be decisive, his reading of Oedipus is quite unlike that of Freud. Where Lévi-Strauss arrests the narrative in order to discover the logic, Freud produces his own narrative within which to situate the one he has received. Lévi-Strauss explains myth; Freud, where he manages to evade the legacy of the Enlightenment, explores and expands myth. The one is interested in abstraction, stasis and system; the other is interested in the dynamics of culture, understood as narrative. In short, unlike Freud at his most interesting, Lévi-Strauss is both a realist and an allegorist. His 'quest for the invariant', his obsession with 'rules', his insistence on 'order': these are indices of a mind which prefers *logos* to *mythos*, and (though without the Christian implication) the Word to words. For in his hands each myth turns out to be about the code of every myth, the metalanguage which informs and constrains all tellings of tales.

That said, structuralism has proved quite fruitful, in a simplified form, in the analysis of popular narrative forms. Its method of decoding has been applied with interesting results to the Western genre of film, a modern variation on hero myth, by Will Wright. He suggests that this genre is structured through certain basic oppositions, which are variants of the culture–nature division. It is through these that we initially situate all those opposites which motivate the plot, the most obvious being heroes and villains.

Wright distinguishes between the 'classic' or naive Western, such as *Dodge City* (1930), and the 'professional' or more sophisticated Western, such as *Butch Cassidy and the Sundance Kid* (1970). In the former, we know where we stand because we know where the hero stands: that is, with civilization, society, the good; and against the wilderness, that which lies outside society, the bad. In the latter, while relying on the essential structure of opposition for our bearings, we are able to entertain the possibility that life may be more complicated. The hero here is more likely to be identified with the wilderness, and to be antagonistic to the society: hence we are no longer sure who is good and who is bad (see Wright 1975). It is important, of course, that the viewer is still relying on the essential structure of opposition, that between culture and nature, for her bearings. Without this paradigm, the film would not be able to explore variations of alignment or to mediate satisfactorily the contradictions of cultural experience itself, which is the focus of myth.

This kind of analysis works well on Westerns, which make a point of displaying their mythic structure. It is perhaps more difficult to read classic literary texts in terms of the nature–culture opposition. Here, we do better if we remain alert to any suggestion at all of contradictions being mediated. Thus, Austen's *Sense and Sensibility* obviously invites a structuralist reading: initially, there is too much 'sense' in Elinor Dashwood and too much 'sensibility' in her sister Marianne; the novel shows us that the human norm lies somewhere between. Another example might be Milton's *Paradise Lost.* On the one hand, God foresees all events, including the fall from paradise; on the other hand, Adam and Eve choose to commit sin quite freely. This epic poem might then be seen as a long and complex mediation, by which necessity and freedom turn out to be aspects of the same divine wisdom. Again, we might even see *Hamlet* as an extended enactment of the opposition between the contradictory impulses of the prince's most famous soliloquy: 'To be' and 'not to be'. The drama resolves these by letting Hamlet 'be' until the time comes 'not to be', when his father's death is avenged: an act which both negates and affirms his own identity. Here a certain strain is evident in the reading, and we might well conclude, after trying out a few examples, that there is a limited potential to such decoding: one cannot help but feel that, in pursuit of the grammar of the mind, one is leaving out almost everything that makes the interpretation of the particular text interesting. The richness of narrative is being reduced to the common denominator of universal 'order'.

Thus, despite the above evidence of a fruitful influence within cultural studies, we might want to agree with the anthropologist Clifford Geertz that the lasting impression of structuralist mythography is its abstraction and its essentialism. Geertz reflects that 'what Lévi-Strauss has made for himself is an infernal cultural machine. It annuls history, reduces sentiment to a shadow of intellect.' His 'search is not after all for men, whom he doesn't much care for, but for Man, with whom he is enthralled'. In short, his structuralism amounts to little more than 'hypermodern intellectualism' (Geertz 1993: 356–9). Geertz himself, by contrast, recognizes the primacy of language without subscribing to a metalanguage. Indeed, his is an anthropology which constantly reflects on its own status as a linguistic construct. Inspired by the thought of Paul Ricoeur and Kenneth Burke, Geertz denies any claim to transcendent objectivity, and views his own interpretation as discourse and rhetoric (Geertz 1993: 19, 29). He knows that reading myth is also mythic reading.

Another anthropologist, Victor Turner, has sought to demonstrate the limits of the very principle of structure. If we think of it not simply as an abstract pattern but as a cultural assumption, we see how dangerous it may become. 'Structure' for Turner can all too often be a closed and static system, 'arid and mechanical'.

Countering this there has to be what he calls 'communitas', a much more 'elusive' concept, but pragmatically important:

> All human societies implicitly refer to two contrasting social models. One . . . is of a society as a structure of jural, political and economic positions, offices, statuses and roles, in which the individual is only ambiguously grasped behind the social persona. The other is of society as a communitas of concrete, idiosyncratic individuals who, though differing in physical and mental endowment, are nevertheless regarded as equal in terms of shared humanity.
>
> (Turner 1974: 166)

Turner associates 'structure' with secular hierarchy and 'communitas' with any religious vision which offers a corrective to that order. He refers us to St Francis of Assisi who, taking a vow of marriage to 'Lady Poverty', rejected both the world of property and an all too worldly ecclesiastical establishment. Significantly, perhaps, he was a near contemporary of Joachim, so his followers, including Dante, tended also to be influenced by the abbot of Fiore.

'Communitas', moreover, being transitional, marginal, 'liminal', corresponds to that moment in what Arnold van Gennep calls a 'rite of passage' when the initiate is placed outside society, on the 'threshold' (Latin, *limen*). The separation of the initiate is thought to coincide with the suspension of normal social rules, so that the 'post-liminal' phase of reintegration involves rebirth not only for the individual but also for the community. Thus, where 'structure' insists on identity and certainty, 'communitas' allows scope for difference and ambiguity, and so for potential (Turner 1974: 81–2). One cannot help but recall here Rickword's case for 'The Returning Hero', for the 'humorous' view of the universe which reinvigorates 'the social mind'. As for the early Rickword, so for Turner: far from being parasitic upon 'structure', or incidental to society, the 'liminality' of 'communitas' is essential to human development. Without such risk-takers as St Francis, the given hierarchy will tend to inertia, rigidifying injustice and inequality; and conversely, spontaneous spirituality has to have some order to test itself against, some threshold to cross. So, we see that Turner's model is analogous not only to 'The Returning Hero', but also to Ricoeur's 'dialectic of ideology and utopia' and to Burke's 'comic corrective'. It assumes myth to be active within history.

One notable thinker who is concerned with collective logic yet who cannot be contained by the terms of structuralist mythography is the literary theorist René Girard. An opponent of Freud (and with him, Frazer) as much as of Lévi-Strauss, he yet begins from both their premises. With Freud, he believes that human culture has its roots in violence; with Lévi-Strauss, he believes that myth is traditionally about 'order'. But Girard goes beyond both, in a direction that aligns him with Turner, Ricoeur and Burke. His decisive break with Freud is over the Oedipus complex, which in *Violence and the Sacred* he rejects in favour of a theory of 'mimetic desire'. He argues that violence threatens wherever one person wants to imitate another person, to have what they have or to be what they are, but is prevented from doing so by lack of resources or status. This desire to imitate the chosen model, if universally expressed, leads to a chronic and 'impure' violence. In order to purge itself of this disease, society decides on an act of abrupt and 'pure' violence. It selects at random a victim, a 'scapegoat', and kills him, thus directing the collective violence away from the group (Girard 1977: 39–51).

Unlike Frazer's model, in which a particular man must be murdered because he is thought to represent the god, for Girard the choice of victim is arbitrary; it is only after the event that the scapegoat is deified. Unlike Freud's model, it is not the son killing the father that matters (except in so far as he wishes to 'imitate' him, and marry the mother), but society preventing its own self-destruction. Hence, Girard reads Sophocles' *Oedipus Rex* as concerning the 'sacrificial crisis': Oedipus is the 'surrogate victim' who is destroyed by his society, not because he is supposed to have done anything wrong, but because it is contriving to hide from itself the real causes of its internal crisis: it needs a scapegoat (Girard 1997: 84–5). Girard's account here owes much to Burke's suggestion that 'perfectionism' taken to the extreme involves systematic aggression.

Thus far, Lévi-Strauss and Girard might agree: myth is about the threat of 'disorder' and the need for 'order'. But Girard parts company with structuralism when, in *The Scapegoat* (1986) and *Things Hidden since the Foundation of the World* (1987), he argues that myths need to be questioned as texts which justify persecution. Against the sacrificial logic of myth, which for Girard always takes the side of victors against victims, he proposes the anti-sacrificial vision of scripture. The God we discover in the Bible is the God of the victims. In particular, the example of Jesus Christ repudiates the sanctification of violence. In effect, it signifies an end to the scapegoat mechanism, the crucifixion being the sacrifice of an entirely innocent victim whose very aim is the end of all sacrifices. The message we receive from the Gospels is that of love, forgiveness and non-violence. With Victor Turner, Girard believes this kind of imaginative thinking involves a crossing of thresholds, a leap into uncertainty. The irony is, of course, that Christianity itself soon became, and for many remains, a sacrificial religion (as noted by Freud in *Moses and Monotheism*). It has always been ready to create scapegoats and to relish 'victimage' (to use Kenneth Burke's term).

This explains why T. S. Eliot in his play *Murder in the Cathedral* (1935) finds it entirely appropriate to fuse Frazerian mythography and Christian doctrine in his celebration of the martyrdom of Thomas Becket. He accepts, that is, the very logic which Girard is repudiating. There can be little doubt that the author concurs with the chorus when, after the event, it thanks God for the 'blood of Thy martyrs and saints' which shall 'enrich the earth' (Eliot 1961: 71). The protagonist, too, confirming the chorus's understanding, speaks very much like the Eliot we already know, taking the 'sign of the Church' to be the 'sign of blood': 'His blood given to buy my life' and 'My blood given to pay for His death' (Eliot 1961: 60–1). This kind of Christianity stands in relation to Girard's as type to anti-type. Its sanctification of violence is mythic, if we agree with the speaker in Geoffrey Hill's poem 'Genesis': 'There is no bloodless myth will hold' (Hill 1985: 16). But perhaps, even given Girard's view that Christianity deconstructs the logic of sacrifice, the faith he espouses may be seen as more than demythologization. For his purpose is not to replace *mythos* with *logos*, if by the latter we mean hierarchical doctrine. Rather, he is correcting one sort of story by means of another. He effectively demonstrates that Christianity is no less a myth than the story of the scapegoat which it rewrites. Thus, Girard may be said to be a demythologizer in that he repudiates the literalism evident in the relish for 'blood' in the lines just quoted. At the same time, Girard may be said to be a remythologizer in that he endorses the symbolic potential of Christian narrative. Hence, he might be aligned with Paul Ricoeur. It is Ricoeur, we recall, who speaks of myth as a 'disclosure' of 'possible worlds'. For him the Gospel story of the resurrection offers 'freedom in the light of hope': it displays a 'logic of surplus and excess' and 'an *economy of superabundance*' (Ricoeur 1974: 410). As such, contra Bultmann, it cannot be demythologized, any more than the profane imagination can cease producing stories of the sacred. In the next chapter we will consider how that imagination has become more important than ever in the present era.

6

HISTORY

CRITICISM AS VISION

The year 1957 saw the publication of two books which have remained deeply influential: *Mythologies* by Roland Barthes and *Anatomy of Criticism* by Northrop Frye. We will consider Barthes's book first, but must begin by recognizing that, though its title seems the more relevant to our discussion, the work itself is less about mythology than about ideology, and that in the pejorative sense of mystification. Or, to be more accurate, for Barthes the two terms are interchangeable. Thus, there is a 'mythology of wine', predicated on certain assumptions about health and social behaviour, which attributes magical properties to the French national drink: 'it is above all a converting substance, capable of reversing situations and states, and of extracting from objects their opposites – for instance, making a weak man strong or a silent one talkative'. But it also serves to distract consumers from the fact that the production of wine is 'deeply involved in French capitalism'. It is a drink which 'cannot be an unalloyedly blissful substance, except if we wrongly forget that it is also the product of an expropriation' (Barthes 1973: 61). Other 'myths' considered include a black soldier saluting the French flag on a magazine cover, Roman haircuts in Hollywood films, the face of Greta Garbo, steak and chips, striptease, the Citroen car, and a wrestling match.

Though we call this kind of analysis structuralist, we should distinguish it from the decoding which we have already encountered. For one thing, the very material studied is different. Lévi-Strauss is concerned with archaic or primitive narratives which reveal something of the workings of a universal human mind. Barthes is concerned with the peculiar workings of contemporary communications and media. Also, they differ as to intentions and interests. Lévi-Strauss sets out to demonstrate that culture and nature are mediated through the logic or grammar of the myth, and concludes that this is a necessary activity of the human mind. Barthes sets out to demonstrate that culture and nature are in effect identified, and concludes that this is a sinister deception. In more detail, we may say of Barthes that he exposes 'mythology' as the systematic presentation of bourgeois thinking as if it were the only possible way of thinking: 'what goes without saying.' Thus, 'myth' is 'depoliticized speech' which represses the 'contingent, historical, in one word: *fabricated*' quality of capitalism' (Barthes 1973: 143). Bourgeois ideology pretends that the cultural construction is a natural phenomenon.

This kind of analysis is necessary and it is impressive; but as *Mythologies* does not offer anything more positive, it has to be seen as a variation on demythologization, propounding its own myth of mythlessnesss. Barthes is implicitly claiming to be able to demystify the forces which hold others in thrall and so, presumably, transcend them. Unlike Bultmann, however, he does not need to locate and then set aside any narrative, since nearly all his subjects are non-narrative images or concepts. So it is not that *mythos* is being replaced by *logos,* rather, it is assumed to be a kind of false *logos* in the first place. Moreover, as each reading only repeats the same point, that beneath the apparently natural there lies the cultural, we might call Barthes's methodology a kind of political allegory. That said, the notion of the denial of history is an interesting one, and we will return to it later.

Those interested in discovering another Barthes, much more concerned with exploration than explanation, might consult the selection of essays written in the 1960s and early 1970s, *Image – Music – Text*. Though his 'Introduction to the Structural Study of Narratives' (1966) turns out to be little more attentive to story as story than is Lévi-Strauss's exposition of Oedipus, 'The Struggle with the Angel' (1971) offers some strikingly new insights. This analysis of Genesis 32: 22–32 relates the encounter between Jacob, the figure chosen by God to be the ancestor of the people of Israel, and an unidentified 'man' or angel, to the structure of folk tale. Ostensibly it is an application of the categories expounded by the Russian formalist critic Vladimir Propp in his *Morphology of the Folktale* (1928), a proto-structuralist work which treats popular narratives as rigidly rule-governed. But Barthes goes much further, trying to account for the sheer strangeness of the episode.

According to Propp's scheme, if this were a standard folk tale concerning 'the Quest', we would expect to distinguish between 'the Originator of the Quest', 'the Hero' who is on the quest, and 'the Opponent'. The crucial factor for Barthes is that in Genesis 32 the first and last of these are revealed to be one and the same. It is God who sends Jacob on his quest; it is God who, in the form of the 'man', wrestles with him at the fords of the Jabbok river, apparently seeking to destroy him. Barthes argues that the reason for this breach of the 'rules' is theological: the affirmation of monotheism. The God of the Israelites has to be thought of as so powerful that there could be no independent force strong enough to hinder one of his chosen servants. Hence, the story is only allowed to be told so long as it does not offend against the hard-won doctrine of one almighty God. This in effect means that, though it is undoubtedly derived from non-Biblical sources, it has to be retold in such a way that it overrides the 'rules' of folk tale or legend. Thus, Barthes's theological insight turns out to be a literary one. To quote John Barton's succinct summary of a complicated argument:

> Genesis 32 is able to have the effect it obviously does have on most readers only because it *first* constrains us to read it as if it were a

> normal folk-tale, and *then* turns the tables on us by illicitly exploiting the conventions of such tales. The result is a surrealistic sense of disorientation. A parallel from modern literature would be a detective novel where the detective himself turned out to be the murderer . . . Consider [also], for example, the Middle English poem *Sir Gawain and the Green Knight*, where in the moment of disclosure we (and Gawain) learn that Sir Bertilak, his host, and the Green Knight, his adversary, are one and the same. The reader is likely to experience just the same shudder as in Genesis 32, and for the same reason: confusion of roles undermines our confidence that we know what we are reading.
>
> (Barton 1984: 118–19)

Thus, Barthes has done more than explain the grammar or structure underlying the narrative expression: he has treated the particular story as an intervention in an inherited discourse. In short, he has stressed that sense of potential which we have associated with radical typology rather than with allegory. His closing comments are, then, particularly significant. He suggests that we pursue the 'dissemination' of the text, 'not its truth'. For the 'problem' Barthes takes to be crucial is 'exactly not to manage to reduce the Text to a signified, whatever it may be (historical, economic, folkloristic or kerygmatic), but to hold its *significance* fully open' (Barthes 1981: 141).

It is the Barthes of 'The Struggle with the Angel', not of *Mythologies*, who has the more affinities with Northrop Frye. But before considering the *Anatomy* as a genuinely mythopoeic work, we should acknowledge that, at first glance, it does look very much like a standard exposition of structuralist principles. Indeed, Frye states explicitly in his introduction that he intends to assert the 'science' of literary criticism and to counter 'appreciation', 'impressionism' and 'naive induction' (Frye 1971: 7, 15). It is written on the assumption that criticism can be scientific precisely because literature itself is 'not a piled aggregate of "works", but an order of words' (Frye 1971: 17). Value-judgements of individual texts are discounted in favour of 'the systematic study of the formal causes of art' (Frye 1971: 29). The form which is the 'cause' of the art of literature is myth: the 'modes' of literary narrative work according to the logic of 'displacement', which is the 'adaptation of myth . . . to canons of morality or plausibility' (Frye 1971: 365). The more literature distances itself from myth, moving from 'romance' through the 'mimetic' modes, the more 'real' it appears; though, as Frye indicates, this appearance is deceptive, as is evident once we reach the self-conscious exposure of device favoured by 'irony'.

Frye defines a narrative mode as a 'conventional power of action assumed about the chief characters in fictional literature', adding that they 'tend to succeed one another in a historical sequence' (Frye 1971: 366). He classifies them according to 'the hero's power of action', which decreases as we proceed from the narrative mode of myth (1) through the four narrative modes of literature (2–5). Hence we get the following scheme:

1. If superior in *kind* both to other men and to the environment of other men, the hero is a divine being, and the story about him will be a *myth* in the common sense of a story about a god. Such stories have an important place in literature, but are as a rule found outside the normal literary categories.
2. If superior in *degree* to other men and to his environment, the hero is the typical hero of *romance*, whose actions are marvellous but who is himself identified as a human being. The hero of romance moves in a world in which the ordinary laws of nature are slightly suspended: prodigies of courage and endurance, unnatural to us, are natural to him, and enchanted weapons, talking animals, terrifying ogres and witches, and talismans of miraculous power violate no rule of probability once the postulates of romance have been established. . . .
3. If superior in degree to other men but not to his natural environment, the hero is a leader. He has authority, passions, and powers of expression far greater than ours, but what he does is subject both to social criticism and to the order of nature. This is the hero of the *high mimetic* mode. . . .
4. If superior neither to other men nor to his environment, the hero is one of us: we respond to a sense of his common humanity, and demand from the poet the same canons of probability that

we find in our own experience. This gives us the hero of the *low mimetic* mode. . . .

5. If inferior in power or intelligence to ourselves, so that we have the sense of looking down on a scene of bondage, frustration or absurdity, the hero belongs to the *ironic* mode. This is still true when the reader feels that he is or might be in the same situation, as the situation is being judged by the norms of a greater freedom.

(Frye 1971: 33–4)

Paradoxically, it is his initial simplification of paradigms, involving the characterization of 'myth' as a narrative about a god, which allows Frye to offer his sophisticated account of the modes. This in turn allows him to accommodate all possible literary genres.

'Romance' covers, for example, legend and folk tale. The two 'mimetic' modes cover what is usually referred to as literary realism, but Frye makes it clear that, where we may think we are witnessing the representation of reality, we are actually enjoying works as conventional and stylized as those of myth or romance. Thus, the 'high mimetic' covers, for example, epic and tragedy, which are, traditionally, highly structured works. The 'low mimetic' covers, for example, comedy, a term which in turn covers the eighteenth- and nineteenth-century novel: what is at work is 'the Cinderella archetype', which Frye describes as 'the incorporation of an individual very like the reader into the society aspired to by both, a society ushered in with a happy rustle of bridal gowns and banknotes' (Frye 1971: 44). That leaves only the 'ironic', which covers, for example, modernist poetry and fiction, satirical fantasy and the theatre of the absurd. This final mode, irony, frequently offers a disturbing parody of romance, as with the abortive quests of *Heart of Darkness* and *The Trial*: thus any illusion of realism we may have had in our experience of the 'mimetic' modes is dispelled.

The system is not completely watertight, however, as the awkward category of epic will indicate. Frye's inclusion of epic along with tragedy in the 'high mimetic' creates some confusion, because the main examples of the genre suggest it is closer to myth, or at least the paradigm of hero myth, than is romance.

Thus, the protagonist of the Babylonian epic *Gilgamesh*, though not a god, is semi-divine: though mortal, he is able to undertake the most marvellous adventures, akin to those of Perseus and Theseus. Frye, having defined myth as a narrative about a god, would have no choice but to place *Gilgamesh* in the sphere of literature rather than myth proper. But there still remains the question of its proximity to myth. Frank McConnell, contradicting Frye, thinks it more logical to place epic above romance, the hero of the former usually being a king with divine authority and the hero of the latter usually being a knight or the equivalent (McConnell 1979: 3–20). In order to justify Frye's categorization, one would have to translate 'epic' as 'secondary' or 'literary epic' (Jenkyns 1992: 53–6). This might be exemplified by Milton's *Paradise Lost*: though the heroism belongs to the son of God, who offers to counteract Satan and undo the results of the fall of Adam and Eve, it is they who are the actual protagonists, strictly speaking. Moreover, their narrative is the occasion of too many elaborate speculations (about predestination and free will, for example) to retain the impact of 'primary epic'.

Another problem with Frye's scheme is that while it seems to offer an insight into literary history, with the four modes following one another chronologically, this sequence runs the risk of abstraction. Thus, though it is broadly true that in English culture romance precedes realism, we might be tempted to infer from the opening paragraphs of the *Anatomy* that this process is universal and inevitable. But of course other cultures form their own histories; and romance can appear after realism, as it has done even in twentieth-century England, with the rise of 'sword and sorcery' narratives, for example. In fact, Frye goes to some trouble later in his book to deny these implications, and to insist on the flexibility of his model. But certainly he frequently had to face the charge of being more synchronic than diachronic, and of being insensitive to particular cultures other than the Anglo-American. However, this charge may miss the point of his enterprise, which Paul Ricoeur describes as a celebration of an endlessly 'productive imagination' (Ricoeur 1991: 244).

We might illustrate the four literary narrative types as follows, by listing some of their more famous protagonists. In romance we find: Robin Hood; Perceval; Chaucer's Aurelius ('The Franklin's Tale'); Spenser's Red Cross Knight; Tarzan; Batman and Superman; Obi-Wan Kenobi and Luke Skywalker (*Star Wars*). In the high mimetic we find: Shakespeare's King Lear, Antony and Cleopatra, Othello and Hamlet; Milton's Adam and Eve. In the low mimetic we find: Shakespeare's Beatrice (*Much Ado about Nothing*) and Viola (*Twelfth Night*); Jane Austen's Fanny Price (*Mansfield Park*); Dickens's Pip (*Great Expectations*). In the ironic we find: Hardy's Tess; Kafka's Gregor Samsa ('Metamorphosis') and Joseph K; the inhabitants of Eliot's *Waste Land*; Orwell's Winston Smith (*Nineteen Eighty-Four*); Beckett's Vladimir and Estragon (*Waiting for Godot*).

So far, we have a dispassionate account of a literary 'system', an 'order of words', of which Lévi-Strauss might approve. But the *Anatomy* is much more than a demonstration of structure. Though Frye has listed his modes, and I have supplemented the catalogue with named characters and texts, we still have only begun. Here the difference from the Barthes of *Mythologies* needs stressing. Barthes in effect equates myth with ideology: it confirms the status quo. Frye's model has utopian implications. For the sequence of modes is not meant to be an arid classification of forms, but is meant to demonstrate what Paul Ricoeur calls 'narrative understanding'. Frye is offering his own reading of myth, which he sees 'displaced' through the four modes of literature, as a mythic reading. With Blake, he is chiefly interested in myth as mythopoeia; and like him, he has his own story to recount. Unlike the early Barthes, who sees myth as culture disguised as nature, Frye wants to tell us about the reconciliation of nature and culture through the power of the mythic imagination.

There are two paradigms implicit in this story of Frye's: the deliverance myth, as given in the Bible; and fertility myth, as given in *The Golden Bough*. The clue to his use of the latter comes at the end of the first of the four essays that comprise the *Anatomy*, in the following unassuming digression, which concerns the way literature not only has myth as its origin, even where it may seem to be concerned with 'verisimilitude', or semblance of actuality, but also as its destiny: 'Reading forward in history, therefore, we may think of our romantic, high mimetic and low mimetic modes as a series of *displaced* myths, *mythoi* or plot-formulas progressively moving over towards the opposite pole of verisimilitude, and then, with irony, beginning to move back' (Frye 1971: 51–2). That is, with the final narrative mode we are forcibly reminded that the first and founding mode, namely myth itself, has been ever-present beneath the apparent realism of literature, and we witness the reaffirmation of its 'formal cause'. Just as literature descends from myth, through romance downwards, so does irony return to myth. Again, as above, we can easily supply our own examples. Indeed, we have discussed the following texts already: *The Waste Land*, *Ulysses*, *Finnegans Wake*, 'The End', *Dispatches* and *Apocalypse Now*. We have even encountered a manifesto of ironic mythopoeia, in the form of Edgell Rickword's essay, 'The Returning Hero'. Looking around for yet one more example, we might seize upon Ted Hughes's poetic work, *Crow* (1970): its hero is a bird which many people dismiss as ugly and sinister, but which Hughes deems worthy to be the focus of the poet's blueprint for a new, darkly humorous kind of myth. The powerful impact of the volume is due not only to Hughes's visceral language, but also to the way it resonates with Native American mythology, in which crows or ravens frequently take the role of the 'trickster' – a figure who is mischievous yet creative, and who, while behaving unpredictably, is yet central to the tribe's identity.

If we accept the principle of the return of irony to myth, then the pattern may be regarded as cyclical, as with Frazer's fertility myth. Significantly, the two central literary modes, the high and low mimetic, are most clearly represented by the genres of tragedy and comedy, respectively. In one, the hero falls from high to low, from life to death: for example, King Lear, Antony or Othello. In the other, the hero rises like Cinderella from low to high, from a kind of death-in-life of obscurity and confusion, to a new way of life: for example, Viola, Fanny Price or Oliver Twist. This pattern of renewal, expanded, forms the cyclical movement of the four literary modes. Frye's 'order of words' is reminiscent of the story of the dying god and the reviving god, representative as they are of the seasonal round. Thus, the four *mythoi* are analogous to the four seasons: romance is the *mythos* of summer, the high mimetic (represented by tragedy) is that of autumn, irony of winter, and the low mimetic (represented by comedy) of spring.

At the same time, however, the cycle is contained by a larger pattern still, the myth of deliverance which is implicit in 'the Great Code' itself. This is a design both cosmic and historical, concerning a heaven above and a hell below, and a creation at the beginning of time and a new creation at the end. Frye indicates this vast, inclusive framework by two kinds of symbolism: 'apocalyptic' and 'demonic'. These are the ultimate terms of the myth which contains, informs and moves literary expression. Their dialectic encompasses the cycle outlined above. Frye's *Anatomy*, his own mythic reading of literature, is an attempt to affirm the 'apocalyptic' vision as the permanent possibility which inspires the secular imagination. For Frye uses the term 'apocalypse' in a wholly positive sense: he means, not the literal expectation of catastrophe, nor even a religious doctrine, but rather a beatific or idyllic revelation, a sense of harmony and reconciliation, an imaginative anticipation of what we have called the 'not yet'. It is the form which reality assumes under the aspect of desire, defined in its broadest sense as the wish for more abundant life. Here we encounter images such as the paradisal garden, the tree of life, the highway, the heavenly city, and the beatific lamb. To make sense, however, it must be balanced by a vision of the world which desire rejects: the 'demonic'. Here we encounter images such as the harsh wilderness or the sinister forest, the tree of death, the labyrinth, the city of destruction, and the serpent or dragon (Frye 1971: 141–50).

It will be clear by now that Frye is telling a story which implies a cosmology. It is the traditional Christian one: 'a heaven above, a hell beneath, and a cyclical . . . order of nature in between' (Frye 1971: 161). But he is reading it literarily not literally. Like literature itself, it is for him a vast, imaginative construct, not a representation of reality. Thus, he gives special status to the first of the four literary modes, romance: with its sense of the marvellous, and its quest structure, it represents the power of the human mind to construct a cosmos according to the imperatives of desire. He tries to convey the significance of the form which he elsewhere calls, in the title of another book, *The Secular Scripture*, as follows:

> The central form of quest-romance is the dragon-killing theme exemplified by the stories of St George and Perseus. . . . A land ruled by a helpless old king is laid waste by a sea-monster, to whom one young person after another is offered to be devoured, until the lot falls on the king's daughter: at that point, the hero arrives, kills the dragon, marries the daughter, and succeeds to the kingdom.
>
> (Frye 1971: 189)

The same pattern is evident in the last book of the Bible, which is the basis for 'an elaborate dragon-killing metaphor in Christian symbolism'. Drawing on suggestions in earlier books, that there is a sea-monster named the Leviathan which is 'the enemy of the Messiah, and whom the Messiah is destined to kill in the "day of the lord"', the author of Revelation identifies the Leviathan, Satan and the serpent of Eden. That is, 'the hero is Christ (often represented in art standing on a prostrate monster), the dragon Satan, the impotent old king Adam, whose son Christ becomes, and the rescued bride the Church' (Frye 1971: 189). Thus, the secular romance, with its roots in the fertility cycle, and the sacred vision, with its dialectic of the apocalyptic and demonic, turn out to be complementary not contradictory. They both bear witness to the persistence and power of mythopoeia.

With Frye, one could not get a more clear reversal of Barthes's position in *Mythologies:* where Barthes stresses the duplicitous and conspiratorial aspects of bourgeois culture, binding us to the status quo, Frye sees the culture of any age as carrying within it the potential for freedom. Again, contrasting Frye with Eliot, we may observe that the sequence of modes recalls the 'ideal order', but the proponent of the latter finally decided to subordinate cultural tradition to religious orthodoxy. Moreover, as Frye himself points out in his study of the poet, Eliot's own view of history was deeply conservative and pessimistic (Frye 1981: 7). It may have been a myth, but it was certainly not a quest.

In a sense, then, the Bible in the *Anatomy* serves a similar function to that of *The Golden Bough*. It provides food for the imagination. Of Frazer's massive mythographic work he remarks that it is, 'as literary criticism, an essay on the ritual content of naive drama': that is, 'it reconstructs an archetypal ritual from which the structural and generic principles of drama may be logically derived'. Thus: 'it does not matter two pins to the critic whether this ritual ever had any *historical* existence or not' (Frye 1978: 125). Frye's Frazer is a non-realist Frazer. As to the Bible: Frye devotes two books to its formal analysis, *The Great Code* (1982) and *Words with Power* (1990), and in the first of these gives an extremely full account of scriptural typology (Frye 1982: 105–38). But it becomes clear long before completing our reading of the first volume that he is treating 'the Great Code' in a manner similar to Blake's: not as a doctrinal constraint, but as an imaginative agenda. Thus, commenting on the Biblical creation myth as an anti-type to existing ancient Near Eastern narratives, he suggests that 'we take the Bible as a key to mythology, instead of taking mythology in general as a key to the Bible' (Frye 1982: 92). An orthodox Christian could not make such a suggestion. Again, thinking no doubt of Dante's own mythopoeic work, he has no qualms about using the Bible as an illustration of a secular narrative form, 'the U-shaped pattern' which is 'the standard shape of comedy':

> The entire Bible, viewed as a 'divine comedy', is contained within a U-shaped story of this sort, one in which each man . . . loses the tree and water of life at the beginning of Genesis and gets them back at the end of Revelation. In between, the story of Israel is told as a series of declines into the power of heathen kingdoms, Egypt, Philistia, Babylon, Syria, Rome, each followed by a brief moment of relative independence. The same U-narrative is found outside the historical sections also, in the account of Job and in Jesus' parable of the prodigal son.
>
> (Frye 1982: 169)

Though the emphasis here is on comedy rather than romance, Frye's point is that both sacred and secular scripture, perceived as a 'total vision of possibilities', or 'total body of imaginative hypothesis', are narrative projections. Neither flatly linear nor deterministically cyclical, they are best seen as negotiating 'the shape of history and as working within the tension between 'temporal movement' and 'revelation' (Frye 1982: 198). The 'order of words' may imply the one 'Word', but what the Bible, mythology, literature and criticism all indicate to Frye is that travelling hopefully towards it may be as good as having arrived.

A SINGLE STORY?

> The greatness of Frye, and the radical difference between his work and that of the great bulk of garden-variety myth criticism, lies in his willingness to raise the issue of community and to draw basic, essentially social, interpretive consequences from the nature of religion as collective representation. . . . The religious figures then become the symbolic space in which the collectivity thinks itself and celebrates its own unity; so that it does not seem a very difficult next step, if, with Frye, we see literature as a weaker form of myth or a later stage of ritual, to conclude that in that sense all literature, no matter how weakly, must be informed by what we have called a political unconscious, that all literature must be read as a symbolic meditation on the destiny of community.
>
> (Jameson 1981: 69–70)

The writer of this commendation of Frye is a Marxist literary critic. In many respects Fredric Jameson's *The Political Unconscious* is a political revision of the *Anatomy*. Certainly, it owes far more to Frye's visionary criticism than it does to the 'scientific' or 'structural' Marxism of the late Louis Althusser. We might almost say that Frye offers Jameson his means of countering Althusser's challenge. That challenge is, in Jameson's summary, the denial that 'a sequence of historical events or texts and artefacts' may be 'rewritten in terms of some deeper, underlying and more "fundamental" narrative'. This is resisted by appeal to the notion of the 'secular scripture':

> Romance now again seems to offer the possibility of sensing other historical rhythms, and of demonic or Utopian transformations of a

> real now unshakably set in place; and Frye is surely not wrong to assimilate the salvational perspective of romance to a reexpression of Utopian longings, a renewed meditation on the Utopian community, a reconquest . . . of some feeling for a salvational future.
>
> The association of Marxism and romance therefore does not discredit the former so much as it explains the persistence and vitality of the latter, which Frye takes to be the ultimate source and paradigm of all storytelling. On this view, the oral tales of tribal society, the fairy tales that are the irrepressible voice and expression of the underclasses of the great systems of domination, adventure stories and melodrama, and the popular or mass culture of our own time are all syllables and broken fragments of some single immense story.
>
> (Jameson 1981: 104–5)

The inspiration of Frye pervades the whole of Jameson's lengthy book, and this intuition of a single story recurs frequently. Thus, we are told that 'the human adventure is one'. Or again, we are told that historical events 'recover their original urgency for us only if they are retold within the unity of a single great collective story' and 'only if they are grasped as vital episodes in a single vast unfinished plot' (Jameson 1981: 19–20). We might say that Jameson represents a new breed of critic, the Marxist myth critic, were it not for the fact that he has been anticipated by the Rickword of 'The Cultural Meaning of May Day'.

The story or 'human adventure' assumed by *The Political Unconscious* is the myth of deliverance. As we know, in its Marxist version it runs from the Eden of primitive communism to the Jerusalem of mature communism, with the 'fall' into class conflict coming between. Unlike Althusser and most other contemporary Marxists, Jameson makes no apology for the mythic structure of this grand narrative. He consistently invokes the collective, class memory of what has been lost (primitive communism) as a prefigurement of the future (mature communism). Memory and desire are indispensable to Marxism.

The argument of *The Political Unconscious* is complex, but makes perfect sense if the above reflections are borne in mind. It may perhaps be summarized, without too much distortion, in five stages. First, Jameson redefines ideology, not as false consciousness but as a 'strategy of containment'. That is, if ideology is illusion, then it is necessary illusion. In order to function within the given social order, we have to 'repress' history. Here Jameson is explicitly politicizing Freud, and also adapting Barthes's analysis of 'myth' (actually, ideology) as the presentation of the cultural and historical as natural and eternal. Second, Jameson sees history as 'what hurts': that is why we repress it. But to this he adds that it is also a site of contradictions. On the one hand, there is the 'hurt' of present class oppression and alienation. On the other hand, there is the 'hope' of a collective, non-oppressive future. The key to both is political revolution, which would remove the oppression and establish the collectivity, but this very need has to be repressed by anyone seeking to survive in her society as it stands. Third, however, Jameson insists that class consciousness itself is by its very nature collective, involving a sense of solidarity. As such, it prefigures, no matter how dimly, the ideal of a communal future. It is, in short, not only ideological but utopian. Fourth, narrative is a 'socially symbolic act'. That is, like Lévi-Strauss's myth, it resolves the real contradictions of history in imaginative form. In doing so, it allows us to deal provisionally with the 'hurt' and the 'hope', neither of which will go away for long. Fifth, interpretation is always able to read any given narrative as articulating not only ideology (the repression of the need for revolution), but also utopia (the anticipation of collectivity).

Now let us situate this argument more exactly in terms of influence. I have already mentioned Frye. But it should also be stressed that Jameson is drawing on the ideas of the German philosopher Ernst Bloch (1885–1977), and in particular his apocalyptic version of the Marxist myth of deliverance. The author of the massive work of speculation, *The Principle of Hope* (1959), Bloch argued throughout his career that Marxism is an unapologetically utopian vision of history. Against vulgar interpretations of Marx's work, which reduced it to a mechanical materialism, his Marxism was explicitly a narrative projection of the future. Basing his thinking on not only Marx but also the Bible, and in particular the Book of Revelation, he was fascinated by the tension between the already and the not yet, and he saw

Marxism as the secular expression of the latter principle. Hence, no matter how oppressive the given political system might be, and no matter how repressed the vision of an alternative might seem to be, the not yet would somehow find expression in collective fantasy. This could take the form of fairy tale, film or fiction, but the seeds of the future were always implicit in them. In other words, mythic thinking was not to be explained away as reactionary, but was to be celebrated for its utopian potential. Jameson endorses this radical approach to genre:

> Thus, for instance, Bloch's reading of the fairy tale, with its magical wish-fulfilments and its Utopian fantasies of plenty and the *pays de Cocagne*, restores the dialogical and antagonistic content of this 'form' by exhibiting it as a systematic deconstruction and undermining of the hegemonic aristocratic form of the epic, with its sombre ideology of heroism and baleful destiny; thus also the work of Eugene Genovese on black religion restores the vitality of these utterances by reading them, not as the replication of imposed beliefs, but rather as a process whereby the hegemonic Christianity of the slave-owners is appropriated, secretly emptied of its content and subverted to the transmission of quite different oppositional and coded messages.
>
> (Jameson 1981: 86)

Nor do we have to confine the utopian dimension of literature to popular narrative. No matter how far a particular literary text might seem to be committed to preserving the status quo, it can always be read with a view to the potential of the not yet.

Jameson, fusing the ideas of both The *Principle of Hope* and Frye's *Anatomy*, declares that 'all class consciousness of whatever type is Utopian in so far as it expresses the unity of a collectivity' in an imaginative form:

> The achieved collectivity or organic group of whatever kind – oppressors fully as much as oppressed – is Utopian not in itself, but only insofar as all such collectivities are themselves *figures* for the ultimate concrete collective life of an achieved Utopia or classless society. Now we are in a better position to understand how even hegemonic or ruling-class culture and ideology are Utopian, not in

> spite of their instrumental function to secure and perpetuate class privilege and power, but rather precisely because their function is also in and of itself the affirmation of collective solidarity.
>
> (Jameson 1981: 291)

Here we might provide our own example: Book I of Edmund Spenser's *The Fairie Queene*, which we have already referred to as a reactionary version of apocalyptic narrative. Jameson would argue that such a text could still be recuperated for revolutionary thought. It celebrates what can be achieved by co-operation: the Red Cross Knight does not work alone, but is aided by Una as much as he aids her, and is also guided throughout his quest by the figure of Prince Arthur. Moreover, any narrative which concerns the victory over the forces of chaos and the reaffirmation of paradisal existence (Eden being saved from the dragon) cannot help but inspire dreams of a better, more equitable world. Again, a modernist work like *The Waste Land*, while it may be seen as the expression of reactionary pessimism, might also persuasively be read, with its evocation of fertility myth and of the quest for the Grail, as a gesture towards a new, non-alienated life.

Thus Jameson affirms 'The Dialectic of Utopia and Ideology', in the words of the title of his concluding chapter. Anticipating the formulations of Paul Ricoeur, he also harks back to those of Kenneth Burke. Indeed, it is to Burke that Jameson owes his concept of narrative as a 'socially symbolic act'. Here is Burke in 1941: 'Critical and imaginative works are answers to questions posed by the situation in which they arose. They are not merely answers, they are *strategic* answers, *stylized* answers.' Thus, literature is 'symbolic action'. It is a 'strategy' deployed in a 'situation'. Of course, 'there is a difference, and a radical difference, between building a house and writing a poem about building a house'. One must distinguish between 'practical' and 'symbolic' acts. But the point is that the latter is still an 'act' (Burke 1989b: 77–9). Here is Jameson forty years later:

> Kenneth Burke's play of emphases, in which a symbolic act is on the one hand affirmed as a genuine act, albeit on the symbolic level, while on the other it is registered as an act which is 'merely' symbolic,

> its resolutions imaginary ones that leave the real untouched, suitably demonstrates the ambiguous status of art and culture.
>
> (Jameson 1981: 81)

Jameson is deploying Burke's terminology in order to correct the vulgar or reductive Marxism which views the literary text as a simple reflection of its social and historical 'context'. What he proposes rather is that the literary text is the rewriting of a 'subtext' (Jameson 1981: 81).

We might extrapolate from Jameson's speculations as follows. Frazer explains the periodic sacrifice of a representative of the fertility god as a 'magical' event. The action is meant to ensure the revival of the crops – in an agricultural society, the community relies on the seasonal cycle of vegetation. Frazer points out that the act does not achieve its end, since magic is a false kind of science. Nevertheless, we might say, it is important imaginatively, since it enables the community to affirm itself through ritual and myth. Moreover, both the ritual and the myth offer a means of dealing with intolerable problems such as scarcity and the threat of death, and also of justifying social hierarchy, the god being embodied in the king. They are 'symbolic acts', respectively acting out and narrating a crucial drama, the subtext of which is the 'hurt' of history, whether under the aspect of survival or of social conflict (Dowling 1984: 124–6).

Jameson is not initially forthcoming with literary examples, but we might think, for example, of Percy Bysshe Shelley's poem 'Adonais' (1821), which is a pastoral elegy for his friend and fellow-poet John Keats. Based on the myth of Adonis, the dying and reviving god, the poem is merely 'symbolic' in the sense that no matter how much Shelley weeps, his friend will not return from the land of the dead; and that is the burden of the poem itself, to an extent. But 'Adonais' is nonetheless an 'action', which asserts Keats's lasting value as a poet in defiance of those reviewers whose hostility contributed to his early death. History, in the form of philistine bourgeois culture, is both acknowledged and opposed. Another example might be Mark Twain's *Huckleberry Finn* (1884), a novel whose very plot concedes that victories over institutional racism are likely to be exceptional, indeed unusual. However, it still acts symbolically upon the problem of oppression by means of the device of the innocent narrator (Huck querying the so-called common sense of his day), the structure of quest romance (Huck and the slave Jim escaping up the Mississippi) and the symbolism of their friendship (Huck preferring damnation with Jim to the salvation favoured by white racists). The 'hope' gets expressed as well as the 'hurt'.

Jameson's 'Dialectic of Utopia and Ideology', then, with its understanding that a challenge to the present and a prefigurement of the future is always implicit, might suggest a position roughly analogous with radical typology. Certainly, in his discussion of traditional interpretations of the Bible, he would seem to reject allegory, in so far as that is perceived as a means of closing off the promise of the scriptures. In Chapter 1 of *The Political Unconscious*, Jameson considers 'the medieval system' of interpretation, that method of analysis formulated by St Thomas Aquinas among others, and thoroughly familiar to Dante. It distinguished between the four 'levels' or 'senses' of meaning to be discovered in any Biblical episode: the 'literal' (the historical event narrated); the 'allegorical' (what it tells us about Christ, 'allegory' here being a synonym for 'orthodox typology'); the 'moral' (the relevance for the individual believer); and the 'anagogical' (the spiritual significance). While the notion of 'levels' implies stasis, the four-stage sequence suggests dynamism. Jameson explicitly emphasizes the latter.

Applying this mode of analysis to the primary myth of deliverance, the story of Moses leading the exodus of the Hebrews, he shows how each level generates the next, running from the past of the Old Testament to the past of the New, and thence via the present of the reader to the future of humanity. The fourth level is thus the final 'horizon' of interpretation. For him, the 'anagogical' does not denote some vague, mystical conjecture, but is the moment 'in which the text undergoes its ultimate rewriting in terms of the destiny of the human race as a whole, Egypt then coming to prefigure that long purgatorial suffering of earthly history from which the second coming of Christ and the Last Judgment come as the final release'. That is, the 'historical or collective dimension' is thereby attained once again; only now, 'from the story of a particular people it has been transformed into universal history and the destiny of humankind as a whole' (Jameson 1981: 30–1). Jameson's stress on 'rewriting' is certainly reminiscent of radical typology, but phrases such as 'universal history' may give us occasion for doubts. These doubts may be confirmed when the medieval system is translated explicitly into Marxist terms, and the senses or levels are made to conform to the theory of the mode of production:

> What our preceding discussion of the medieval levels suggests . . . is that this is by no means the whole story, and that to grasp the full degree to which this schema projects an essentially allegorical operation, we must enlarge its master code or allegorical key to the point at which the latter becomes a master narrative in its own right; and this point is reached when we become aware that any individual mode of production projects and implies a whole sequence of such modes of production – from primitive communism to capitalism and communism proper – which constitute the narrative of some properly Marxian 'philosophy of history'.
>
> (Jameson 1981: 33)

Though the motto of *The Political Unconscious,* announced on its first page, is 'Always historicize!', it needs to be read in tension with the above quotation, where temporal sequence is immediately translated into one dominant 'philosophy of history'.

In this context, we might consider another statement which is made barely a page into the book, concerning 'metacommentary': 'Interpretation is here construed as an essentially allegorical act, which consists in rewriting a given text in terms of a particular interpretive master-code.' Specifically, 'Marxism is here conceived as that "untranscendable horizon" that subsumes such apparently antagonistic or incommensurable critical operations' as psychoanalysis, myth criticism and structuralism, 'at once cancelling them and preserving them' (Jameson 1981: 10). That is, however Bloch may rewrite Marxism as a myth of the 'not yet', of permanent possibility, Jameson ultimately insists on closure and finality. There may be many fascinating ways of imagining the future within history, but only Marxism can comprehend history. As Robert Young comments on Jameson:

> Even though Marxist criticism must now enter the marketplace as interpretation rather than, as in the old days, through an invocation of its higher knowledge in the form of History and Truth, it is still a superior form of interpretation. For unlike all the others it does not actually have to compete with its rivals because, according to its dialectical logic, it can both incorporate them and transcend them. What at first, then, looked like an abandonment of traditional Marxist notions of History and Truth was in fact only a first move in bringing them back via the meta-claim of interpretive absolutism and history as transcendence.
>
> (Young 1990: 103)

In short, just as with orthodox Christianity, 'the meaning precedes the interpretation', and all interpretation is 'simply a matter of translation into a master code' (Young 1990: 107). Jameson's Marxist myth of deliverance is paradoxically at odds with his commitment to Marxist allegory.

In this light, Jameson may be seen to differ not only from Bloch, but also from Burke and Frye. Burke argues that 'hierarchy' is always open to the 'comic corrective', and that there is no system which is not susceptible to 'perspective by incongruity'. He further argues that such a corrective or perspective must always be immanent, since there is no transcendent position from which to look down on the whole of history. Perfection is always a projection. There being no absolute truth, we are each of us only able to view the world through a particular 'terministic screen', which sets limits to what can be seen (Burke 1966: 45). This phrase is surely echoed in Jameson's 'strategy of containment', the difference being that Jameson believes that his own 'strategy', namely Marxism, is exempt from the historical limits it depicts and diagnoses. Similarly, where Frye gives priority to 'the order of words', Jameson gives priority to the sequence of modes of production. Deferring to Althusser on this point, he accepts that history might best be conceived as 'an absent cause' which, like

Freud's unconscious, cannot be known directly but only through its effects:

> We would therefore propose the following revised formulation: that history is *not* a text, not a narrative, master or otherwise, but that, as an absent cause, it is inaccessible to us except in textual form, and that our approach to it and to the Real itself necessarily passes through its prior textualization, its narrativization in the political unconscious.
>
> (Jameson 1981: 35)

Reading this quotation in isolation, we might hesitate to label Jameson's position as either realism or non-realism, but the above insistence on Marxism as 'allegory' and on the need for a 'master-code' must surely rule out non-realism. What we have here, then, is a variant on realism which avoids literalism but which will concede the minimum to pragmatism and perspectivism.

But it would be unfair to dismiss Jameson's Marxist myth-criticism on the grounds that its assumption of totality is in itself totalitarian. Jameson's skill as an interpreter of narrative is such that we take away from *The Political Unconscious* and his other works the sense, not of remorseless reduction, but of continuing surprise. His understanding of myth is profound, and his ability to read literary texts mythically is agile and endlessly suggestive. We have already referred in Part I to his reading of *Ulysses.* The later chapters of *The Political Unconscious* itself contains long and intriguing interpretations, too long and intriguing to be summarized neatly here, of classic texts such as Conrad's *Lord Jim.* It is as if, despite his adherence to the letter of Marxism, with its attendant allegorical master-code, the spirit of his criticism is permanent possibility – that of radical typology.

Thus, in his response to the phenomenon of postmodernity, given initially only three years after the publication of *The Political Unconscious,* he does not simply reassert the validity of Marxism in the face of what he calls 'the cultural logic of late capitalism'. He diagnoses the condition with the same enthusiasm as he might want to reserve only for the utopian aspect of traditional and modern narratives. Richard Kearney suggests that the postmodern condition brings with it a shift to the metaphor of culture as 'a labyrinth of mirrors', in which nothing is stable or certain: a continuing intertextual play of images (Kearney 1988: 253). Jameson knows and understands this, and he acknowledges the radical difference between Van Gogh's painting of peasant shoes, redolent of authenticity and depth, and Warhol's 'Diamond Dust Shoes', self-referential and wilfully superficial (Jameson 1991: 6–10). His answer is not to invoke the 'reality' of class struggle and the 'truth' of Marxism, but to risk a wager, to propose a tentative clue to the labyrinth, potentially no less effective than Ariadne's thread. He calls this clue an 'aesthetic of cognitive mapping': that would be a 'new political art' which would have to begin to negotiate 'the world space of international capital' at the same time as it attempts 'a breakthrough to some as yet unimaginable new mode of representing this last' (Jameson 1991: 54). It is as if we were being reminded that the Marxist myth of deliverance, that 'vast unfinished plot', is nothing without the permanent potential of creative rewriting and radical improvization.

TESTAMENTS OF DELIVERANCE

It is in the midst of the postmodern 'labyrinth of mirrors' that Marina Warner begins the second of her 1994 Reith Lectures, *Managing Monsters.* She recalls her recent experience at the 'Future Entertainment Show', where she found herself to be one of the few female visitors. The place was packed with teenage boys and young men playing video games: games like 'Streets of Rage', 'Mortal Kombat', 'Street Fighter', 'Zombie Apocalypse' and 'Splatterhouse'. In each of these 'the hero slays monsters': 'Just as Jason and his Argonauts did or Hercules and his Twelve Labours – indeed some of the games quote classical adventures and their pantheons.' What more is involved is hard to discern: the narrative richness of the ancient paradigm of hero myth has been forgotten, and all we have is the moment when 'the hero busts his way through' (Warner 1994: 17–18). Sophisticated technologically, we seem to have become naive mythologically. In the face of this chaos of perfunctory narratives, Warner thus has to attempt her own kind of 'cognitive mapping'.

From the Babylonian creation myth, featuring Marduk's battle with Tiamat, through Greek hero myths such as Theseus and the minotaur, to the romance of St George and the dragon, myth and monstrosity have always been linked. Warner traces the word 'monster' back to two Latin words, one of which means 'show' and the other of which means 'warn':

> [A] myth shows something, it's a story spoken to a purpose, it issues a warning, it gives an account which advises and tells often by bringing into play showings of fantastical shape and invention – monsters. Myths define enemies and aliens and in conjuring them up they say who we are and what we want, they tell stories to impose structure and order.
>
> (Warner 1994: 19)

That being so, what do contemporary monsters tell us about ourselves, particularly the role of men? Warner's lecture is called 'Boys Will Be Boys: The Making of the Male', and it explores a disturbing shift in attitudes. If the key narrative is that of hero myth, then we have witnessed a change in our conception of heroism. Moving back from the contemporary model of the hero as unthinking aggressor, she demonstrates the relevance of other models, one modern and one ancient. Her texts are *Frankenstein* and the *Odyssey*.

Though Warner's focus is on hero myth, she is also interested in variations on paradigms: thus her choice of *Frankenstein* (1818) is interesting because it is itself a radical exploration of two inherited models. It is both a modern hero myth, with its protagonist as scientific experimenter, and a modern creation myth, with its story of the construction of a new creature by human agency. Thus, it rewrites two stories: that of Prometheus, maker of humanity, as told in ancient Greece (in the eighth century BC) by Hesiod and that of the Book of Genesis, as mediated by Milton's *Paradise Lost*. Warner, acknowledging this dual legacy, explores the central shift of emphasis from antiquity to modernity, whereby the human being arrogantly takes all the initiative. But she demonstrates that Mary Shelley's achievement is not only to rewrite ancient myths, but to challenge modern thinking. In particular the novel queries the supremacy of male rationality: 'Mary Shelley grasped the likelihood that a man might make a monster in his own image and then prove incapable of taking responsibility for it.' Thus, a crucial episode is that in which the 'creature' demands its independent rights, above all that to a mate, and his appalled creator refuses, declaring that he and the monster are 'enemies'. Shelley exposes this modern double-bind: the monster is an emanation of the male mind, but the male mind can only cope with it by hostility. And it is this hostility, Warner reminds us, which alone gets expressed in contemporary video narratives; whereas the novel presents us with the monster's own poignant case. 'Current tales of conflict and extermination never hear the monster say: "I am malicious, because I am miserable." Or, "Make me happy, and I shall again be virtuous." The phrases sound absurd, because we're so accustomed to expect the hero to have no other way of managing monsters than slaying them' (Warner 1994: 21–2). We are thus invited to read Mary Shelley's modern, exploratory myth not only as a rewriting of ancient paradigms, but also as a challenge to our own complacency and aggression.

Similarly, Warner reminds us that what has been taken over from Greek hero myth and epic has been the model of the brutal combatant. We have to reread the ancient paradigm in order to see how far we have simplified the notion of heroism:

> In Homer, Odysseus tells the Cyclops that his name is Nobody. So, when Odysseus blinds the Cyclops in his one eye, the giant howls for help to his father the god of the sea and the other Olympians. But all the gods hear is his cry, 'Nobody has blinded me.' And so they do nothing.
>
> This trick from the *Odyssey* is literally one of the oldest in the book. The hero who lives by his wits survives in countless hard luck, Puss in Boots-style stories. . . . Charlie Chaplin, and even Woody Allen have worked this groove, the heroic pathetic. But a gleeful use of cunning and high spirits against brute force, a reliance on subterfuge have almost faded from heroic myth today. In the prevailing popular

> concept of masculinity, as reflected in comics, rock bands, street fashion, Clint Eastwood or Arnold Schwarzenegger movies, the little man, the riddler or trickster has yielded before the type of warrior hero, the paradigm of the fittest survivor.
>
> (Warner 1994: 25)

Moreover, where Greek heroes did slavishly follow the logic of violence, they were not presented as ideal figures but as 'tragic warnings'. They were 'objects of debate, not models' (Warner 1994: 27). This possibility is not allowed for in the scope of 'Splatterhouse' and 'Cannon Fodder'.

However, Warner is not pessimistic. The title of her lecture series suggests that we need not think of monsters as things to 'manage' simply by slaying. Her point is that we have the choice, indeed the obligation, to 'manage' them in another sense: that is, acknowledge them, negotiate with them, interpret them, query them. Here we may think of Jung's process of individuation, which involves facing and incorporating the power of the shadow, our own repressed psyche. Or we may think of Lévi-Strauss's analysis of the resolution of contradictions in the Oedipus story, with the monstrous signifying the earthly origins with which humanity has to come to terms. But Warner differs from them in her insistence that monsters, like myths, are primarily historical. That is to say, the most important thing to do is to interrogate the form which monstrosity is taking in our time. In so far as it becomes merely the alien enemy, the object of mindless terror and violence, we need to remember that 'if monsters are made, not given, they can be unmade, too' (Warner 1994: 31). Here we get some sense of Warner's overall purpose, not only in the Reith Lectures, but throughout her career.

In *Alone of All Her Sex* (1976), she considers, as promised by her subtitle, 'The Myth and Cult of the Virgin Mary' in relation to early goddess-worship as well as the courtly myth-making of the twelfth-century Troubadour poets. *Monuments and Maidens* (1985) includes a reading of Margaret Thatcher, the 'iron lady' of British politics, as Boadicea. In *From the Beast to the Blonde* (1994), she encompasses Rapunzel, Marilyn Monroe and (the pop singer) Madonna in the space of a few paragraphs. That is, she offers a history of myth in terms of its rereading, its rewriting, its re-creating. She is deeply conscious of the ambiguous power of stories: their capacity to enchant can be both life-affirming and destructive. Our obligation is to be both receptive and vigilant. Realizing that myth is always going to be open to change, we must participate in the operation:

> I believe the process of understanding and clarification . . . can give rise to newly told stories, can sew and weave and knit different patterns into the social fabric and that this is a continuous enterprise for everyone to take part in
>
> (Warner 1994: xiv)

What for others may be a source of regret, namely the loss of a sense of originality and authenticity, is for her a sign of constant renewal, of cultural life. She states this clearly as follows: 'Every telling of a myth is a part of that myth; there is no Ur-version, no authentic prototype, no true account' (Warner 1994: 8). Again:

> Myths offer a lens which can be used to see human identity in its social and cultural context – they can lock us up in stock reactions, bigotry and fear, but they're not immutable, and by unpicking them, the stories can lead to others. Myths convey values and expectations which are always evolving, in the process of being formed, but – and this is fortunate – never set so hard they cannot be changed again.
>
> (Warner 1994: 14)

That is a fair summary of the principle we have been calling radical typology. We must trust, we are told, in the very power of myth to change and, in the process, to change us. 'Intertextuality' is not the problem but the solution, if positively understood. For, unlike Lévi-Strauss and Barthes, she does not believe that myth is something that happens behind our backs, as it were: she insists that we have the capacity, as tellers and retellers, interpreters and reinterpreters, to maintain the interaction of myth and history.

Looking in slightly more detail at *Alone of All Her Sex*, we can see Warner refusing merely to 'expose' a set of stories or symbols.

While enlisting Barthes in her repudiation of an essentially and eternally feminine principle, she may be seen even here to be prevented by her fascination with Christian iconography from offering a reductive reading of Christian mythology. Indeed, it is precisely in developing her historical approach that she demonstrates the residual power of the female image. She celebrates what we might call 'the everchanging feminine'. Thus, she moves with ease from Inanna, the Mesopotamian goddess of fertility, to the 'beloved' in the The Song of Solomon, to the 'bride' of the Book of Revelation, to the worshipped lady of Troubadour poetry, and so to Dante's Beatrice. The unifying factor is the Virgin Mary herself, who is either anticipated by, or anticipates, each of these figures. Indeed, Warner is able to make such transitions in the spirit of the Christian witness itself, with its dynamic structuring in relation to previous scriptures.

For it is clear that her concern with time, with the interaction of past and present, derives from her own early Catholicism. A good deal of *Alone of All Her Sex* focuses on Mary as 'the second Eve'. Though she does not use the term, what she is addressing is the principle of 'typology', whereby the 'type' (Adam, Eve) is temporally related to the 'antitype' (Jesus, Mary). As she has explained in interview:

> The New Testament is the book, the Old Testament is the prefiguration of the book, there is an Old Covenant and a New Covenant, and the New Covenant exists as not just a continuum but as a recapitulation in an actual form of the promise of the past
>
> (Tredell 1995: 246)

As she further explains, this is the principle behind much of her own fiction. She mentions her novel *Indigo* (1992), which is based on Shakespeare's *The Tempest* and which is informed by 'the sense that we reenact what was prefigured, that, without it being deterministic, there's some sort of divine plan, that the structures repeat' (Tredell 1995: 247). Here she is using 'divine plan' figuratively, but with the deference that is due to Christianity's ambitious attempt to read history as a narrative of redemption.

Thus, though *Indigo* is a reworking of *The Tempest* rather than the Testament, the idea that myths gain resonance in time, through imaginative reworking, is a lesson learnt from scripture, with its dimensions of prefiguration and fulfilment, foreshadowing and realization. Interestingly, Warner's volume of short stories, *Mermaids in the Basement* (1993), is essentially an audacious series of 'antitypes', with the tales of the fall and of the flood, of the encounter of Susannah with the elders and of the visit to Solomon by the Queen of Sheba, among others, acquiring new life in the contemporary world. If the original idea was that the Christian scriptures were the completion of earlier ones, Warner implies that the best stories are those which never exhaust their promises. In effect, what she is about is the secularization of the scriptural pattern, in such a way that the closure of conventional typology is translated into the endless possibility of transformation (see Coupe 2006).

Myths will always need retelling and reinterpreting, and the women's movement, feminist and post-feminist, has made striking contributions to this process. Thus, Elinor W. Gadon views the myth of Theseus and the minotaur as a story justifying the destruction of Minoan matriarchy and goddess-worship. When the patriarchal Mycenaeans invaded Crete, bringing their sky father Zeus with them, they sought to discredit, but also incorporate, such rituals as 'bull leaping', which the Cretans had conducted in a 'labyrinth' sacred to the goddess. In telling the tale of the killing of the minotaur (half-bull, dwelling in the womb of the earth) they celebrated the suppression of Minoan female-centred religion (Gadon 1989: 97–107). Again, Hélène Cixous takes the figure of monstrosity in the undoubtedly male-oriented Perseus myth, and celebrates the female monster whom the hero has to behead. For her, 'The Laugh of the Medusa' is an emblem of a bisexuality which evades sexual distinction and domination, and she proposes a new kind of writing which subverts essentialism and expresses the multiplicity of desire (Cixous 1980: 253–4).

Similarly, interpretation must be reinterpreted. On the whole, Freud's influence has been an anxious one. Kate Millett set the agenda when she declared him to be 'beyond question the strongest individual counterrevolutionary force in the ideology of sexual politics' (Millett 1969: 178); but Juliet Mitchell, Jacqueline Rose and others have argued in favour of the theory of the Oedipus complex in so far as it implies that sexual identity is a cultural construct rather than a stable, biological essence (Moi 1985: 28). Jung has had an easier passage, given his more positive view of the female. But 'feminist archetypal theory' has had to acknowledge such regrettable tendencies as that of associating the male with 'thought' and the female with 'feeling'. Again, in case of misunderstanding, the term 'archetype' has had to be redefined as the 'tendency to form and reform images in relation to certain kinds of repeated experience', and so as varying from culture to culture and from individual to individual, rather than as an eternal and universal form (Lauter and Rupprecht 1985: 13–14).

Some of the most important acts of mythic reading inspired by the women's movement have been works of fiction. In the novels of Margaret Atwood, for instance, mythopoeia (forging new possibilities of narrative for women) and mythography (interrogating the dominant male narrative) are brilliantly achieved at the same time. Particularly impressive is *The Handmaid's Tale* (1985). This is presented as the memoir of 'Offred', or 'Of-Fred', the eponymous female hero, who lives in the near-future fundamentalist republic of Gilead, in what was New England, where her job is to bear children for state officials whose marriages are barren. There the Bible, particularly the Old Testament, is taken literally, and used to justify the oppression of women. Offred tell us about her 'placement' at the home of 'the Commander', a high-ranking government official, where she has to substitute for Serena, the commander's wife, during the act of sexual intercourse. While recounting this part of her life, she also wonders what has become of her own husband Luke and their child. We also hear about her friend Moira, who rebels against the system, only to end up working in the state-run brothel, 'Jezebel's'. Offred herself dreams of getting away from Gilead, and at the end of the memoir we are not sure whether the commander's chauffeur Nick has effected her flight over the Canadian border. For, entering the van which he has brought for her, she herself does not know whether she is escaping or going to prison: 'And so I step up, into the darkness within; or else the light' (Atwood 1996: 307).

The novel concludes with some 'Historical Notes', a partial transcript from an academic conference on Offred's narrative, held in 2195, when her world is already past. The keynote address by 'Professor Pieixoto' consists of a brusque and insensitive commentary on the text we have just read, which shows he scarcely understands it. But his last sentence, which for the participants in the conference is simply a conventional token, also significantly forms the last sentence of Atwood's novel: 'Are there any questions?' (Atwood 1996: 324). This open-ended novel invites us to query the way in which narratives are constructed and interpreted, and above all how one narrative gains precedence over others.

Thus, though we can easily categorize *The Handmaid's Tale* in literary-critical terms, what merits attention is the way it deconstructs and reconstructs myth. Strictly speaking, Atwood's novel belongs to the category of 'dystopia' or 'anti-utopia'. As Northrop Frye observes, this form of satire carries its own mythic directive: it 'presents human life in terms of largely unrelieved bondage. Its settings feature prisons, madhouses, lynching mobs, and places of execution.' That is, with this form of narrative, which Frye takes to be an extreme form of the ironic mode, we are granted a full-scale 'demonic' vision, the contrary of the 'apocalyptic'. This ironic myth, of which Orwell's *Nineteen Eighty-Four* is the most famous representative, depicts 'the nightmare of social tyranny, often featuring the use of parody-religious symbols suggesting some form of Satan or Antichrist worship' (Frye 1971: 238). Atwood, who studied under Frye at the University of Toronto, would seem to have taken the full measure of this insight, and her novel may be seen as a conscious exercise in ironic mythopoeia.

For 'Gilead', named after the place where the patriarch Jacob set up his 'heap of stones' and established his household, is dedicated to the worship of God the Father, the deity of law and male authority – Blake's Urizen. In the name of this patriarchal God, Offred and her fellow Handmaids are held, pending 'placements', in a prison camp which was once part of Harvard

University: they are denied knowledge and given dogma. The Bible is reduced to arid formulae, mainly concerning the necessity for women to obey men and the obligation to breed. The soldiers of Gilead's army are called 'Angels', and the policemen are called 'Guardians of the Faith'. Apart from mass-religious ceremonies known as 'Prayvaganzas', Handmaids are expected to participate in the violence of public, mob executions, euphemistically known as 'Salvagings'. And all the while, for every 'Offred' there is an 'Ofglen' who has instructions to spy on her counterpart for signs of deviance from, or doubt about, the state. The republic of Gilead, then, is a fictional instance of how the myth of deliverance may be appropriated in order to justify social hierarchy, despite its future-orientated trajectory. Specifically, the novel reminds us that the 'salvation history' narrated in the Bible may be put to patriarchal use, justifying the subjugation of women. Deliverance has become domination.

But parodying oppressive religion is not the only point of *The Handmaid's Tale*. What is being interrogated is the imposition of the Word upon words, of the illusion of truth on the power of imagination. The enemy is totalitarianism, the attempt to subject people to a perverse form of perfectionism. What Atwood shows us in Offred is someone struggling to maintain a vision against the dead weight of doctrine, sacred or otherwise. Significantly, the Handmaids are told that the slogan 'From each according to her ability; to each according to his needs' comes from St Paul, when it actually comes from Marx (Atwood 1996: 127). The two grand narratives, the Marxist and the Biblical, are equally false when turned into absolute truth. So Offred, in resisting the deadly totality of Gilead, has to reaffirm the permanent possibility of myth.

The promise that the oppressive regime of Gilead might one day be overcome is figured for Offred in the garden of the Commander's wife, Serena. Here she gains a sense of the 'apocalyptic' dimension of existence, in Frye's sense: that is, she experiences a beatific revelation:

> The summer dress rustles against the flesh of my thighs, the grass grows underfoot, at the edges of my eyes there are movements, in

> the branches: feathers, flittings, grace notes, tree into bird, metamorphosis run wild. Goddesses are possible now and the air suffuses with desire.
>
> (Atwood 1996: 161–2).

This is not the paradisal garden of Biblical myth, which for Offred can only be seen now as serving patriarchal ideology. What she enjoys here is a pre-Biblical, pagan delight in nature itself as sacred. What her imagination responds to is the vitality of the fertility goddess, not the hierarchical order of the one and only God.

Let us not overlook, either, that use of the word 'metamorphosis', which is hugely resonant. The ancient Roman poet Ovid (43 BC–AD 18) produced a poetic compendium of myths which he called *Metamorphoses*, because every narrative included was about transformation: from animal to man, from woman to tree, from mortal to god or, less dramatically, from one season to another. It was his conviction that myths were there to be retold, thus giving life to culture, just as endless alteration was what gave life to nature. In *Tales from Ovid* (1997), Ted Hughes's rendition of selected passages from *Metamorphoses*, we read of the 'Golden Age', in which human beings understood and respected the workings of nature: this first era of human development, we are told, was 'without law, without law's enforcers', for 'Listening deeply, man kept faith with the source'. Falling from the 'Golden' and eventually declining into the 'Iron Age', humanity failed to hear 'the harmony of the whole creation': 'Earth's natural beauty no longer sufficed. / Man tore open the earth, and rummaged in her bowels' (Hughes 1997: 8, 12). Jonathan Bate has drawn attention to the 'profoundly ecological' quality of Hughes's version of *Metamorphoses*, which he achieves while remaining brilliantly true to the original. Nor is the lament for 'Mother Earth' an attempt by Hughes to please a feminist readership: 'Language which identifies all-conquering humankind as male and the ravaged earth as female is as old as Hesiod' (Bate 2000: 28–9).

Bearing Ovid's work in mind, and returning to *The Handmaid's Tale*, we may say that Gilead represents the loss of this wisdom of the earth: it wishes to impose a sterile stasis on nature, both internal and external. More generally, we may say that the relationship between mythology and ecology, and their common debt to the idea of transformation, is crucial to understanding Atwood's work. Barbara Hill Rigney sees it as informed by a vision of 'the green world', which is inseparable from her fascination with myth. The myth that seems to mean most to the author is the ancient Greek story of Persephone, which is an interesting variation on the pattern documented by Frazer: instead of the god dying and reviving, it is the goddess who does so. Persephone, a young maiden, is captured by Hades, lord of the underworld, and taken down to his kingdom to be his queen. Her mother, Demeter, the goddess of corn, mourns her, and so the crops begin to fail. Zeus eventually intervenes, ruling that Persephone be released from the underworld each spring, as long as she returns each autumn. Rigney tells us: 'All Atwood's heroines . . . incarnate the mythological Persephone's part-time residence in the underworld.' To return like Persephone 'from the underworld to her mother's meadow, is to achieve a special knowledge': that is, 'to assume the role of artist, which is synonymous with "seer", to become . . . the shaman' (Rigney 1987: 7). We have met the figure of the shaman before: s/he has the power to enter into the sacred mystery of nature and return to tell the tale; s/he crosses boundaries; s/he undergoes metamorphosis. *The Handmaid's Tale* celebrates, as with Offred in the garden, the power of a transformative imagination that is rooted in a mythically intense response to natural beauty. We may take this as our cue to consider, in our final chapter, the relationship between the myths we tell one another and the earth on which we live.

7

EARTH

THE WAR ON NATURE

Taking our cue from Coppola's film, *Apocalypse Now*, throughout this book we have found the term 'apocalypse' to be an important source for speculation about the nature of the mythic imagination. Let us remind ourselves of the most famous apocalyptic narrative of all, that recounted in the last book of the Christian Bible. The Book of Revelation concerns the victory over the 'beast' and over the 'whore of Babylon', along with 'the dragon, that old serpent, which is the Devil, and Satan', by the Messiah and his angels (Revelation 20: 2). After plague and pestilence have ravaged much of the earth, the Messiah establishes 'a new heaven and a new earth' (Revelation 21: 1). Thus, the creation myth narrated in the first chapter of the first book of the Bible, Genesis, is retold with an 'apocalyptic' turn. Where Adam and Eve fell from the garden, their descendants, or at least those who have remained faithful to God and have recognized his Son, the 'second Adam', are allowed to enter the heavenly city of Jerusalem. We have progressed from creation to re-creation, from Eden to Jerusalem, from 'fall' to redemption.

The original readers of the final book of the Christian Bible had reason to hope that it announced imminent events, and in particular the 'second coming' of the Messiah. But we surmized in an earlier chapter that it would also have been gratefully received as an encouragement to stand firm in the face of violent and barbaric oppression by the Roman emperor. As a 'symbolic act', it offered a strategy for dealing with the situation of relentless persecution. In other words, it illuminated the darkness of the present as much as it announced specific future events. In the centuries following its composition, the contents of the book had to be interpreted less and less exactly, as the Messianic moment seemed less and less likely. However, the literal interpretation of Revelation has retained a residual power, and has periodically reasserted itself. As might be expected, the recent transition to a new millennium has led to a heightened investment in the apocalypse as literal truth. Revelation has been read under the sign of 'realism', with the presupposition that the text can afford access to the hidden meaning of history. As we have explained previously, 'realism' encourages an allegorical reading, since it claims to be able to crack the code underlying the myth and to translate exactly its symbolism and structure. It discovers that the very 'last day' which John the Divine foretold is close at hand. The Antichrist is the specific enemy one's nation is facing now; the battle of Armageddon will be the culmination of the war it is waging now. Against such dangerous certainty, it is far better to opt for 'non-realism' and to put one's trust in the liberating power of 'revelation', which is what 'apocalypse' means, after all. In short, we should let the 'possible world' of myth remain possible.

However, the consequences of literal interpretation need to be addressed. In an article on 'end-time' thinking, the novelist Ian McEwan notes how central apocalyptic myth has been to North American civilization, and how exactly it was drawn upon right from the beginning: 'When Christopher Columbus arrived in the Americas . . . he believed he had found, and was fated to find, the Terrestrial Paradise promised in the Book of Revelation. He believed himself to be implicated in God's planning for the millennial kingdom on earth.' Indeed, the evidence is there in

Columbus's record of his first journey, which is quoted in the article: 'God made me the messenger of the new heaven and the new earth of which he spoke in the Apocalypse of St John . . . and he showed me the spot where to find it' (McEwan 2008: 2). Though McEwan does not pursue this theme, it is worth reminding ourselves that Columbus's conviction of a God-given mission, informed by apocalyptic myth, was shared by the early settlers of North America, and that it persisted right through to the nineteenth century and beyond. In the 1840s, the phrase 'manifest destiny' was coined to justify the pioneers' settlement of the western part of the continent; later, it was used to vindicate the United States' expansionist and imperialist policy in the global arena. The settlers had believed themselves to be the chosen people of God, who were fulfilling the words of scripture; their descendants, even if secularly inclined, perpetuated their apocalyptic way of thinking, which in times of crisis would take on a religious form.

An obvious instance of this is the response to the destruction of the twin towers of the World Trade Center in New York by Muslim terrorists on 11 September 2001, which resulted in the death of nearly 3,000 innocent people. This provoked a perfectly understandable anger and a sense of desperation; but what we need to note is that, in turn, it also exacerbated the increasingly apocalyptic mood of American fundamentalists. The idea of revenge merged with that of divine justice, encouraging an accompanying expectation of a final battle of Armageddon. In this scenario, the enemy, an equivalently fundamentalist Islam, would be overcome once and for all. The President of the United States, George W. Bush, significantly revived the phrase that had been used by the allies in the Second World War to describe the triple foe of Germany, Italy and Japan. He referred to three apparently unrelated nations, namely Iraq, Iran and North Korea, as constituting an 'axis of evil'. A believer in a literal apocalypse, Bush knew that a great many citizens of the United States would understand the implicit identification of those other countries with the demonic powers depicted in the Book of Revelation.

If the nation itself was founded on a Biblical promise, interpreted literally, then it need not surprise us that in the present situation, when it has felt itself to be the victim of terrorist assault, it turns back to Revelation. McEwan reflects more generally on the function of literal apocalypticism:

> Periods of uncertainty in human history, of rapid, bewildering change, and of social unrest appear to give these old stories greater weight. It does not need a novelist to tell you that where a narrative has a beginning, it needs an end. Where there is a creation myth, there must be a final chapter. Where a god makes the world, it remains in his power to unmake it. When human weakness or wickedness is apparent, there will be guilty fantasies of supernatural retribution. When people are profoundly frustrated, either materially or spiritually, there will be dreams of the perfect society where all conflicts are resolved, and all needs are met.
>
> (McEwan 2008: 23)

Bringing this perspective to bear on the contemporary mood, he reflects that even when there is a sizeable minority which is sceptical of the claims of religion, 'the problem of fatalism remains'.

According to McEwan, this problem is intensified by the rise of Islamic fundamentalism which, though it derives from another scriptural source, yet nurtures a 'sense of an ending' which complements Christian fundamentalism:

> In a nuclear age, and in an age of serious environmental degradation, apocalyptic belief creates a serious second order danger. The precarious logic of self-interest that saw us through the cold war would collapse if the leaders of one nuclear state came to welcome, or ceased to fear, mass death. The words of Ayatollah Khomeini are quoted approvingly in an Iranian 11th grade textbook: 'Either we shake one another's hands in joy at the victory of Islam in the world, or all of us will turn to eternal life and martyrdom. In both cases, victory and success are ours.' And if we let global temperatures continue to rise because we give room to the faction that believes it is God's will, then we are truly – and literally – sunk.
>
> (McEwan 2008: 23)

Extrapolating from McEwan's article, it is fair to say that the fundamentalists' apocalypse, whether Christian or Islamic, is curiously non-literal when it comes to the actual catastrophe that is looming ahead of us, implicit in his allusion to 'environmental degradation'. There is always a danger that an apocalyptic myth may encourage a fixation on the anticipated new order at the expense of the actual planet we live on. Indeed, the Book of Revelation itself conveys the fate of the earth after the opening of 'the seventh seal' in an alarmingly dismissive fashion: 'there followed hail and fire mingled with blood, and they were cast up on the earth: and the third part of trees was burnt up, and all green grass was burnt up' (Revelation 8: 7). Even the beatific world which will emerge out of catastrophe sounds alarmingly unnatural: 'and there was no more sea' (Revelation 21: 1). This last detail is understandable in a mythological context where the primordial waters were traditionally associated with the threat of chaos, as in both the Babylonian and the Israelite creation narratives. But in our own era, when the seas have been polluted by garbage and sewage, and need vigorously protecting, the words ring hollow, no matter how far we try and read them symbolically. Again, the heavenly city of Jerusalem is described as having a street of 'pure gold, as it were transparent glass'; moreover, 'the city had no need of the sun, neither of the moon, to shine in it; for the glory of God did lighten it' (Revelation 21: 21–23). This celebration of divine artifice, with its implicit denial of nature, hardly makes for environmental responsibility. Indeed, Kenneth Burke in his later years drafted a blueprint for a satire, to be entitled 'Helhaven', in which he rewrote Revelation so that the rich, or 'saved', lived in a luxurious, synthetic 'heaven' well away from the very real 'hell' they had created through industrial pollution, which was populated by the poor, or 'damned' (see Coupe 2005: 164–80).

The link between apocalyptic myth and ecological catastrophe in turn brings us back to *Apocalypse Now.* The contempt for the fate of the earth which McEwan associates with apocalyptic fundamentalism is represented at the very start of the film. Here is the opening sequence, as it is set out in the original screenplay:

> FADE IN: A SIMPLE IMAGE OF TREES – DAY
>
> Coconut trees being VIEWED through the veil of time or a dream. Occasionally coloured smoke wafts through the FRAME, yellow and then violet. MUSIC begins quietly, suggestive of 1968–69. Perhaps 'The End' by the Doors.
>
> Now MOVING through the FRAME are skids of helicopters, not that we could make them out as that, though; rather, hard shapes that glide by at random. Then a phantom helicopter in FULL VIEW floats by the trees – suddenly without warning, the jungle BURSTS into a bright red-orange glob of napalm flame.
>
> The VIEW MOVES ACROSS the burning trees as the smoke and ghostly helicopters come and go.
>
> (Milius and Coppola 2001: 1)

With this sequence in mind, we may say that *Apocalypse Now* is about a war waged by a predominantly Christian nation, convinced of its 'manifest destiny', against not only a demonized human enemy, but also against the earth itself. The film is as much about the destruction of nature as it is about the 'horror' which the United States projects onto an alien culture. If in the Book of Revelation, a protracted catastrophe precedes the creation of 'a new heaven and a new earth', Coppola does not flinch from depicting ecological disaster, which his film reveals to be the inevitable consequence of literal apocalypticism. The land of Vietnam is the inevitable casualty, along with the people of Vietnam, of a supposedly God-given mission.

NATURE NOW AND THEN

We related Coppola's film to fertility myth and its complementary ritual by way of the scholarship of Sir James Frazer. In *The Golden Bough*, Frazer, of course, was mainly concerned to expose the ignorance of 'savage' people who thought of nature as expressing itself through fertility gods and goddesses. Nature as such was not his sphere of interest. His theoretical stance was that of cultural evolutionism, a rather clumsy extrapolation from Charles Darwin's theory of the evolution of species through the mechanism of natural selection. Cultures which regarded the land in terms of either magic or religion were, for Frazer, irrevocably primitive: his ideal was the clarity and certainty apparently afforded by modern science. However, whatever his intentions, Frazer made the study of fertility myth and ritual accessible to writers such as T. S. Eliot, thus affording them the conceptual framework within which to compose the major literary works of modernism.

Here we come up against a paradox: an anthropologist (Frazer) who was not sympathetic to the material he documented, and who had little interest in the status of nature, aroused in a poet (Eliot) a fascination with 'magic and religion' and an opportunity to make imaginative sense of nature. However, the conventional assessment is that, Lawrence apart, the modernist writers tended to treat nature merely as a source of metaphors for a spiritual state. The obvious instance is *The Waste Land* itself: while indebted to Frazer's documentation of vegetation ceremonies, the title is usually taken to be wholly symbolic, intended to convey to the suitably erudite reader a sense of being lost in a 'wasteland' of cultural and religious decline rather than of being concerned about a literal state of drought and desiccation. Words, it is assumed, need not be taken to refer to the natural world.

But what if we were to read the poem with a deliberate *naïveté*, post-critical rather than pre-critical, taking the title on its own terms? Obviously, we would have to bear in mind the cultural significance of the poem: the wealth of allusion, the ironic juxtaposition of images from glorious past and squalid present, the sophisticated experimentalism. That said, we might infer that the title of Eliot's great modernist work is open to another, equally interesting and vital reading: the poet may not only be drawing on symbolism from *The Golden Bough*, but may also be thinking of the way that unbridled technological progress renders the earth arid and inhospitable. The critic Robert Pogue Harrison encourages this approach in the course of his fascinating study of the literary treatment of nature, *Forests: The Shadow of Civilization*:

> Poetry does not only monitor spiritual states of being, or what one used to call the 'spirit' of an age; it also registers the spiritual effects of a changing climate and habitat. As the external environment undergoes transformations, poets often announce them in advance with the clairvoyance of seers, for poets have an altogether sixth

> sense that enables them to forecast trends in the weather, so to speak. Like oracles, they may couch their message in the language of enigma. And like oracles, the meaning of their message becomes fully manifest only after the events it foretells have unfolded. Modern poetry at its best is a kind of spiritual ecology. The wasteland grows within and without . . .
>
> (Harrison 1993: 148–9).

In this light, the whole poem would then reveal a sense of malaise expressive not only of cultural impoverishment, but also of alienation from the earth itself. It is worth following up Harrison's insight by noting that Eliot himself indirectly encouraged such a reading in subsequent years: first, by lamenting in prose writings such as *After Strange Gods* (1934) and *The Idea of a Christian Society* (1939) the damage which agrarian capitalism was doing to the land; and second, by celebrating particular locations as redolent of sacred presence in his poetic sequence, *Four Quartets* (1944). Moreover, *The Waste Land* has inevitably acquired greater relevance over the decades, as more and more of the planet has been 'laid waste'.

To read a poem which is rooted in myth as though it were about the relationship between humanity and the earth should not strike us as odd. Nor need such reading be confined to the modern era, in which the awareness of the need to respect nature is especially acute. The ancient Mesopotamian epic of *Gilgamesh*, which is so close to myth that it is frequently defined as such, centres on that very theme. Early written versions date back to the Sumerian period (late third millennium BC), with the epic beginning to take shape during the 'old Babylonian' period (early second millennium BC). It is interesting that *Gilgamesh* should have reached its final form at about the time that the *Enuma Elish* was being narrated annually, with its account of a creation effected apparently by violence done to nature. It is as if the epic is exploring the issues that the myth cannot, given that the latter has to fulfil its purpose of glorifying the Babylonian ruler by glorifying the Babylonian state god.

The story goes as follows. Gilgamesh, the king of Uruk, has been born of the union between a goddess and a man, and being semi-divine, he is obsessed about achieving immortality. He is an arrogant and unpopular ruler. The city walls which he has built define his sense of his own importance and his desire for permanence, but he knows that the world beyond is not under his control. The people of Uruk, whom he mistreats, ask the gods to send a rival who could challenge Gilgamesh's power. The wild man, Enkidu, arrives, but in their struggle, the two come to respect each other, and so become firm friends. Still anxious for immortality, Gilgamesh goes on various adventures with Enkidu. The most famous is the journey to the cedar-forested mountain owned by the giant Humbaba; arriving there, they kill the giant and cut down all the trees. This is a terrible offence, however, and so Gilgamesh is only storing up trouble for himself. Nor is he helped by his refusal of the amorous advances of the fertility goddess Ishtar (the Babylonian equivalent of the Sumerian Inanna), even though he has good reason. He knows that succumbing to her charms would mean he would have to undergo the annual descent into death and the underworld that is the destiny of her mate Tammuz (the Babylonian equivalent of the Sumerian Dumuzi), who is a classic instance of the dying god of vegetation In her anger, Ishtar sends the Bull of Heaven to defeat Gilgamesh and Enkidu, only to see it slaughtered by the seemingly invincible pair.

Finally, the assembly of gods decides to punish Gilgamesh by giving his friend a mortal illness. When Enkidu dies, Gilgamesh is not only grief-stricken, but also more conscious than ever of his own mortality. He travels to see Utnapisthtim, who with his wife survived the great flood which the gods had caused in order to punish humanity for its disobedience (this story forming a type of the later, Biblical story of Noah's ark). Utnapishtim gives Gilgamesh a plant which bestows the gift of immortality, but on the way home a snake steals it from him while he is bathing (this story forming a type of the later, Biblical story of Adam and Eve being forced to endure mortality after being tempted by the serpent in the garden of Eden). Gilgamesh has to accept that his might is nothing compared with that of nature, and that he has to pay for his offence, an offence that consists of not only destroying the forest, but also presuming to desire immortality. We might draw again on Harrison's *Forests*, in which Gilgamesh's fate is read as implicit in his early reputation, as builder of the walls of Uruk:

> Walls, like writing, define civilization. They are monuments of resistance against time, like writing itself, and Gilgamesh is remembered by them. Walls protect, divide, distinguish; above all, they abstract. The basic activities that sustain life – agriculture and stock breeding, for instance – take place beyond the walls. Within the walls one is within an emporium; one is within the jurisdiction of a bureaucracy; one is within the abstract identity of race, city, and institutionalized religion; in short, one is within the lonely enclosure of history. Gilgamesh is the builder of such walls that divide history from prehistory, culture from nature, sky from earth, life from death, memory from oblivion.
>
> (Harrison 1993: 14–15)

In order to define himself, to render his name immortal and his reputation immutable, Gilgamesh pits himself against the cedar-forested mountain, that is, against nature and against the natural fact of death. But the epic of *Gilgamesh* reminds humanity to know its mortal place in the cosmic order, and to treat the earth with respect. We may note in passing that it therefore relates to the creation myths which we associate with ancient Mesopotamia, both Sumerian and Babylonian. It relates to the Sumerian insofar as it suggests that nature is the benign source of our being, violence against which is offensive. It relates to the Babylonian in that we are left in no doubt of the superiority of deities to men, and of the right of the former to punish the latter at will. Either way, it offers an unequivocal warning against human arrogance.

Thus, looking retrospectively over the centuries, from *Apocalypse Now* via *The Waste Land* right back to *Gilgamesh*, the question may always be asked: how does the given work refer to the natural world? Obviously, Coppola's work has the advantage here, since film can represent visually the impact of human behaviour on nature; moreover, being a film about a war, it can emphasize the physical violence done to the earth. It might be interesting to consider briefly two other significant works of cinema which explore related themes.

The Wachowski brothers' *Matrix* film trilogy (1999–2003) depicts a world in which technology has finally severed humanity from the natural environment. If the earth was once thought of as a 'mother', the 'Matrix' (womb) is now a computer program which generates an illusory world to occupy the minds of human beings while machines feed off the energy of their bodies. The series comprises a powerful dystopia about the end of nature, in which reality has been replaced by systematic illusion. It might be said to take the contemporary condition, as outlined by the philosopher Jean Baudrillard, to its logical extreme. With the emergence of 'digitality', or 'virtual reality', he tells us, we are witnessing 'the collapse of reality into hyperrealism, in the minute duplication of the real'. Machines, he tells us, can now generate 'a completely imaginary contact-world of sensorial mimetics and tactile mysticism' (Baudrillard 1983: 140–1). Their trilogy poses the question: what are the possibilities for humanity if the machine has reached the point of entirely laying waste the earth? In the process, it reworks narrative patterns that will by now be familiar to us.

If the *Matrix* series amounts to a hero myth, then the hero is 'Neo', a computer hacker who joins up with a father-figure called 'Morpheus' and a female contact, with whom Neo becomes enamoured, called 'Trinity'. If it amounts to a fertility myth, then the protagonist, or fertility god, is again Neo: he is killed by the agents of the Matrix, only to be brought back to life by the kiss of Trinity, who in this respect stands in for the goddess. The mythic quality of the trilogy does not stop there, however. We would also be entitled to read it as a myth of deliverance: Neo is the 'One' ('Neo' being an obvious anagram), whose task it is to lead imprisoned humanity to 'salvation'. The Biblical echoes in the films would seem to endorse this interpretation: for example, the resistance movement to the Matrix is centred in a city known as 'Zion', at the centre of which lies 'the Temple'. Again, the very name Trinity suggests the Christian version of monotheism, and the doctrine of three persons in one God. However, we have to be careful in reading a film in which nothing is what it seems.

By the end of the series a less hopeful version of events has emerged: the suggestion is that the struggle between Neo and his antagonist Agent Smith, who is busy occupying the minds of all those imprisoned by the Matrix, is all part of the Matrix's plan, which involves Neo going through his sacrificial moment again and again. That is, far from the structure being one of deliverance, with Neo as Messiah, the trilogy endorses the cyclical pattern of fertility myth, with Neo as dying god. The trilogy does not finish with a neat resolution, but hints at further, endless incarnations of Neo and of the struggle in which he has to recurrently engage. Eliade's 'eternal return' and Nietzsche's 'eternal recurrence' come to mind. The central theme, then, would not be that of victory over the forces of evil, but the need to come to terms with what our own technology, which now seems to possess a will of its own, is doing to the planet. All in all, this is an intriguingly bizarre fable which forces us to ask just what is 'natural' if indeed we really have brought about the end of nature.

By way of contrast, we might consider Peter Jackson's cinematic trilogy, *The Lord of the Rings* (2001–3), based on J. R. R. Tolkien's monumental work of fiction (1954). Thanks to the success of the film, there can be few people who have not heard of the main protagonist, Frodo Baggins, or of his mentor, Gandalf the wizard. Again, the plot is now widely familiar: Frodo, Gandalf and their allies have to undertake a daunting, seemingly endless journey across 'Middle-Earth' in order to prevent the dreaded 'Ring' of the title falling into the hands of the 'Dark Lord', named Sauron. But it is perhaps easier to sum up the plot than it is to categorize it. Strictly speaking, it is a romance, in the sense used by Northrop Frye: that is, a literary genre which borders on the realm of the mythic and which involves a quest, a confrontation with monsters or monstrous forces, and the triumphant moment of recognition for the hero. Given the depth and scope of the narrative, however, we might even be entitled to claim that Tolkien has created a full working mythology. *The Lord of the Rings* expands the essential quest structure to include all sorts of character-groupings, alliances, sub-plots, dramatic changes of scene, evocations of locality and invocations of legend, so that we have the sense of being immersed in a complete world. Central to this mythopoeic vision is the celebration of a culture which lives in harmony with nature, for that is what the region of Middle-Earth known as the 'Shire' represents. The rural setting from which Frodo sets off is beautifully green and lush, a paradisal place, celebrated in the film by stunning cinematography. The same attention is paid to the landscape of Mordor, which is the blighted territory which casts its shadow over the pastoral idyll. The one is presented as exquisitely natural; the other is presented as grossly unnatural. Deeper themes are being explored than in the standard 'sword and sorcery' entertainment.

Not long before the film was commissioned, there appeared Patrick Curry's timely reading of *The Lord of the Rings*. In *Defending Middle-Earth*, he argued that the significance of Tolkien's text is primarily ecological. It is about the need to prevent our world, idealized as Middle-Earth, from being destroyed by the nightmare of darkness and destruction, rationalized by an ideology of industrialism, which is Mordor. To briefly convey the flavour of his approach to Tolkien's myth, I will summarize what Curry has to say about the importance of trees. First, Middle-Earth derives from Tolkien's childhood memories of the English countryside, in his exploration of which he came to have a profound love of trees. Second, the focus on the need for trees throughout the book relies on English iconography of the wood or forest as the realm of healing and renewal (as in Shakespeare's comedies, such as *A Midsummer Night's Dream* and *As You Like It*). Third, the tree symbolism is rooted in the archetype of the Tree of Life: Curry lists variations on this, such as the World Tree of Scandinavian saga, the Biblical Trees of Life and of Knowledge, the Bo Tree under which the Buddha meditated until he gained spiritual liberation, and the May Tree of rural festival. No doubt we could elaborate on Curry's insight by tracing allusions to the 'Golden Bough' documented by Frazer; nor would this be irrelevant, since the narrative lays great stress on willingness to sacrifice oneself for the good of the community. Taking all these associations that trees have, it is significant that Sauron's forces effectively wage a war on trees, felling them to feed the furnaces which sustain his monstrous military-industrial state. Again, the ideology of Mordor is implicit in the Ring itself, which represents a sinister force that functions by the unleashing of technology against nature itself (see Curry 1997: 59–72).

All in all, then, one would hope that the appeal of the film trilogy at the beginning of a new millennium goes deeper than its special effects, its endless battle-scenes, or even its magical atmosphere. One would hope that its audiences are responding, whether consciously or unconsciously, to its celebration of a culture that is rooted in nature, in the face of what Kenneth Burke calls 'technological psychosis'. *The Lord of the Rings*, then, is surely one of the most important mythic works of our era. Not only does Tolkien succeed in producing a distinctly English kind of myth, but he puts myth to work on one of the most serious tasks we can have, to defend the earth from pollution and plunder. Confronting the accusation that *The Lord of the Rings* is based on Tolkien's idealization of the English countryside of his childhood, Curry defends nostalgia as a necessary and valid dimension of Tolkien's mythmaking, in that it offers an image of a world in which human beings know what it is like to feel that nature is one's 'home'. He deploys a phrase coined by the critic and nature writer Fraser Harrison, 'radical nostalgia': 'far from encouraging a passive retreat from political and social realities, such ideals have real power' (Curry 1997: 53–4).

'Radical nostalgia' may be seen as complementary to what I call 'radical typology': both of them challenge the given culture, opening up the present to other possibilities of seeing and, therefore, of being. Tolkien's mythopoeic imagination appeals to the human need, in the depths of the psyche, to feel some bond with the earth. It identifies modernity with the unrestrained growth of technology, and unashamedly evokes an English, rural past. In this respect, it belongs to the same ethos as William Morris's 'green' socialism, with its cult of medieval craftsmanship and its belief in the healing power of both natural and artistic beauty (see Coupe 2000: 32–6). Or again, we may be reminded of F. R. Leavis's protest against the displacement of the 'organic community', which fostered a 'human naturalness', a way of life in accord with the rhythms of nature, by the ugliness and squalor of industrialization (see Coupe 2000: 73–6). Such stances may be dismissed as sentimental, but it has to be said that the critique of the present through evocation of the past is a powerful and recurrent form of rhetoric. The word 'nostalgia', coming from two ancient Greek words, *nostos* and *algos*, really means 'home-sickness', so the association of an earlier era with the feeling of being at 'home' on the earth is not an idle one. Nor is it a coincidence that the root of the word 'ecology' is *oikos*, 'house': it is the study of nature, based on the assumption that the earth is our true dwelling-place. It is as though the collective memory of a more harmonious relationship with nature than exists now fuels the desire for a future reconnection, so that we can 'return home'. As environmental degradation intensifies, perhaps 'radical nostalgia' will prove necessary to our survival on the planet.

NATURE AS REVELATION

It is important to emphasize here that claiming that poems, films and myths have nature as their ultimate referent does not mean that we have to resort to 'realism', as previously defined. They are not statements about nature; nor are they keys to some coded, absolute truth about 'Nature'. In Burke's terminology, they are 'symbolic acts' which have the power to change or intensify our sense of responsibility to our natural environment. Thus, what we have called 'non-realism' becomes all the more important in this context, the word 'nature' being notoriously complex and varied in its usage (see Soper 1995). Here I want to consider four perspectives on our relationship with the earth that draw on myth and that avoid a naive literalism. The reader is not being asked to choose between them, nor to try and reduce all four to one basic message. It is sufficient that they each raise possibilities. Perhaps we should remind ourselves first that myth is a living force when it is understood as imaginative *exploration*; it becomes sterile and oppressive when it is read as literal *explanation*. To return to issues raised at the beginning of this chapter, we may say that all myth is apocalyptic in that it offers the possibility of 'revelation'. Blake's famous dictum is itself apocalyptic in a sense that we need to bear in mind when trying to link mythology and ecology: 'If the doors of perception were cleansed, everything would appear to man as it is, infinite' (Blake 1971: 154). What is exciting about bringing nature into the equation is that we begin to see that the earth itself may become a source of revelation: 'For every thing that lives is Holy' (Blake 1971: 159).

The first perspective is that of a poet who came to fame in association with the 'Beat' movement of the 1950s and 1960s, namely Gary Snyder. The provocative title for Snyder's selection of his own work is *No Nature.* At first, the reader might think Snyder is espousing the view that reality or, more specifically, nature does not exist, being no more than a 'cultural construction'. Soon, though, it becomes apparent that his position is much closer to 'non-realism'. As we have seen previously, non-realism does not deny reality: rather, it draws attention to the distance between the words we use and the world to which they refer. As he explains in his preface:

> [W]e do not easily *know* nature, or even know ourselves. Whatever it actually is, it will not fulfil our conceptions or assumptions. It will dodge our expectations and theoretical models. There is no single or set 'nature' either as 'the natural world' or 'the nature of things.' The greatest respect we can pay to nature is not to trap it, but to acknowledge that it eludes us and that, our own nature is also fluid, open, and conditional.
>
> (Snyder 1992: v)

Far from nature being a linguistic creation, it is that which language can never succeed in containing. Far from there being *no* nature, there is no *known* nature, in that whatever we say about it will never quite do justice to its infinite beauty and mystery. But that does not mean that the poet has no obligation to try and use words to speak about the natural environment. Thus, he concludes with this affirmation: 'An open space to move in, with the whole body, the whole mind. My gesture has been with language' (Snyder 1992: v). I have elsewhere characterized Snyder's as an 'eco-Zen' vision: that is, his Buddhist sense of the interrelatedness of all life, which involves a respect for the 'Buddha-nature' underlying the manifest world, complements his sense of environmental responsibility, both as poet and as activist (see Coupe 2007: 164–9).

Throughout his work, Snyder reminds us of the need to respect not only nature but also any culture which shows us how to respect nature, such as that of the Native Americans. For Snyder, this respect extends to drawing on their myths. He even uses their original, mythic name for North America as the title of one of his volumes of poems: *Turtle Island* (1974). In the introductory note, reprinted in *No Nature*, Snyder explains the appeal of the phrase:

> Turtle Island – the old-new name for the continent, based on many creation myths of the people who have been living here for millennia, and reapplied by some of them to 'North America' in recent years. Also, an idea found worldwide, of the earth, of cosmos even, sustained by a great turtle or serpent-of-eternity. . . . The poems speak of place, and the energy pathways that sustain life. Each living being is a swirl in the flow, a formal turbulence, a 'song'. The land, the planet itself, is also a living being – at another pace. Anglos, black people, Chicanos, and others beached up on these shores all share such views at the deepest levels of their old cultural traditions. Hark again to those roots, to see our ancient solidarity, and then to the work of being together on Turtle Island.
>
> (Snyder 1992: 204).

What Snyder takes from the name 'Turtle Island' is the realization that the mythological and ecological dimensions of existence are complementary. The poet's job is to help keep the ancient myths alive, in the service of the planet as 'living being'. Like the songwriter Jim Morrison, discussed in an earlier chapter, Snyder sees this task as bringing the poet close in spirit to the figure of the shaman, since it is the shaman who knows how to enter into the spirit of nature on behalf of the tribe.

Included in this volume is one of his most celebrated poems, 'Front Lines', the very title of which is meant to remind us that there is a war going on, waged by global capitalism against the earth. Here, he rejects the rapacious logic of 'development', summed up in a scene set in rural California. We see 'landseekers' driving up in their four-wheel vehicles: 'they say / To the land, / Spread your legs.' We see a bulldozer 'grinding and slobbering' on top of 'The skinned-up bodies of still-live bushes'. This outrage against the environment is seen for what it is in the context of the earth's beauty and intrinsic value, which for Snyder has been long understood by the Native American inhabitants: 'Behind is a forest that goes to the Arctic / And a desert that still belongs to the Piute / And here we must draw / Our line' (Snyder 1992: 218).

Snyder invokes native culture, which he associates with respect for the sacredness of the earth. In doing so, he implicitly rejects the apocalyptic narrative which, interpreted literally, justifies expansionism and imperialism. He may, of course, be criticized for idealizing Native American culture, but he is not the only environmental activist to invoke 'the ecological Indian' (see Garrard 2004: 120–7). That need not detract from his overall purpose, to counter the destructive use of myth with the creative use of myth. He resists the vision of the earth as an alien realm which is there to be conquered by promoting a vision of the earth as our true home. That is, he aligns *mythos* and *oikos.*

The second perspective is that of Theodor Adorno, the Marxist thinker whose *Dialectic of Enlightenment*, co-written with Max Horkheimer, we referred to briefly in Chapter 3. He is especially relevant here on account of his posthumously published work, *Aesthetic Theory* (1997). To appreciate its significance, we have to realize that his approach to nature in that book stems from the early, visionary Marx, not from the later, social-scientific Marx. The latter notoriously reduced nature to the status of a 'tool house', that is, a supply of resources to be put to whatever use human beings see fit (Marx 1977: 285). Adorno rejects this conceptualization of nature; he rejects too, the Marxist cult of industrial progress which, deriving from the Enlightenment project, anticipates the victory of humanity over nature. Rather, he emphasizes the urgent need for contemporary humanity to have some sense of a realm that stands outside of the given culture, offering a challenge to it and also a promise of a different mode of being. Natural beauty represents 'the not-yet-existing, the possible', which technocratic modernity, whether capitalist or communist, has denied.

Summarizing Adorno's complex argument, we might say that for him 'nature' is a 'critical' term in the fullest sense. For to invoke nature is to provide the grounds of a 'critique' of our culture, which is in a state of 'crisis', alienated as it is from the earth: 'The shame felt in the face of natural beauty stems from the damage implicitly done to what does not yet exist by taking it for existent. The dignity of nature is that of the not-yet-existing; by its expression it repels intentional humanization.' Hence, the beauty of nature carries the promise of 'what is reconciled' (Adorno

1997: 73–4). Or, more cryptically but more relevantly to our context: 'Natural beauty is myth transposed into the imagination and thus, perhaps, requited.' As such, it is deeply ambiguous: 'no feeling person . . . fails to be moved by the sound of a robin after a rain shower'; but insofar as we are far from what such beauty promises, we will also hear 'something frightening' in the song of birds, associated with 'ancient divinations' which presage 'ill fortune'(Adorno 1997: 66). What is promised, a state of harmony between humanity and nature, and within human society, is by definition 'not yet', and so remains intangible and, to that extent, a source of anxiety.

Thus Adorno may be said to be articulating something very like 'radical typology'. Myths carry within them the promise of those further myths which will rework them, with the 'type' always finding fulfilment in the 'anti-type' which itself becomes a 'type' in its turn. Similarly, for Adorno, natural beauty, which always exceeds aesthetic conventions and can never be adequately represented, invites us to see beyond the given cultural order which, though provisional, must always present itself as permanent. Nature is 'not yet' in the dual sense of awaiting an end to its own exploitation by humanity and of offering humanity a glimpse of what a non-alienated existence might be like. Either way, the dimension of nature is associated with apocalyptic hope. If a 'new earth' is to come about, it will be, in Blake's words, by cleansing 'the doors of perception' and realizing that we are already living on it: 'For every thing that lives is Holy.' Indeed, this very earth becomes 'new' if only we are open to the 'not yet': such is the nature of revelation and the revelation of nature. To invoke Blake once more, we may ask ourselves: 'How do you know but ev'ry Bird that cuts the airy way / Is an immense world of delight, clos'd by your senses five?'

It might sound odd to say that a mythic imagination is also required to understand a scientific theory, but that is true of our third perspective. Myth and science meet most famously in James Lovelock's 'Gaia theory'. The technical name for this is 'Earth System Science', but it is to Lovelock's credit that he knew immediately, when the novelist William Golding suggested it to him, that the name 'Gaia' was perfect for his rediscovery of something that he felt the archaic mind had intuitively understood.

The earth, he tells us, is a self-regulating organism; or, more exactly, the biosphere (the part of the earth where life exists) is a kind of grand ecosystem, involving subtle interactions of the different parts. Accused by some fellow-scientists of being unscientific because of his decision to use a mythic name for the earth, he still sees no need to apologize:

> I know that to personalize the Earth System as Gaia . . . irritates the scientifically correct, but I am unrepentant because metaphors are more than ever needed for a widespread comprehension of the true nature of the Earth and an understanding of the lethal dangers that lie ahead
>
> (Lovelock 2007: 188).

In trying to bring home to fellow-scientists and to the public the disastrous consequences of the way we are polluting and plundering the earth, Lovelock has at various times tried to spell out the importance of mythology to human thought:

> In times that are ancient by human measure, as far back as the earliest artefacts can be found, it seems that the Earth was worshipped as a goddess and believed to be alive. The myth of the great Mother [*sic*] is part of most early religions. The Mother is a compassionate, feminine figure; spring of all life, of fecundity, of gentleness. She is also the stern and unforgiving bringer of death. . . . At some time not more than a few thousand years ago the concept of a remote master God, an overseer of Gaia, took root.
>
> (Lovelock 1989: 208)

Taking our cue from Lovelock, we ought here to remind ourselves of the Greek creation myth in which Gaia plays so important a part. From Hesiod's *Theogony* we can distil the following basic narrative. In the beginning there was Chaos, the formless void. From Chaos there eventually emerged Eros (Love) and Gaia (the Earth-Mother). Gaia produced Uranus (the Sky-Father). Then Gaia coupled with her son Uranus; their children included the twelve Titans, among whom were Oceanus and Cronus. Uranus resented his children and wished them harm, so Gaia hid them within herself for as long as she could. Eventually, they began to cause her too much discomfort, so she then arranged for her son Cronus to castrate Uranus, so that he could rule in his father's place.

It is by hearing this story again that we realize how shrewd Lovelock has been in choosing the name of Gaia: she encompasses both life and death, both maternal affection and violent revenge, both reward and punishment. As the destruction of the natural environment worsens, so Lovelock has emphasized more and more the dark side of the earth mother. His latest book is called *The Revenge of Gaia*, in which he warns humanity that it will very likely not survive the ecocastrophe to come; and that it may be in the best interest of the planet that we do not, so that Gaia can regain her balance once more.

Even if we confine ourselves to the subject of myth, it is fascinating to see how an ancient story (and we may assume that it was told long before Hesiod set it down) can be rediscovered in our time and found to have acquired new significance and relevance. It is as if we know unconsciously that we have lost that sense of the 'whole' as 'holy' and as if the Gaia myth is springing up afresh to serve our urgent needs. This exemplifies dramatically the principle of 'radical typology': the myth is not merely recovered, but it is also recreated, acquiring intensely new significance. This significance may only be appreciated, however, if we are prepared to trust in what Coleridge called the 'shaping spirit of imagination'. Lovelock himself has stated that it is about time we acknowledged how little we can understand reality if we rely on rational categories and systems:

> The universe is a much more intricate place than we can imagine. I often think our conscious minds will never encompass more than a tiny fraction of it all and that our comprehension of the Earth is no better than an eel's comprehension of the ocean in which it swims.
> (Lovelock 2007: 49)

Gaia, then, is not an absolute 'truth' which can be stated once and for all by the rational mind: it is much closer to *mythos* than it is to *logos*.

Someone who agrees with Lovelock about the need to go beyond or beneath the rational mind in order to appreciate Gaia is Theodore Roszak. In his early days a cultural historian associated with the counterculture of the 1960s, he has now developed a discipline known as 'ecopsychology', which gives us our fourth perspective. Roszak believes that, given the damage we are doing to external nature, we will eventually have to come to terms with the damage that is thereby being done to our own internal nature. His aim is to help people recognize the profound link between psyche and planet, between soul and earth. In doing so, he has to assume the existence of an 'ecological unconscious'. In his *Voice of the Earth* (2001), Roszak argues that 'repression of the ecological unconscious is the deepest root of collusive madness in industrial society'; by the same token, 'open access to the ecological unconscious is the path to sanity' (Roszak 2001: 320). Summarizing the significance of 'ecopsychology', he states:

> Just as it has been the goal of previous therapies to recover the repressed contents of the unconscious, so the goal of ecopsychology is to awaken the inherent sense of environmental reciprocity that lies within the ecological unconscious. Other therapies seek to heal the alienation between person and person, person and family, person and society. Ecopsychology seeks to heal the more fundamental alienation between the person and the natural environment.
>
> (Roszak 2001: 320)

The ostensible source of the term is psychoanalysis; but Roszak is highly critical of Freud's fixation on the individual sexual subject and his view of nature as an alien, hostile realm. Roszak argues that the psyche does not exist in an environmental vacuum, any more than it lives in a domestic or social vacuum. If the earth is our ultimate home (*oikos*), then we cannot uproot ourselves from it without there being psychological consequences.

In keeping with Lovelock's realization that only myth and metaphor can do justice to Gaia, Roszak traces the idea of nature as a sacred whole back to the earliest form of religious consciousness, namely 'animism'. The *OED* defines this as follows: '1. the attribution of a living soul to plants, inanimate objects, and natural phenomena. 2. belief in a supernatural power that organizes and animates the material universe. [Latin *anima* life, soul' + ISM]' Animism preceded mythology, which personalized those natural phenomena in the form of gods and goddesses, but which retained the idea of nature as a living, sacred whole. This may seem to be an abstruse, pedantic point, but Roszak is interested in the way that, over the centuries, poets have instinctively been drawn to animism, just as they have been instinctively drawn to mythology. Essentially, he regards it as the same instinct, in terms of 'ecopsychology'. Thus, he draws on Wordsworth's 'Tintern Abbey' (1798) in order to refute the offensive pronouncement in a well-known nineteenth-century hymn, that 'The heathen in his blindness bows down to wood and stone':

> The blindness is ours. No people, regardless of the simplicity of their culture, ever took a stone carving to be divine. Modern anthropological scholarship now tells us as much. We have lost some quality of experience that would allow us to see the world as they did – or rather to see through it as they did. I take the animist worldview to be just that: things were once transparent to the human eye; greater realities moved behind and within them, were seen in this and that, here and there as if through a lens. This is where the concept of 'spirit' comes from, this once-homely, utterly normal sense that something other than matter moves behind matter, animates it, sustains it. Of that 'something,' tribal people stood in awe, as Wordsworth still did when he reached back to salvage the remnants of a visionary childhood in language that can still speak to us:
>
> And I have felt
> A presence that disturbs me with the joy
> Of elevated thoughts; a sense sublime
> Of something far more deeply interfused,
> Whose dwelling is the light of setting suns,
> And the round ocean and the living air,
> And the blue sky, and in the mind of man;
> A motion and a spirit, that impels
> All thinking things, all objects of all thought,
> And rolls through all things.
>
> (Roszak 2001: 91–2)

Roszak not only identifies this 'sense sublime' with archaic consciousness, but he also, by implication, offers it as a guide for our troubled times. If we can regain the connection between 'the light of setting suns' and 'the mind of man', he implies, then both nature and humanity might have a future.

A RELIGION OF THE WORLD

We can infer a broad consensus among the four theorists we have just discussed: that, if there is such a thing as the sacred, it is manifest in the profane; and that *oikos*, our true home, merits our profound reverence. Obviously, they differ in the ways they articulate the importance of having an ecological sense. For example, Snyder's 'Buddha-nature' may have much in common with Lovelock's 'Gaia', but they come from different discourses, and from different disciplines, so cannot be treated simply as synonymous. What links them is the interest in mythology as a means to understanding ecology. The same may be said of Adorno and Roszak. But it is with that conjunction that things get slightly more complicated. Adorno's apocalyptic myth is Marxist, and therefore materialist in the philosophical sense, while Roszak, as a prophet of the 'New Age', advocates a recovery of archaic spirituality as the answer to the contemporary world's problems. Granted, Adorno's Marxism is unorthodox, being far more 'green' than 'red', and being sympathetic to the religious worldview; but it is not strictly compatible with Roszak's assumption that 'something other than matter moves behind matter'.

Rather than revisit Adorno's work, which would take us into the farther reaches of dialectical materialism, I want to devote this closing section to the work of Michel Serres, a scientist who turned to philosophy in order to develop a new kind of 'materialism'. This is one which recognizes the miraculous dimension of matter rather than one which explains away all phenomena according to inflexible laws. It is also one which seeks to approach *oikos* by way of *mythos*. Much of Serres's work remains untranslated: here I will rely on two short volumes in English, *Hermes: Literature, Science, Philosophy* (1982), and *The Natural Contract* (1995); interested readers who want an accessible overview might also consult his extended dialogue with Bruno Latour, published as *Conversations on Science, Culture, and Time* (1995).

Serres's thinking has had a delayed but profound influence on what I call 'green studies', particularly by alerting scholars to the inseparability of ecology and mythology. Perhaps more than Lovelock, it is Serres who insists that modern science needs to regain touch with humanity's archaic past, for in so doing it may regain a sense of reverence for the material world:

> We are constantly losing our memory of the strange acts that priests used to practise alone in sombre and secret nooks, where they would dress the statue of a god, adorn it, ready it, raise it up or take it out, prepare a meal for it and talk to it constantly. They would do this every day and every night, at dawn and at dusk, when the sun and the shade reached their apogee. Were they afraid that a single pause in this continuous, infinite upkeep and conversation would open the door to tremendous consequences?
>
> Amnesiacs that we are, we believe that they adored the god or goddess sculpted in stone or wood. No: they were giving to the thing itself, marble or bronze, the power of speech, by conferring on it the appearance of a human body endowed with a voice. So they must have been celebrating their pact with the world.
>
> (Serres 1995a: 47)

In that we have lost our ability and, worse still, our desire to make this 'pact', terms such as 'atheist' or 'unbeliever' are insufficient, says Serres. Rather, our crime is 'negligence':

> Modernity neglects, speaking in absolute terms. It cannot and will not think or act toward the global, whether temporal or spatial.
>
> Through exclusively social contracts, we have abandoned the bond that connects us to the world, the one that binds the time passing and flowing to the weather outside, the bond that relates the social sciences to the sciences of the universe, history to geography, law to nature, politics to physics, the bond that allows our language to communicate with mute, passive, obscure things – things that, because of our excesses, are recovering voice, presence, activity, light. We can no longer neglect this bond.
>
> While we uneasily await a second Flood, can we practice a diligent religion of the world?
>
> (Serres 1995a: 47)

If we agree with the eighteenth-century philosopher Jean-Jacques Rousseau that human culture only became possible through a 'social contract', a pact between individuals to respect one another's rights, then we have to take the next step now. We have to enter into a 'natural contract', by which human culture itself makes a pact with the earth:

> Back to nature, then! That means we must add to the exclusively social contract a natural contract of symbiosis and reciprocity in which our relationship to things would set aside mastery and possession in favour of admiring attention, reciprocity, contemplation, and respect; where knowledge would no longer imply property, nor action mastery, nor would property and mastery imply their excremental results and origins. An armistice contract in the objective war, a contract of symbiosis, for a symbiont recognizes the host's rights, whereas a parasite – which is what we are now – condemns to death the one he pillages and inhabits, not realizing that in the long run he's condemning himself to death too.
>
> (Serres 1995a: 47)

In simultaneously invoking myth, putting humanity in its place and stressing the need for a new reverence for nature, Serres is in agreement with his fellow-scientist Lovelock. However, for Serres the mythic figure he prefers is the ancient Greek god Hermes; and in choosing him, he perhaps differs in emphasis from Lovelock. For Hermes testifies less to the sacred whole than to the way all the parts meet and come together. He is a god of mediation, of journeys and meetings, of mysterious connections. Here is one of Serres's many accounts of him:

> Psychopompus: this is one of the names under which Antiquity venerated Hermes; by this title they meant that he accompanied dead souls to hell. He watched in silence over our mortal agonies, guide of messengers, bonds and cords, angel flying in limpid air, nimble as a rocket, then led us toward the other world. His name, his acts, his myth sum up all these stories.
>
> He was honoured, as well, as an innovator: he had invented objects, the lyre and the panpipe, named for his son [Pan, god of flocks and herds, and also of wild, secluded places], but also the letters and

> signs of writing; and perhaps, too, road milestones, those tall rocks that in ancient Greece bore his name as well as a face and a sex, organs of communication that symbolize roads.
>
> Constructor of relations, of objects, conductor after death, god of messages and productive passages, his silent and translucent presence could be divined at the two twilights of dawn and dusk.
>
> (Serres 1995a: 117–18)

Hermes is the very model of what Serres himself attempts to do: to cross boundaries between disciplines, such as science, myth and literature; to understand the relationship between culture and nature, between spirit and matter, and between life and death.

If Hermes is his model, then the ancient Roman poet Lucretius (*c.* 100–*c.* 50 BC) is his source. It is Lucretius' six-volume work, *On the Nature of Things*, that provides his main evidence that science has much to learn from poetry and myth. For it was Lucretius who put into verse the philosophy of Epicurus, and in so doing made a powerful case for the idea that the origin of the earth, and so of humanity, lay in the motion of minute particles, or atoms. Though Epicurus's reputation is for hedonism, his main contribution to human thought, according to Lucretius, and so to Serres, is his 'atomist' theory of creation. According to this theory, the reason why there is something rather than nothing is that in the dim past there came about within the 'void' a subtle variation in the movement of atoms, a variation which Lucretius called the *clinamen*. The new contact made between atoms because of this swerving movement generated life, resulting eventually in the world we know. It is an important insight for Serres, because it anticipates such modern scientific spheres of knowledge as thermodynamics, atomic physics and quantum mechanics. Thus, it demonstrates that the wisdom of the past may anticipate the knowledge of the present. Lucretius is our contemporary, in that he knew already that life proceeds from turbulence, that order comes from disorder, that cosmos comes from chaos.

However, we have to distinguish Lucretius's creation myth from the Babylonian, for Lucretius's *clinamen* is a wholly benign process: no conflict or violence is involved. For what *On the Nature of Things* tells Serres is that life proceeded from the joyous dance of atoms, with its capacity for spontaneous variation of motion. Thus, we should respect chance and diversity, not try and impose abstract ideas of necessity or hierarchy upon the rich variety of existence, the sheer beauty of things. We may even read Lucretius's poem as a prefigurement of 'chaos theory', first put forward by Edward Lorenz in the course of experiments in meteorology in the early 1960s. It has become popularly known as the 'butterfly effect', in the light of the rhetorical question habitually posed by Lorenz: 'Does the flap of a butterfly's wings in Brazil set off a tornado in Texas?' Unpredictability is part of the overall pattern, as with Lucretius's notion of creation through divergence. Rather than impose order, says Serres, the poet is telling us to discover the organic order that underlies apparently random events and entities; but this order is so subtle that it cannot be understood through the unaided reason. Hence, Serres insists that science needs poetry in order to appreciate the 'orderly disorder' of the world.

Poetry in turn needs myth, and Serres has much to say about the opening of *On the Nature of Things*, in which Lucretius offers his tribute to Venus, the Roman fertility goddess. This may seem odd, given that in the rest of the poem he goes to some pains to repudiate religious beliefs, but it makes imaginative sense when we see that he is praising Venus by contrast with Mars, the god of war. By way of background, we need to know that Venus is the equivalent of the Greek goddess Aphrodite and that Mars is the equivalent of the Greek god Ares. However, where Aphrodite had greater powers than Ares, the militaristic Romans made Mars a more dominant figure than Venus. Thus, it is all the more remarkable that in the relevant myth Venus manages to subdue Mars, temporarily at least, by virtue of her female charms. It is this aspect of their story that no doubt encouraged Lucretius to eulogize the goddess and to denigrate the god. Let Serres explain:

> The hymn to Venus is a song to voluptuousness, to the original power, victorious – without having fought – over Mars and over the death instinct, a song to the pleasure of life, to guilt-free knowledge. The knowledge of the world is not guilty but peaceful and creative. It is generative and not destructive.
>
> (Serres 1982: 98)

What Venus represents is the fruitful 'disorder' that is actually an order so subtle and so complex that we are usually not aware of it: in that sense, she goes way beyond the doctrines of religion. From her we learn a mythic reverence for plurality and process, rather than a rigid religious hierarchy. Her vision is one of immanence, by which the whole proceeds from the part, the global from the local, forming a 'fragile synthesis'.

Mars, on the other hand, represents the violent 'order' that is all too often associated with religion. Instead of honouring the diversity of life, it imposes a deadly uniformity on everything. The religion of Mars leads in turn to the aggressive rationality of 'science, or what we call science'. Serres characterizes this way of thinking as 'the order of reasons', since it rationalizes away the miraculous creativity of nature:

> The order of reasons is repetitive, and the train of thought that comes from it, infinitely iterative, is but a science of death. A science of dead things and a strategy of the kill. The order of reasons is martial. . . . The laws are the same everywhere; they are thanatocratic [i.e., imposing the rule of Thanatos, god of death]. There is nothing to be learned, to be discovered, to be invented, in this repetitive world, which falls in the parallel lines of identity. . . . Nothing is new under the sun of identity and nothing is kept under the same old sun. Nothing new and nothing born, there is no nature. There is death forever. Nature is put to death or it is not allowed to be born. And the science of all this is nothing, can be summed up as nothing. . . . And identity is death. Everything falls to zero, a complete lack of information, the nothingness of knowledge, non-existence. The Same is Non-Being.
>
> (Serres 1982: 100)

Against the dead knowledge of Mars, which reduces all natural phenomena to one 'identity', Serres affirms the living vision of Venus, which celebrates randomness, chance, and infinite potential. The 'angle of inclination', the *clinamen*, 'breaks the chain of violence, interrupts the reign of the same' and so 'gives birth to nature as it really is' (Serres 1982: 100). The alternative to Mars is not to posit a world of spirit that might transcend matter altogether, but rather to renew our understanding of materialism:

> The chosen model is a fluid one. The nature of Mars, of martial physics, is one of hard, rigid, and rigorous bodies; the physics and nature of Venus are formed in flows. . . . We misunderstood Lucretius because we were the children of Plato and the Stoics, because the fundamental facts of Epicurean nature remained marginal in traditional science. . . . Moreover, we put their nature [i.e., that of the 'flows', of 'random events' and 'disequilibria'] outside nature, placing them in the soul and the subject. On the contrary, however these facts are the foundation of materialism. Atoms are not souls; the soul itself is atomic.
>
> (Serres 1982: 103)

It will be clear by now that Serres does not set out simply to discredit the scientific urge to enquire into the 'nature of things'. As hinted above, he respects Lucretius because he anticipates recent scientific hypotheses, such as chaos theory. What he opposes is the legacy of the Enlightenment, with its equating of science with rationality, and its naive faith in the ideal of human progress by means of the control and manipulation of nature. Knowing this, we may be surprised to learn that in *The Natural Contract* he acknowledges the benefits of space exploration. It is hard to do justice to the subtleties of that book in paraphrase, but he seems to view this development as a secular variant upon the theological principle of the 'fortunate fall'.

According to this principle, the rebellion of Adam and Eve in eating the fruit of the tree of knowledge of good and evil, which led to their expulsion from paradise, is ultimately justified because it necessitated the supreme sacrifice of Christ, the son of God, which delivered Adam and Eve's descendants into the eternal bliss of heaven. Serres's implicit narrative, deploying his motif of 'casting off', would then run roughly as follows. When modern humanity decided to 'cast off' from nature, by means of technology, it began a long process of detachment which eventually became one of complete alienation from the earth. But just at that point of alienation, advances in that technology made it possible for humanity to 'cast off' from the planet itself, by means of spacecraft. In doing so, it was given the opportunity to see the earth from afar. In seeing the earth from afar, it was given the opportunity to revere it once more, only now with an added intensity, a deeper sense of urgency. Thus, with a new sense of reverence came a new sense of responsibility. Serres does not go so far as to say that the alienation from the earth is justified; the 'fall', we may say, is not so much 'fortunate' as 'revelatory'. He is looking for a light amid the darkness. Here is the moment of the fall, as he describes it:

> From the nature we used to speak about, an archaic world in which our lives were plunged, modernity casts off, in its growing movement of derealization. Having become abstract and inexperienced, developed humanity takes off toward signs, frequents images and codes, and, flying in their midst, no longer has any relation, in cities, either to life or to the things of the world. . . . We are no longer *there*. We wander, outside all places.
>
> (Serres 1995a: 120)

Here is the moment when the fall produces its own revelation:

> Cast off far enough from our Earth, we can finally look at her whole. The farmer with his bent back lived on the furrow and saw nothing else; the savage saw only his clearing or the trails across the forest range; the mountain dweller, his valley, visible from the mountain pastures; the city dweller, the public square, observed from his floor of the building; the airplane pilot, a portion of the Atlantic. . . . Here is a hazy ball surrounded by turbulence: Planet Earth as satellites photograph her. Whole.
>
> How far up must we be flying to perceive her thus, globally? We have all become astronauts, completely deterritorialized: not as in the past a foreigner could be when abroad, but with respect to the Earth of all humankind.
>
> In bygone days, each individual, at once a soldier and a tiller of the soil, used to defend his plot of earth, because he lived off it and because there his ancestors lay: the plough and the gun had the same local meaning as the tomb, object-bonds to the soil. Philosophy invents the being there, the here-lies, at the very moment when this localness is disappearing, when the earth comes together and moves from plot of ground to universe, when its name is adorned with a capital letter. From this small local port and its ordinary objects we have cast off. Our most recent voyage brought us from earth to Earth.
>
> (Serres 1995a: 120)

Recalling a phrase from an earlier chapter, we might describe Serres's narrative as a 'circuitous quest'. In the words of Eliot's *Four Quartets*, 'the end of our exploring' shall be 'to arrive where we started / And know the place for the first time' (Eliot 1963: 222). But however we choose to comprehend the idea of a vision that comes at the end of a journey, we need to be clear about what his 'natural contract' involves, and how it takes us beyond the literal apocalypticism which we discussed earlier. We noted two main dangers of this 'realist' use of myth. First, there is the assumption that one group of humans may regard themselves as the 'saved' and its enemy as the 'damned'. Second, there is the assumption that the Biblical promise of 'a new earth' absolves humanity from its responsibility to the earth which we inhabit – the earth from which we were born and which has nurtured us. Against such a reductive version of apocalypse, we might turn with relief to Serres, who proclaims a new sense of 'love'. Love, he tells us, has two laws: 'Love one another' is the first. However, this is not enough: 'This first law remains silent about mountains and lakes, for it speaks to men about men as if there were no world. Here then is the second law, which asks us to love the world' (Serres 1995a: 49). Hence the importance of that view of the whole Earth from afar, which takes us back in imagination to the garden of Eden:

> Seen from above, from this new high place, Earth contains all our ancestors, indistinguishably mingled: the universal tomb of universal history. What funeral service do all these vapour plumes herald? And since, from up here, no one perceives borders, which are abstract in any case, we can speak for the first time of Adam and Eve, our first common parents, and thus of brotherhood. One humanity at last.
>
> (Serres 1995a: 121)

Without subscribing to a literal interpretation of the opening chapters of the Book of Genesis, Serres draws on the imaginative potential of the myth, to reflect on our current situation:

> Here is where our expulsion from earthly paradise led us: this, then, is the provisionally final result of hominization and history, of our work, of the painful generations drawn forth by individual death. To

> the universe-object corresponds, then, in all its meanings, universal death: of course it threatens us here, but it is also lying in wait everywhere else; what I called the other world [i.e., the world of abstraction, alienation and pollution] now covers the whole planet.
>
> (Serres 1995a: 121)

But now the task before us is neither to seek the Eden we have lost nor to seek the Jerusalem we have been promised. Rather, it is to recover a sense of place, and to learn to love the earth we inhabit in the place where we find ourselves. It is to recover the spiritual materialism of Lucretius.

In so doing, we will inevitably draw on our knowledge of both ecology and mythology, but there will be no one dominant myth, just as there can be no one dominant form of life. Hermes himself is intriguingly indefinite: his identity is amorphous, his functions are various. When Serres offers his eulogy to the earth, equivalent to Lucretius's eulogy to Venus, he does so in a mixture of 'pagan' and Biblical mythology, both subordinated to the imperatives of ecology. Taking his cue from the image of 'the lovers' apple, a token exchanged between our first parents', that is, the forbidden fruit eaten by Adam and Eve, he offers us a meditation that reads more like poetry than philosophy:

> . . . The largest apple. The most beautiful sphere or turbulent ball. The most ravishing boat, our caravel [i.e., small ship] new and eternal. The fastest shuttle. The most gigantic rocket. The greatest space ship. The densest forest. The most enormous rock. The most comfortable refuge. The most mobile statue. The complete clod of earth open at our feet, steaming.
>
> Indescribable emotion: mother, my faithful mother, our mother who has been a cenobite [i.e., religious woman] for as long as the world has existed, the heaviest, the most fecund, the holiest of maternal dwellings, chaste because always alone, and always pregnant, virgin and mother of all living things, better than alive, irreproducible universal womb of all possible life, mirror of ice floes, seat of snows, vessel of the seas, rose of the winds, tower of ivory, house of gold, Ark of the Covenant, gate of heaven, health, refuge, queen surrounded by clouds, who will be able to move her, who will be able to take her in their arms, who will protect her, if she risks dying and when she

> begins her mortal agony? What have we not destroyed with our scientific virtuosity?
>
> (Serres 1995a: 121–2)

This kind of writing is mythopoeic: it draws on existing myths in order to develop a new ecological myth, founded on a new materialism. It links *mythos* inseparably with *oikos*, and it tells us that *oikos* offers us as much sense of the sacred as we will ever need. Looking back to an archaic bond with the earth in a spirit of 'radical nostalgia', it simultaneously looks forward, in a spirit of 'radical typology', to what Serres has called 'a diligent religion of the world'.

Putting this another way, we might say that we have to learn to remythologize nature so that we can rediscover nature; and in that way we can learn to respect nature anew. But of course, as stated earlier, we can never 'know' nature: a bird's song is, and should remain, a source of wonderment. So we may say, by way of conclusion, that it is by re-reading and re-telling myths, that is, by keeping myths alive, that we can gain some sense of the sacred dimension of profane experience, and revere the earth as a source of continuing revelation. Perhaps *mythos*, which has the power to release us from the limits of the given *logos* and to restore us to *oikos*, acts rather like the figure celebrated in one of Wallace Stevens' later poems: 'I am the necessary angel of earth, / Since, in my sight, you see the earth again, / Cleared of its stiff and stubborn, man-locked set' (Stevens 1986: 127).

Bibliography

Abrams, M. H. (1971) *Natural Supernaturalism: Tradition and Revolution in Romantic Literature*, New York: Norton.

Ackerman, Robert (1990) *J. G. Frazer: His Life and Work*, Cambridge: Cambridge University Press.

Adorno, Theodor (1997) *Aesthetic Theory* (eds Gretel Adorno and Rolf Tiedemann), London and Minnesota: Athlone Press/University of Minnesota Press.

Allen, Don Cameron (1970) *Mysteriously Meant: The Rediscovery of Pagan Symbolism and Allegorical Interpretation in the Renaissance*, Baltimore: Johns Hopkins University Press.

Altizer, Thomas J. J. (1963) *Mircea Eliade and the Dialectic of the Sacred*, Westport, Connecticut: Greenwood Press.

—— (1967) *The New Apocalypse: The Radical Christian Vision of William Blake*, Ann Arbor: Michigan State University Press.

—— (1985) *History as Apocalypse*, New York: Albany.

—— (1990) *Genesis and Apocalypse: A Theological Voyage toward Authentic Christianity*, Louisville, Kentucky: John Knox Press.

Atwood, Margaret (1996) *The Handmaid's Tale*, London: Virago.

Auerbach, Erich (1968) *Mimesis: The Representation of Reality in Western Literature*, Princeton: Princeton University Press.

—— (1984) *Scenes from the Drama of European Literature*, Manchester: Manchester University Press.

Barnaby, Karin and Pellegrino D'Acierno (eds) (1990) *C. G. Jung and the Humanities*, London: Routledge.

Barthes, Roland (1973) *Mythologies* (ed. Annette Lavers), London: Paladin.

—— (1981) *Image – Music – Text* (ed. Stephen Heath), New York: Hill & Wang.

Barton, John (1984) *Reading the Old Testament: Method in Biblical Study*, London: Darton, Longman & Todd.

Bate, Jonathan (2000) *The Song of the Earth*, London: Picador.

Baudrillard, Jean (1983) *Simulations*, New York: Semiotext.

Bell, Michael (1997) *Literature, Modernism and Myth*, Cambridge: Cambridge University Press.

Beltz, Walter (1983) *God and the Gods: Myths of the Bible*, Harmondsworth: Penguin.

Bertens, Hans (1995) *The Idea of the Postmodern: A History*, London: Routledge.

Blackwell, Trevor and Jeremy Seabrook (1988) *The Politics of Hope*, London: Faber & Faber.

Blake, William (1971) *Complete Writings* (ed. Geoffrey Keynes), London: Oxford University Press.

Brown, Norman O. (1973) *Closing Time*, New York: Random House.

Bultmann, Rudolf (1953) 'The New Testament and Mythology', in H. W. Bartsch (ed.), *Kerygma and Myth: A Theological Debate*, London: SPCK.

Burke, Kenneth (1966) *Language as Symbolic Action: Essays on Life, Literature and Method*, Berkeley: University of California Press.

—— (1970) *The Rhetoric of Religion: Studies in Logology* (1961), 2nd edn, Berkeley: University of California Press.

—— (1971) 'Doing and Saying: Thoughts on Myth, Cult and Archetype', *Salmagundi* 7: 100–19.

—— (1984a) *Permanence and Change: An Anatomy of Purpose* (1935), 3rd edn, Berkeley: University of California Press.

—— (1984b) *Attitudes Toward History* (1937), 3rd edn, Berkeley: University of California Press.

—— (1989a) 'Revolutionary Symbolism in America' (1935), in Herbert W. Simons and Trevor Melia (eds), *The Legacy of Kenneth Burke*, Madison: University of Wisconsin Press, 1989, pp. 267–80.

—— (1989b) *On Symbols and Society* (ed. J. R. Gusfield), Chicago: University of Chicago Press.

Calasso, Robert (1994) *The Marriage of Cadmus and Harmony*, London: Vintage.

Campbell, Joseph (1988) *The Hero with a Thousand Faces*, London: Paladin.

Cantor, Paul A. (1984) *Creature and Creator: Myth-making and English Romanticism*, Cambridge: Cambridge University Press.

Cixous, Hélène (1980) 'The Laugh of the Medusa', in E. Marks and I. de Courtivron (eds), *New French Feminism*, Brighton: Harvester.

Clifford, James (ed.) (1986) *Writing Culture: The Poetics and Politics of Ethnography*, Berkeley: University of California Press.

Cohn, Norman (1970) *The Pursuit of the Millennium*, London: Paladin.

—— (1993) *Cosmos, Chaos and the World to Come*, New York: Yale University Press.

Coleridge, S. T. (1971) *Select Poetry and Prose* (ed. Stephen Potter), London: Nonesuch Press.

Conrad, Joseph (1973) *Heart of Darkness* (1902; reprint), Harmondsworth: Penguin.

Coppola, Francis Ford (1979) *Apocalypse Now*, USA: Zoetrope Studios.

Coupe, Laurence (2005) *Kenneth Burke on Myth: An Introduction*, New York: Routledge.

—— (2006) *Marina Warner*, Tavistock: Northcote House.

—— (2007) *Beat Sound, Beat Vision: The Beat Spirit and Popular Song*, Manchester: Manchester University Press.

—— (ed.) (2000) *The Green Studies Reader: From Ecocriticism to Romanticism*, London and New York: Routledge.
Cowie, Peter (1990) *Coppola*, London: Faber & Faber.
Cupitt, Don (1982) *The World to Come*, London: SCM Press.
—— (1986) *Life Lines*, London: SCM Press.
—— (1990) *Creation Out of Nothing*, London: SCM Press.
—— (1995) *The Last Philosophy*, London: SCM Press.
—— (1997) *After God: The Future of Religion*, London: Weidenfeld & Nicolson.
Curry, Patrick (1997) *Defending Middle-Earth: Tolkien, Myth and Modernity*, Edinburgh: Floris Books.
—— (2008) 'Nature Post-Nature', *New Formations* 64: 51–64.
Dante Alighieri (1995) *The Portable Dante* (ed. Mark Musa), London and New York: Penguin/Viking.
Derrida, Jacques (1976) *Of Grammatology*, Baltimore: Johns Hopkins University Press.
—— (1982) 'Of an Apocalyptic Tone Recently Adopted in Philosophy', *Semeia* 23: 63–97.
—— (1994) 'Spectres of Marx', *New Left Review* 205: 31–58.
Dickens, Charles (1971) *Bleak House* (1852–3; reprint), Harmondsworth: Penguin.
Docherty, Thomas (ed.) (1993) *Postmodernism: A Reader*, New York and London: Harvester.
The Doors (1992) *The Doors: Lyrics 1965–1971*, London: Omnibus.
Doty, William G. (2000) *Mythography: The Study of Myths and Rituals*, Tuscaloosa: University of Alabama Press.
—— (2004) *Myth: A Handbook*, Tuscaloosa: University of Alabama Press.
Dowling, William C. (1984) *Jameson, Althusser, Marx: An Introduction to 'The Political Unconscious'*, London: Methuen.
Eco, Umberto (1989) *The Middle Ages of James Joyce*, London: Hutchinson Radius.
Eliade, Mircea (1958) *Patterns in Comparative Religion*, London: Sheed and Ward.
—— (1968) *Myths, Dreams and Mysteries*, London: Fontana.
—— (1971) *The Myth of the Eternal Return: Or, Cosmos and History*, Princeton: Princeton University Press.
Eliot, T. S. (1948) *Notes Towards the Definition of Culture*, London: Faber & Faber.
—— (1961) *Murder in the Cathedral*, London: Faber & Faber.
—— (1963) *Collected Poems 1909–1962*, London: Faber & Faber.
—— (1964) *The Use of Poetry and the Use of Criticism*, London: Faber & Faber.
—— (1970) *For Lancelot Andrewes: Essays on Style and Order*, London: Faber & Faber.
—— (1975) *Selected Prose* (ed. F. Kermode), London: Faber & Faber.

Feldman, Burton and Robert D. Richardson (1972) *The Rise of Modern Mythology*, Bloomington: Indiana University Press.
Ferguson, John (1980) *Jesus in the Tide of Time: An Historical Study*, London: Routledge & Kegan Paul.
Fiorenza, Elisabeth (1985) *The Book of Revelation: Justice and Judgement*, Philadelphia: Fortress Press.
Fowlie, Wallace (1994) *Rimbaud and Jim Morrison: The Rebel as Poet*, London: Souvenir Press.
Frazer, Sir James George (1978) *The Illustrated Golden Bough* (ed. Sabine McCormack), London: Macmillan.
Freud, Sigmund (1950) *Collected Papers*, Vol. V, London: Hogarth Press.
—— (1974) 'The Interpretation of Dreams', in *Complete Works*, Vols IV–V, London: Hogarth Press.
—— (1985) *The Origins of Religion* (ed. Albert Dickson), Harmondsworth: Penguin.
Frye, Northrop (1971) *Anatomy of Criticism: Four Essays*, Princeton: Princeton University Press.
—— (1978) *Northrop Frye on Culture and Literature* (ed. Robert Denham), Chicago: University of Chicago Press.
—— (1981) *T. S. Eliot: An Introduction*, Chicago: University of Chicago Press.
—— (1982) *The Great Code: The Bible and Literature*, London: Routledge & Kegan Paul.
Gadon, Elinor W. (1989) *The Once and Future Goddess: A Symbol for Our Time*, New York: Harper Collins.
Garrard, Greg (2004) *Ecocriticism*, London: Routledge.
Geertz, Clifford (1993) *The Interpretation of Cultures: Selected Essays*, London: Fontana.
Girard, René (1977) *Violence and the Sacred*, Baltimore: Johns Hopkins University Press.
Gould, Eric (1981) *Mythical Intentions in Modern Literature*, Princeton: Princeton University Press.
Graf, Fritz (1993) *Greek Myth: An Introduction*, Baltimore: Johns Hopkins University Press.
Harrison, Robert Pogue (1993) *Forests: The Shadow of Civilization*, Chicago: University of Chicago Press.
Hellmann, John (1986) *American Myth and the Legacy of Vietnam*, New York: Columbia University Press.
Herr, Michael (1978) *Dispatches*, London: Pan.
Hill, Geoffrey (1985) *Collected Poems*, Harmondsworth: Penguin.
Hopkins, Jerry and Danny Sugerman (1980) *No One Here Gets Out Alive*, London: Plexus.
Hughes, Ted (1997) *Tales from Ovid: Twenty-Four Passages from the Metamorphoses*, London: Faber.

Jackson, Peter (2001–3) *The Lord of the Rings* (trilogy), New Zealand: Camperdown Studios.
Jameson, Fredric (1981) *The Political Unconscious: Narrative as a Socially Symbolic Act*, London: Methuen.
—— (1982) 'Ulysses in History', in W. J. McCormack and A. Stead (eds), *James Joyce and Modern Literature*, London: Routledge & Kegan Paul.
—— (1991) *Postmodernism, or, The Cultural Logic of Late Capitalism*, London: Verso.
Jenkyns, Richard (1992) *Classical Epic: Homer and Virgil*, London: Duckworth.
Jewett, Robert and John Shelton Lawrence (1977) *The American Monomyth*, New York: Doubleday.
Jones, Derek and Graham Handley (1988) *The Modern World: Ten Great Writers*, London: Channel Four Publications.
Joyce, James (1960) *Ulysses* (1922; reprint), London: Bodley Head.
—— (1966) *Finnegans Wake* (1939; reprint), London: Faber & Faber.
Jung, Carl G. (1966) 'Instinct and the Unconscious', *Collected Works*, Vol. 15, Princeton: Princeton University Press.
—— (ed.) (1990) *Man and His Symbols*, London and New York: Arkana.
—— (1992) *The Gnostic Jung* (ed. Robert A. Segal), London: Routledge.
Kafka, Franz (1970) [1925] *The Trial*, Harmondsworth: Penguin.
Kane, Sean (1998) *Wisdom of the Mythtellers*, Peterborough, Ontario: Broadview Press.
Kearney, Richard (1988) *The Wake of Imagination*, London: Hutchinson.
—— (1991) *Poetics of Imagining: From Husserl to Lyotard*, London: Harper Collins.
Kermode, Frank (1967) *The Sense of an Ending: Studies in the Theory of Fiction*, London and New York: Oxford University Press.
—— (1973) *Lawrence*, London: Fontana.
—— (1990) *Modern Essays*, London: Fontana.
King, Martin Luther, Jr (2001) *A Call to Conscience: The Landmark Speeches* (ed. Clayborne Carson and Kris Shephard), New York: Grand Central Publishing.
Kirk, G. S. (1970) *Myth: Its Meaning and Function in Ancient and Other Cultures*, Cambridge: Cambridge University Press.
—— and J. E. Raven (eds) (1960) *The Presocratic Philosophers*, Cambridge: Cambridge University Press.
Larkin, Philip (1983) *Required Writing: Miscellaneous Pieces 1955–1982*, London: Faber & Faber.
—— (1988) *Collected Poems*, London: Faber/Marvell Press.
Lauter, Estella and Carol Schreier Rupprecht (1985) *Feminist Archetypal Theory: Interdisciplinary Revisions of Jungian Thought*, Knoxville: University of Tennessee Press.
Lévi-Strauss, Claude (1968) *Structural Anthropology*, Harmondsworth: Penguin.
—— (1978) *Myth and Meaning*, London: Routledge.

Lovelock, James (1989) *The Ages of Gaia: The Biography of Our Living Earth*, Oxford: Oxford University Press.
—— (2007) *The Revenge of Gaia: Why the Earth is Fighting Back – and How We Can Still Save Humanity*, London: Penguin.
Lyotard, Jean-François (1984) *The Postmodern Condition: A Report on Knowledge*, Manchester: Manchester University Press.
—— (1992) *The Postmodern Explained to Children*, London: Turnaround Press.
McConnell, Frank (1979) *Storytelling and Mythmaking: Images from Film and Literature*, New York and London: Oxford University Press.
McEwan, Ian (2008) 'The Day of Judgment', *Guardian Review* 31 May 2008, pp. 2–4, 23.
McLuhan, Marshall (1967) *The Medium is the Message*, Harmondsworth: Penguin.
Mali, Joseph (1992) *The Rehabilitation of Myth: Vico's 'New Science'*, Cambridge and New York: Cambridge University Press.
Manganaro, Marc (1992) *Myth, Rhetoric and the Voice of Authority: A Critique of Frazer, Eliot, Frye and Campbell*, New Haven: Yale University Press.
—— (ed.) (1990) *Modernist Anthropology: From Fieldwork to Text*, Princeton: Princeton University Press.
Manuel, Frank E. (1965) *Shapes of Philosophical History*, London: Allen & Unwin.
Marx, Karl (1977), *Capital*, Vol. I, New York: Vintage.
—— and Friedrich Engels (1973) *Selected Works*, London: Lawrence and Wishart.
Milius, John and Francis Ford Coppola (2001) *Apocalypse Now Redux: An Original Screenplay*, London: Faber.
Millett, Kate (1969) *Sexual Politics*, London: Virago.
Moi, Toril (1985) *Sexual/Textual Politics*, London: Methuen.
Moltmann, Jurgen (1967) *Theology of Hope*, New York: Harper & Row.
Morris, Brian (1987) *Anthropological Studies of Religion: An Introductory Text*, Cambridge: Cambridge University Press.
Morrison, Jim (1985) *The Lords and The New Creatures*, London: Omnibus.
—— (1991) *The American Night: The Writings of Jim Morrison*, Harmondsworth: Penguin.
Munz, Peter (1973) *When the Golden Bough Breaks: Structuralism or Typology?*, London: Routledge & Kegan Paul.
Nietzsche, Friedrich (1977) *A Nietzsche Reader* (ed. E. J. Hollingdale), Harmondsworth: Penguin.
—— (1979) *Philosophy and Truth: Selections from Nietzsche's Notebooks of the Early 1870s* (ed. Daniel Breazeale), Brighton: Harvester, 1979
Primavesi, Anne (2000) *Sacred Gaia: Holistic Theology and Earth System Science*, London: Routledge.
—— (2003) *Gaia's Gift: Earth, Ourselves and God After Copernicus*, London: Routledge.

Rée, Jonathan (ed.) (1992) *Talking Liberties*, London: Channel Four Publications.
Reeves, Marjorie (1976) *Joachim of Fiore and the Prophetic Future*, London: SPCK.
Rickword, Edgell (1937) 'The Cultural Meaning of May Day', *Left Review* 3: 130–1.
—— (1974) *Essays and Opinions 1921–1931* (ed. Alan Young), Cheadle: Carcanet Press.
—— (1976) *Behind the Eyes: Selected Poems and Translations*, Manchester: Carcanet Press.
Ricoeur, Paul (1965) *History and Truth*, Evanston: Northwestern University Press.
—— (1967) *The Symbolism of Evil*, Boston: Beacon Press.
—— (1974) *The Conflict of Interpretations* (ed. Don Idhe), Evanston: Northwestern University Press.
—— (1986) *Lectures on Ideology and Utopia* (ed. George H. Taylor), New York: Columbia University Press.
—— (1991) *A Ricoeur Reader: Reflection and Imagination* (ed. Mario J. Valdes), New York and London: Harvester/Wheatsheaf.
—— (1995) *Figuring the Sacred: Religion, Narrative and Imagination*, Minneapolis: Fortress Press.
Rieff, Philip (1951) 'The Meaning of History and Religion in Freud's Thought', *Journal of Religion* 31: 114–31.
Rigney, Barbara Hill (1987), *Margaret Atwood*, London: Macmillan.
Rose, Jacqueline (1986) 'Hamlet – the Mona Lisa of Literature', *Critical Quarterly* 28: 35–49.
Roszak, Theodore (1972) *Where the Wasteland Ends: Politics and Transcendence in Postindustrial Society*, New York: Doubleday.
—— (2001) *The Voice of the Earth: An Exploration of Ecopsychology*, Grand Rapids: Phanes Press.
Rowland, Susan (2005), *Jung as a Writer*, London: Routledge.
Russell, D. A. and M. Winterbottom (eds) (1972) *Ancient Literary Criticism: The Principal Texts in New Translations*, Oxford: Clarendon Press.
Scarborough, Milton (1994) *Myth and Modernity: Postcritical Reflections*, Albany: SUNY.
Segal, Robert A. (1987) *Joseph Campbell: An Introduction*, New York: Garland.
—— (1992) *Explaining and Interpreting Religion: Essays on the Issue*, New York: Peter Lang.
—— (2004) *Myth: A Very Short Introduction*, Oxford: Oxford University Press.
Serres, Michel (1982) *Hermes: Literature, Science, Philosophy* (eds Josue V. Harari and David F. Bell), Baltimore and London: Johns Hopkins University Press.
—— (1995a), *The Natural Contract*, Michigan: Michigan University Press.

—— (1995b), *Conversations on Science, Culture, and Time* (with Bruno Latour), Michigan: Michigan University Press.
Snyder, Gary (1992) *No Nature: New and Selected Poems*, New York: Pantheon Books.
Soper, Kate (1995) *What is Nature? Culture, Politics and the Non-Human*, Oxford: Blackwell.
Spenser, Edmund (1966) *Poetical Works* (eds J. C. Smith and E. de Selincourt), London: Oxford University Press.
Spretnak, Charlene (1991) *States of Grace: The Recovery of Meaning in the Postmodern Age*, New York: HarperCollins.
—— (1999) *The Resurgence of the Real: Body, Nature and Place in a Hypermodern World*, New York: Routledge.
Steiner, George (1969) *Language and Silence*, Harmondsworth: Penguin.
Stevens, Wallace (1984) *The Necessary Angel: Essays on Reality and Imagination*, London: Faber & Faber.
—— (1986) *Selected Poems*, London: Faber & Faber.
Tredell, Nicholas (1995) *Conversations with Critics*, Manchester: Carcanet.
Trubshaw, Bob (2003) *Explore Mythology*, Loughborough: Heart of Albion Press.
Turner, Victor (1974) *The Ritual Process*, Harmondsworth: Penguin.
Vernant, Jean-Pierre (1982) *Myth and Society in Ancient Greece*, London: Methuen.
Wachowski, Andy and Larry Wachowski (1999–2003), *The Matrix* (trilogy), USA: Warner Brothers Studios.
Warner, Marina (2000) *Alone of All Her Sex: The Myth and the Cult of the Virgin Mary*, London: Vintage.
—— (1994) *Managing Monsters: Six Myths of Our Time*, London: Vintage.
—— (1996) *The Inner Eye: Art Beyond the Visible*, London: National Touring Exhibitions.
—— (2002) *Fantastic Metamorphoses, Other Worlds*, Oxford: Oxford University Press.
Weston, Jessie L. (1920) *From Ritual to Romance*, Cambridge: Cambridge University Press.
Winstanley, Gerrard (1973) *The Law of Freedom and Other Writings* (ed. Christopher Hill), Harmondsworth: Penguin.
Wright, Will (1975) *Six Guns and Society: A Structural Study of the Western*, Berkeley: University of California Press.
Young, Robert (1990) *White Mythologies: Writing History and the West*, London and New York: Routledge.

INDEX